(continued from front flap)

under Dizzy Gillespie, Thelonious Monk, and Miles Davis, culminating in the saxophonist's classic quartet that played to steadily increasing audiences throughout America, Europe, and Japan.

The author has drawn on the recollections of those who knew Coltrane best—boyhood friends, band members like Elvin Jones, spiritual mentors like Ravi Shankar, and the women who loved him. *Chasin' The Trane* is the story of a man who struggled against drug addiction, studied African and Eastern music and philosophy, admired Einstein's expanding universe and the shimmering sounds a harp makes, and left behind the enduring legacy of a master musician who was also a beautiful man.

With 16 pages of black-and-white photographs and a complete discography.

CHASIN' THE TRANE

DOUBLEDAY & COMPANY, INC.
GARDEN CITY, NEW YORK
1975

Chasin' The Trane

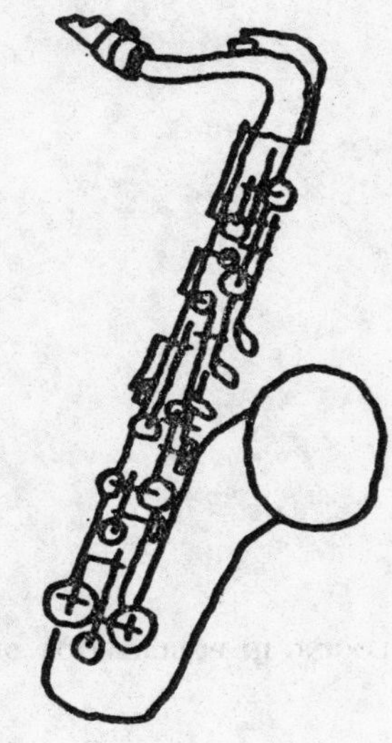

The Music and Mystique of John Coltrane

J. C. THOMAS

PHOTO PROCESSING BY LEXINGTON LABS,
NEW YORK, NEW YORK

LIBRARY OF CONGRESS CATALOGING IN PUBLICATION DATA
Thomas, J. C.
Chasin' the Trane.
Discography: p. 233
1. Coltrane, John, 1926–1967. I. Title.
ML419.C645T5 788'.66'0924 [B]
ISBN 0-385-09604-6
Library of Congress Catalog Card Number 74-2526

Printed in the United States of America
BOOK DESIGN BY OLE AND BENTE HAMANN

DEDICATION

To all the musicians, those in the music business, and music lovers who gave so generously of their time and knowledge—my gratitude.

And, my special thanks to:

Franklin Brower, who recalled more about Trane's boyhood than I could ever remember of my own.

Paul Jeffrey, who knows ever so well what it's like to hang a horn around his neck and play, night after night.

Gerald "Spliby" McKeever, the secret sharer of Trane's long dark nights—and some truly beautiful days.

John Signorelli, for his invaluable assistance in researching the history of the saxophone and its creator.

Rashied Ali, who always knows what time it is.

Earl and Lucy Grubbs, for being beautiful people; their sons, Earl and Carl, for being beautiful musicians.

Naima Coltrane, just for being her own beautiful self.

CHASIN' THE TRANE

In the Negro melodies of America I have discovered all that is needed for the creation of a great and noble school of music. These beautiful and varied themes are the product of the soil. They are the folk songs of America, and your composers must turn to them. All the great musicians have borrowed from the songs of the common people.

ANTON DVORAK

Little of beauty has America given the world save the rude grandeur God himself stamped on her bosom; the human spirit in this new world has expressed itself in vigor and ingenuity rather than beauty. And so by fateful chance the Negro folk song—the rhythmic cry of the slave—stands today not simply as the sole American music, but as the most beautiful expression of human experience born this side of the seas. It has been neglected, it has been persistently mistaken and misunderstood; but notwithstanding, it still remains as the singular spiritual heritage of this nation and the greatest gift of the Negro people.

W. E. B. DU BOIS

The large man with the luminous eyes walks rapidly down the street, his shoulders sagging as if pulled by the weight of the saxophone case he carries in his right hand. He quickly glances at his wrist watch; he frowns, and increases the tempo of his footsteps as though he is late for an important engagement.

As he moved along Bleecker Street in New York's Greenwich Village, two shabbily dressed men huddle in a doorway just a few steps away from the Village Gate, chattering aimlessly and passing a bottle of wine between them. The walking man and the drinking men spot each other simultaneously.

"Hey," *says one of the latter. "Do you think that's . . ."*

"I don't think so, man," mumbles the other. "Pass the bottle, huh?"

The large man with the luminous eyes stares at the two winos for a few seconds, his eyes registering compassion and concern. Instinctively, he reaches for his wallet, pulls out some money, and presses a bill into both men's hands.

As the walking man continues on his way, heading toward the entrance of the Village Gate, the man who spoke first looks at the cash in his hand, turns to his companion and says, with great frustration, "Hey, *man . . . that* was *Trane . . . giving me a* ten *. . . when I got a* million *questions to ask him . . . about* music. . . ."

The Trane ride starts here.

In a southern village, an undisturbed enclave that still showcases an exact replica of an antique steam locomotive, *The Tornado.* A bucolic pastureland of dark loam soil, where peaches, cotton, corn, and tobacco sprout like grass after a gentle rain. The centerpiece of the Seaboard Airline Railroad's $12 million classification yard, handling more than three thousand freight and six hundred passenger cars each day. And a quiet place that spawned a master musician, a man so thoroughly attuned to the sensitivities of the human soul that he suffered all his life from a melancholy as profound as Shakespeare portrayed in his character of the same name.

Hamlet.

North Carolina.
Where John William Coltrane was born.

John Coltrane was three years old when I first met him. His grandfather, Reverend Walter Blair, had a house here in High Point, where he was the pastor of St. Stephen's African Methodist Episcopal Zion Church. The Coltranes were living in Hamlet at the time. But the Reverend was often traveling to other ministries, and he had a big two-story house, so he talked John's family into moving into High Point. In fact, John's father set up his dry-cleaning business and tailor shop right next door to my funeral home here at 600 East High Street. I remember John stopping by many times after talking with his daddy next door. We often had corpses being embalmed or waiting to be worked on, and John used to look at them with about as much curiosity as any other boy would have for a stray dog.

WALTER HOOVER

John Coltrane was born on September 23, 1926, in Hamlet, 100 miles away from High Point. This latter city, today famous as a furniture and hosiery center, was then a small town with a population of 35,000 and an area of thirty-one square miles, with Guilford County being the next highest governing body. The British Isles were the source of its ancestral immigrants, with cabinetmakers from Scotland, miners from England and Wales, and weavers from Ireland pouring into the territory. The English settlement of the South is well documented, as is the custom of giving the family slaves the same surname. So, if tracing family trees was a matter of great importance, the Blairs (Mrs. Coltrane's family, whose predecessors wandered from Virginia to North Carolina with Daniel Boone) and the Coltranes (already indigenous to the area) could count their heritage back more than just a few centuries to medieval England.

The city was not incorporated as such until 1859, but, a century before, some Quakers had settled there and built a Meeting House, circa 1750. The first church, of Methodist persuasion, would not be constructed until 1858, and both of these denominations would exert no small influence on John Coltrane at a later date, as they would on all the black population—about one-third—of High Point.

The history of black people in High Point goes back almost to the founding of the city, with a fellow named Willis Hinton coming to town in 1868 and opening a cafe on South Main Street in 1883; five years later, he established a hotel on East Washington under his own name. Dr. Gerran, the first black physician in town, set up his practice in 1898, following the 1870–85 purchase of substantial property between Wrenn and Perry, High and Commerce streets by blacks. After World War I and up to 1929, when the Great Crash halted many other matters besides migration, blacks were flocking in five-figure numbers to High Point from poorer areas in South Carolina and Georgia.

In the All-American Triad (Chamber of Commerce Ad)

And John Coltrane would explore the triad, the traditional three-note chord, like no other musician before him and few, if any, after.

> I lived on Hoover Street, just a few blocks away from John. His family and mine were very close. Every Monday we'd get together, either at their house or ours, and have dinner. We'd really have a feast. We'd have hominy grits, rice, oatmeal, fried chicken, corn bread, collard greens—and my favorite, sweet potato pie.
>
> BETTY LEACH

High Point supported not one but two all-black neighborhoods, and the difference between them was the same as that between white areas—money. The poorer blacks were located on the South Side. About two or three miles away, on the East Side, was where the more affluent blacks resided, separated from the even more affluent whites by only one street. Some of the streets on the East

Side were paved; none on the South Side could claim that distinction.

Most of the East Side homes date from the 1920s, thus making them new indeed when John Coltrane lived at 118 Underhill, a street that was almost the exact center of that black community. His home, a two-story frame house, with an open porch supported by wooden pillars, sat almost at the top of a gently sloping hill. The front yard was small, the back yard smaller. But an adjoining carport and gravel driveway, plus the paved street itself, testified to the better-than-average status of the house's owner and occupants.

The front door opened into a foyer, followed by a large living room, dining room, country-style kitchen, and downstairs toilet. Upstairs were three bedrooms and a large bath with an old-fashioned four-footed tub.

This was Walter Blair's house, where the Blairs and the Coltranes both lived.

The reverend was born in Edenton, and John Coltrane's father, John Robert Coltrane, came from Sanford. He was called J.R., and he had married Alice Blair while in Hamlet. He was a medium-sized man, five-seven, slim and dapper, with a boyish, open face, and played violin and ukulele when he wasn't busy tailoring. His wife was the taller by at least two inches, a large-boned lady, with a handsome tapered face and long straight hair.

While attending school in the neighborhood, John noticed a boy named James Kinzer who lived at 305 Underhill, a couple of blocks from Franklin Brower, whose Underhill address was 218. John, Franklin, and James grew up to be friends and near look-alikes. But Franklin and John were friends first. James met John through Franklin, who shared James's fascination with reading about major-league baseball scores in out-of-town newspapers. Then John became interested in baseball, too.

On Sundays, these three, among others, would be in temporary residence at Reverend Blair's church. It was a two-story brick building with a gabled roof, fronting a tapered spire, with a basement where John and his buddies attended Sunday school. Later, they'd troop upstairs to the main room with its straight-backed wooden pews and plastered walls to hear the reverend, a charismatic man who often embellished his biblical rhetoric with concrete examples from the lives of prominent people in the community.

During the week, John, Franklin, and James would put in their six hours at the Leonard Street Elementary School, a public school adjacent to the church and built around 1921 through the efforts among others, of the reverend himself. Also a brick building, it was the first public school in High Point for black children. But it was more like a one-room schoolhouse, with various devices used as room dividers, and space was at a premium for the five hundred students in attendance and their sixteen teachers.

In the school, there was a sort of segregation even among students; an A and B section, the former reserved only for those with the best grades. John was A, all the way; though in high school the opposite would be true, when his interests changed and his grades dropped.

> I once looked over a Real Estate Survey of North Carolina cities that was made up in the 1930s by a WPA unit. They surveyed every house in High Point in the Negro neighborhood. According to their findings, 81 per cent of the community rented their homes and less than 10 per cent of the houses were two-story. So in that respect, the Coltrane home was exceptional in both categories.
>
> FRANKLIN BROWER

When the Depression came to High Point, it brought an unemployment rate of nearly 20 per cent, with a doubling of that figure for black people.

However, as a "family" city the inhabitants tended to rally around each other and share the wealth in as fair a manner as possible. Guilford County issued scrip money, acceptable at most retail establishments; the WPA and CCC set up projects and let some Federal money flow into the city. And a surprising number of back-yard gardens were planted and crops harvested during the eight-month warm-weather season in that section of the state.

As Betty Leach said, "My daddy only made a dollar fifty a week and still bought a house, sent two of us to college, and gave us hot food on the table and hot water in the tub."

John Coltrane had a cousin named Mary. (Readers of record album liner notes would learn of her later; the song of the same name in the *Giant Steps* album is his musical dedication to her.) She moved, with her parents, Golar and Betty Lyerly, into the Coltrane household while he was in elementary school. The Reverend Blair and his wife were still living there and, with the Coltrane threesome, that totaled eight in a three-bedroom house. But they were all in the family, so they managed. Unfortunately, John, who had acquired his quiet and private persona early, rarely had a room to himself then, or ever.

Mary was a pert, cheerful, and vivacious girl who was John's polar opposite in most matters. But they shared a mutual drive for excellence and desire for knowledge, and they posted elementary school grades near the top of their class.

J. R. Coltrane worked late and long hours at his tailor shop, so if John spent time with anyone at home it would most likely have been his mother. She was stern, but she made sure he was as well dressed as behaved, providing him with neat clothes and good manners.

John's father, more convivial and outgoing, was known in the community as a good family man and a genial host, when late evening business was slow. Friends would drop by, J.R. would pass around the bourbon bottle, and, hoisting himself up on the counter, his legs dangling, his arms fondling his ukulele (his violin was reserved for more serious moments), he would pluck out a few accompanying chords and his pleasant baritone would embellish the words of his favorite song, "The Sweetheart of Sigma Chi." If John was around, he would naturally be made welcome with everything except the alcohol. Standing quietly by his father, he'd look around shyly, eyes downcast, then slowly raise his vision until his father's head and shoulders were straight in front of him, like a prime photo subject filling a camera's viewfinder. Even at that age, around ten or twelve, his eyes had already achieved a quality of luminosity, of absorption, that made some wonder if John could see in the dark like an owl. His eyes, when focused on someone, gave that person such complete attention that a corresponding transfer of equal interest and attention was called for. In fact, such reciprocity was virtually compelled by the steadiness (and possibly innocent sweetness) of those large and curious brown eyes.

"John always said he wanted to play like his father," Walter Hoover recalls. "He liked his father's favorite song because it was a waltz, and waltzes were very popular at that time."

John Coltrane? Wayne King? An unlikely combination then; but that was well before "Greensleeves" and "My Favorite Things."

And in "The Sweetheart of Sigma Chi" there is also an implied sadness, a strain of unadmitted melancholy, an evocative and possibly incantatory refrain that would sink into John's psyche and was, perhaps, the beginning . . . of the sadness that was well beyond the blues. . . .

Then his father died.

It happened when John was twelve, and had just become a boy scout. J.R. went into the hospital for an undisclosed, if not undiagnosed, illness. A few days later, he died. During that same year, Reverend Blair's wife and Cousin Mary's father also died. James Kinzer recalled that some close friends of the Coltrane family also passed away within a two- or three-year time span. James Gates, a friend and classmate of both John and Mary, remembers that Mary was emotionally and outwardly upset for days after J. R. Coltrane's death, then threw herself into several activities, such as acting in class plays. But John seemed as calm, unruffled, and quiet as always, as if not wishing to reveal his feelings to anyone, hiding his sorrow within his own heart and nurturing it in private.

John Coltrane had no nickname in High Point; he was simply called John. But Brower and Kinzer were known as, respectively, Snookie and Poche. Franklin would discuss baseball and movies with James, but it was John with whom he shared his obsessive collection of Doc Savage comics.

Doc Savage, whom Brower described as a "tall, blond Nordic type who ran an organization dedicated to solving crimes the cops couldn't or wouldn't, and was always too much the devoted nemesis of evildoers to have any room for women in his life." The two main characters were Doc and Monk, the latter a tough, Neanderthal type who assisted the more glamorous Savage in snuffing out the opposition.

For kids in a small Carolina town, this was heady stuff indeed, inspiring more than the usual spate of bedtime fantasies. John and Franklin often stuck their heads inside these harmless publications day and night. They read them while walking to and from school, in class concealed behind a large note tablet or textbook, during lunchtime in the cafeteria, even in the middle of a Saturday afternoon matinee at the movies. Perhaps it seems odd that two black boys would seemingly identify with such WASPish Social Register scions. But at that time, how many blacks of stature would they ever have had the opportunity to learn about? The radio, too, would have been far more likely to fill their young ears full of Amos and Andy rather than the down-home blues of Count Basie's band.

For physical exercise, there was always touch football in the streets and baseball in the sandlots. Walter Williamson, a neighbor and classmate of John's, recalls roller skating on the obstacle course that the spiraling hills of Underhill presented. Betty Leach remembers playing tag and hide-and-seek. Once, John hid himself so well that while everyone concerned was calling his name and loudly proclaiming that he had won, a visitor in the neighborhood started his car and John came darting out from beneath the vehicle, where he'd concealed himself, coughing from the exhaust.

Coltrane and Brower also developed an interest in automobiles, since they were such esoterica in the neighborhood. They persuaded their parents to purchase some of the popular magazines—*Time, Newsweek,* even *True Story* or *Good Housekeeping*—so they could look at the car ads. They hung out in the library and drug and grocery stores, flipping pages and perusing Ford Model As and Chevrolet sedans until chased away by prissy librarians or irate shopkeepers.

Looking over the pictures of the cars, the boys didn't speak much; they mostly pointed, either nodding or shaking their heads, depending on their agreement or disagreement.

They drew cars, too. If someone had made them a present of a magazine, or if they'd pooled their allowances and saved their pennies, they took the publication home and traced the automobile designs on paper, adding their own interpretations and trying to make the vehicles as modernistic and sleek-looking as possible. Franklin was the better of the two; John's penmanship was horrendous even at that early age, and from High Point on he would laboriously print rather than write, signing only his name, and that only if absolutely necessary.

"John wasn't much of a reader then," Franklin says. "It was mostly comics with him. That was really a shame, because Reverend Blair had an excellent library in a built-in bookcase in the dining room of the Coltrane house. I remember reading some things from a fine *History of the South*, published by Duke University."

In later years, as if to make up for lost time (or perhaps intuitively knowing then that he wouldn't have much time left), John joined several book clubs and, when not involved in musical matters—precious little time, it seemed—he read incessantly, the more serious the subject matter the better.

For other harmless diversions in High Point, however, there was always Mrs. Drake's Confectionery Store.

Located in the Henley Hotel, where Underhill and Washington meet, the store was open as late as 10 P.M. and attracted black children from third grade up to young adults. If the kids couldn't afford the tab, they'd stand on the corner or by the window ledge, talking among themselves, looking inside the window, and sometimes calling greetings to those friends within who were too cheap to treat them. If they had a few pennies in their pockets, they'd buy a Baby Ruth or Powerhouse for two cents or ice cream at a nickel a scoop. Mrs. Drake, a goodhearted lady, never threw anyone out; everyone was welcome, whether wealthy or not.

The proprietress also thought highly enough of John to give him a job as soda jerk during his last two years in high school. Mrs. Coltrane had gone to work after J.R. died, hiring herself out as a domestic in white households, and then working in a posh position at the Country Club, thus keeping her household financially together. So John never really experienced the soul-grinding poverty that was the fate of many black children, in good times or bad.

Baseball became John's favorite sport; later, during intermissions while working club dates, he'd check out scores from whoever possessed a portable radio. In High Point, however, it was John and Franklin and James, staking out their diamond on any open and available space, from the cluttered fields behind the school to an unused patch of ground across the street from the Brower home.

There, they dug their Buster Brown shoes into the grass and scratched out a fresh chunk of ground for the bases. Out would come the tennis balls (considerably cheaper than regular baseballs) and the junior model bats that cost only a half dollar apiece. James always headed for the outfield, Franklin the pitcher's slot, and John, with no special preference for position, simply played whatever spot was left open for the sheer sport of it.

On occasion, they would temporarily break the subtle segregation barriers of High Point by sauntering into a white neighborhood, usually by invitation, to play against their hosts. It was never a scheduled attraction, never preplanned; the white kids might wander into the East Side and simply say, "Hey, you guys want to play some ball?"

While John preferred baseball, Franklin turned to movies for more enjoyment. And since it was not the norm for unchaperoned young blacks in those days to attend the films alone, Franklin often persuaded John to accompany him to either the Broadhurst on North Main, just around the corner from the all-white Methodist church, or the Paramount on Hamilton near the Furniture Exhibition Building. The latter was the classier of the two, reserved for Clark Gable and Bette Davis, Humphrey Bogart and Lauren Bacall, and was more for a Sunday family outing than a casual drop-in. It was also segregation-in-the-sky, for the balcony was black only, angling up at such a perilous 45 degrees that Brower believes "a whole generation before Cape Kennedy, we caught our own version of astrophobia just by climbing to the Paramount balcony."

It was at the Broadhurst where these two spent most of their Saturday afternoons, chewing gum, crunching popcorn, and cheering on Johnny Mack Brown and Buck Jones to gun down the bad guys, but don't kiss the girl, you might catch something. Then, for future shock, there was Flash Gordon, blond and beautiful, trying to turn his atomic blaster on the merciless and mad Dr. Ming, looking suspiciously like Chiang Kai-shek.

There was pool, too, a favorite pastime for young men everywhere. John's neighborhood had a few parlors, where each game went for a nickel. He and Franklin played eight-ball with each other; Franklin usually won.

At home, there was that imaginative medium, later supplanted by television—radio.

Once in a while Jimmy Lunceford or Duke Ellington would sneak through the airwaves, basic black rhythm and blues causing some involuntary foot tapping, hip shaking, and "let's boogie" smiles. But Louis Armstrong, more acceptable to white advertising agency executives, was the black artist heard most frequently in High Point. Most of the music black people listened to, as one might expect, was played by white musicians.

Still, when Charlie Barnet's Ellington-influenced crew came blasting out with "Cherokee," that was all right. Another Charlie —Charlie "Bird" Parker—would follow a dozen years later with his own mind-shattering version, and American music would never be the same again.

Nor would black culture; or John Coltrane.

> All of the Negro children in High Point grew up under the strictest discipline. Our parents really watched out for us. We didn't have much chance to get into trouble with our parents and grandparents and great-grandparents always around.
>
> FLOYD PHIFER, JR.

John Coltrane sits quietly in the back row of the high school auditorium, dressed neatly and listening attentively to the chorus. On his right, Mrs. Coltrane; on his left, Cousin Mary. He is still a grammar school student, but his family often brought him to hear the chorus, so smartly dressed in their dark suits, so clear-voiced in their outpouring of song. It was always a treat for him. Though he had not yet dreamed that music would become—and obsessively so—his life and life's work, he still felt an instinctive bond between these vocalists and himself. He had once tried to become one of them, but his voice was too hesitant, too off pitch to join their group. No; to vocal music he would remain a spectator, but not a passive one. He would listen and learn this great vocal music, especially the spirituals; later, he'd recreate some of these fluid melodic lines on his instrument, making his horn sing as intensely and exquisitely as any William Warfield or Paul Robeson.

John is especially quiet, especially attentive now. His great luminous eyes are absorbing the visual and aural magnificence, his coffee-brown skin tingling and the hairs rising on the back of his neck. He is becoming an integral part of the crescendo and diminuendo, the rich and complex counterpoint, the lean harmonies and flowing melodic lines of his favorite song. It is the bass part, striking deep within him, the notes seeping into the soles of his shoes, always touching his soul so much.

The composer: J. S. Bach.

The song: "Jesu, Joy of Man's Desiring."

On Sunday mornings, John Coltrane was an active communicant in that beautiful blend of music and religion so typical of southern churches. He worshiped at the St. Stephen Metropolitan African Methodist Episcopal Zion Church, where the services usually included the following:

Order of Worship: Prelude, Congregation Seated and Bowed in Meditation.
Processional: Hymn #1, Call to Worship: The Lord Is in His Holy Temple: Let All the Earth Keep Silence Before Him. Amen.
Invocation, with Choral Response: Hymn #31, Responsive.
Reading: First Reading, 591, Law of Christ.
Gloria Patria: Lesson from Holy Scriptures.
Pastoral Prayer with Choral Response.
Anthem: The Heavens Are Telling.
The Affirmation of Faith, with Choral Response #597.
The Ministry of Kindness, Choral Response #606.
Special Music: Ain't Got Time to Die.
Offering and Prayer of Consecration.
Acknowledgments and Announcements.
Inspirational Selection: Hymn #212.
Sermon.
Invitation to Christian Discipleship.
Benediction: Congregation Seated and Bowed Prayerfully.
Postlude: Congregation Remains Seated.

John and I played together in Reverend Steele's Community Band. We both played alto horn, and we sat next to each other. Reverend Steele was our scoutmaster, and when he formed his band he tried to get all the scouts in it first.

JAMES KINZER

I was sitting right by John, playing alto horn, when Reverend Steele switched him to clarinet. I guess he got some extra clarinets and only wanted the best musicians in the band to play them. Of course John got first crack at the clarinet, and he seemed to like it. He bought some sheet music written for clarinet, a popular song called "A Dream of Two Blue Orchids." A few weeks later, he was playing it note for note. It was an Artie Shaw arrangement and featured Shaw on clarinet. You could sure tell where John was coming from whenever he played that piece.

JOHN INGRAM

At St. Stephen's church, Sunday morning and Tuesday evening had something in common, from the spiritual to the secular. In the basement that was utilized for Sunday school, many of the same participants would be gathered there each Tuesday, this time for musical education, dispensed by Rev. Warren Steele.

It was band rehearsal for the Community Band.

Reverend Steele was a tall, shambling man who truly believed that idle hands were if not the devil's workshop then at least a cause for concern if both the individual and his peer group were not receiving blessed benefit from a community or cultural activity designed for both moral and mental uplift. He was also a musician himself, a clarinetist, who rather singlehandedly decided that what the black community of High Point most needed at that moment, with the ominous vibrations of World War II rapidly approaching, was some music of character and quality. The opportunity was there for his charges, the outstanding young men comprising his Boy Scout troop, to get themselves involved.

The reverend was not without influence on the East Side; politicians and preachers are, or were then, two of the professions most respected by black people and whose leaders usually received plenty of attention. So he got his troopers out knocking on doors as if for a paper drive, imploring the parents that a community band was badly needed. Reverend Steele also delivered a similar message in several of his sermons. In addition, he conducted some after-hours bargaining with local businessmen, and thus managed to obtain about a dozen used but still serviceable instruments, the majority being alto horns and clarinets, with a few euphoniums, trumpets, and one lowly bassoon thrown in to balance out the band.

Reverend Steele taught the musicians-to-be as a group, not individually. But he had practice books for each instrument, and could show his students the proper fingerings to start with.

John Coltrane, as previously noted, did not claim the first clarinet chair at the beginning. Some pressing personal business at home caused him to miss the first rehearsal, with the result that only an unclaimed alto horn was left by the time he showed up. But the lessons were free, and since so many of his friends were already signed up, John decided to take the alto horn and see what he could do.

At that moment, he was only mildly inclined toward music and, at thirteen, was hardly of a mind or maturity to choose a lifetime career, with or without the influence of the Community Band. The making of music was just something of casual interest to him, a pleasant community pastime.

Reverend Steele, by the way, didn't like jazz.

He didn't like classical music, either; what he had in mind was of a more "respectable" nature yet not too complex for his young students, either. Basic band music, such as Sousa marches; and to popularize things more, some familiar spirituals, straight from the church songbooks.

One day, a clarinetist didn't show, due to sickness, and John asked the reverend if he could "just hold it for a while; it's such a nice-looking horn."

Reverend Steele stood, studying the boy. Their eyes met; John's bright and eager gaze began to work its burgeoning magic on

Reverend Steele's thoughts. He had noticed that John was often the first to arrive and the last to leave band practice. And, his ears informed him that John was also one of the best, if not *the* best, budding musician in the band.

What harm could happen if he let the lad see what he could say on clarinet? He handed over the horn.

John had not been listening to Artie Shaw and Woody Herman for nothing. (Later, Herman would credit Coltrane with influencing him toward trying soprano saxophone, after which he would claim that the soprano was his favorite instrument.) Nor had he been unobservant of the way Floyd Phifer and others were building up their embouchure, adjusting the grip of their teeth and lips to the demands of a reed mouthpiece. John's workouts on alto horn had toughened his lips and powered his lungs; he was ready.

He took the clarinet in his hands, his fingers stroking the wood surface, his fingertips pressing against the metal rings. He placed the mouthpiece half an inch inside, cradling the lower lip over the teeth as he had watched the others do, bringing down the top row of teeth in direct contact with the metal mouthpiece. He didn't hold the horn at the popular 45° angle, however; instead, as if shyly experimenting, he pointed it toward the floor, looking down, and brought a great gust of air up from his diaphragm through his lungs and throat, culminating in a surging release from mouth to mouthpiece, filling the clarinet's two-and-one-half-foot length with air to spare.

And music charged the air.

Just a few brief notes, deep and woodsy in the lower register, fingered themselves through the outcurved bell. Nothing special. Yet, most of the children swiveled their heads toward him. As for Reverend Steele, he had never taken his eyes away from John.

"Can you play that again, John?"

"Well . . . I don't know. . . . I don't really know what I played. . . ."

"Then play anything you like. Just finger the keys, please. I want to hear that sound again."

John did; and Reverend Steele heard.

"Hm," he said.

This time, the boy had altered his attack, had plucked some

Shavian riffs from the upper register; he took care however, with his amateur status on the instrument, to avoid offending the Reverend by any display of popular song style.

"You get a fine tone on clarinet, son."

"Thank you."

"Have you been learning on the side? Watching somebody special playing?"

"Well . . . maybe watching you teach the other clarinet players, Reverend Steele."

The reverend nodded, saying no more, and dismissed the band minutes later.

The next Tuesday evening, the clarinet section was increased by one. Reverend Steele had just "happened to find another clarinet lying around" and a new face was holding down John's former alto horn position, also due to the leader just happening to find another young fellow around who looked as if he should be playing alto horn.

So it was John Coltrane, clarinetist.

John was very much the quiet type, but very creative. We'd come over to his house and have jam sessions in the basement, just us kids fooling around. But John was not only practicing and running scales, he'd also learned several popular tunes and he could play them, note for note. He played a version of "Margie" that I swear was just as fine as Jimmy Lunceford's.

John Ingram

The success of Reverend Steele's Community Band encouraged us to put together a band at William Penn High School. We worked with the PTA in raising money to purchase our instruments. We held socials and teas and rummage sales, and we earned enough money to buy six clarinets. One boy brought his own set of drums, and a few had trumpets, so that's really how we started. The instruments were the property of the school, and that's where they were kept when not in use. Later, the school system purchased some more and rented them out on a fee basis. They were new instruments, but for students, not high-priced professional models.

SAMUEL BURFORD

Samuel Burford was the principal of William Penn High School from 1933 until 1968, when the school was closed and demolished because of urban renewal.

A lean, athletic man of medium build, a dapper dresser and an affable negotiator of personal problems between the students and himself, he was brought to High Point from Lynchburg, Virginia. It was his custom to greet all the students upon arrival at 8:30 A.M. and departure at 3:30 P.M. With 350 students, that's really hustling, and such a personal touch would assist him in becoming a two-term member of the High Point City Council forty years later.

He does not recall John Coltrane as being a particularly distinguished student in high school; in fact, John's grades dropped to a "C" average and stayed there during his time at William Penn. Why, no one seems to know. Perhaps music was too much on his mind, or possibly he had already given up the idea of a college career. For whatever reasons, that was the way things were for him in high school.

The school, originally founded by Quaker financial contributions in 1898, was a two-story brick building located on East Washington Drive. A few additional quickly constructed wooden structures gave it the appearance of a college campus, and its sixteen teachers rarely had a class of more than twenty-five students. Among its facilities were a basketball court and a stage convertible into a gymnasium; not among its facilities were an extensive library or an indoor swimming pool, which the white school had.

And John, like almost every other student, just put in his time there.

He would talk, though; quiet and reserved, self-contained and sometimes withdrawn, he conversed with John Ingram, nicknamed Red, about music, Snookie about movies, Poche about baseball . . . and a few more with whom he might on occasion seek out to share a few pleasant moments.

He was now living with relatives. His mother had moved to Atlantic City, New Jersey, since opportunities for earning income during the wartime 1940s were better up north than down south. One of his grandmothers and a few of her family were residing in the Coltrane home. Since the death of J.R., John had been closest to his mother; he had shared more of his young adult secrets with her than anyone else, including Mary. He was, in a way, a loner; yet he was not lonely, nor had he ever minded being by himself. It was just that he was used to being part of an extended family structure, and now that situation was somewhat fragmented, indeed gradually dissolving under the double strains of death and distance.

He owned some choice clothes, purchased with his savings from the soda-jerk job. Smooth, single-breasted suits with wide lapels and cuffs; soft, patterned shirts; bright ties and black shoes. He often attended Friday night parties at his friends' homes; there, aged bourbon and underaged girls were in attendance, and he was sampling a bit of both.

For John could get the girls when he wanted to. His own growing mystique, that of the isolated yet creative loner, was to his high school crowd what Miles Davis would be to music/sensation seekers a dozen years later.

John's friend Franklin had eyes for one girl in particular, but John was the one who scored. Her name was Dorothea Nelson; her cute figure and upturned nose were among her most attractive assets. The three of them shared most classes; Franklin winked at her, but John whistled phrases to her from his clarinet. She chose John, and he went with her for nearly a year.

She left school, though, in her senior year, passing a special Civil Service test that qualified her to hold down a $25-per-week clerking position at the War Department in Washington, D.C.

Thus ended John Coltrane's first affair.

A tall, aristocratic lady with music in her soul and a teaching certificate came from Durham to High Point in the Fall of 1938 to teach music in the black secondary schools. The Superintendent of Schools, Charles Carroll, had expressed a desire to offer the gift of musical training to all who might never have otherwise had the chance. The lady, Grayce Yokley, who was primarily a piano and theory teacher, soon found it necessary to return to Michigan State University to learn the fundamentals of other instruments, for many students wanted horns, and few exclusively the piano.

When she returned in September 1942, John Coltrane was a high school senior and a well-established member of the Community Band. It seemed only logical and proper that he was one of the first students she brought into the William Penn High School Band. That was an additional assignment for Miss Yokley, to get a high school musical group going; and in that newly formed ensemble the first clarinet chair was occupied by Alice Blair Coltrane's only son.

Twice each week, on Tuesday and Thursday, the band rehearsed in the high school auditorium. Their charts were not much different from the marching music that had filled their stands in Reverend Steele's Community Band. The primary difference was that by now most of the musicians, especially those recruited directly from the Community Band, could sight read and blow their horns like paraprofessionals, after the past few years of constant rehearsal and occasional performances.

The new orchestra was integrated, too; at least, sexually speaking. For Grayce Yokley brought girls into the band, such as Maxine Bostic, who sat next to John in the clarinet section. Ironically, John would later occupy the tenor chair next to altoist Earl Bostic—no relation—in his band, while Maxine's brother Rufus later became one of the first black disc jockeys in the South, using Earl Bostic's theme song, "That's a Groovy Thing," as his opener. He'd also play Coltrane records, too, whenever he could get them.

During his final year in high school, John Coltrane got involved with an alto saxophone.

This is not unusual; clarinet students often progress to alto or tenor saxophone. But in this case, John had no extra money to purchase one; his clarinet belonged to the school, not to himself. He had been listening to Willie Smith of the Lunceford band and naturally Johnny Hodges with Duke Ellington, the latter's version of "Warm Valley" a showcase for Hodges' velvety vibrato.

A fellow named Haygood, who owned a restaurant on Perry Street, also had an alto that he noodled on back in the kitchen when business was slow. John had heard him running scales a few times and, intrigued by the wailing vocal qualities of the horn that he was finally hearing for real and not on record, persuaded Haygood to let him borrow it on occasion for practice at home.

Without Haygood, his complicity and co-operation, there might never have been a John Coltrane, saxophonist. Without Hodges, also, for his influence was a hundred times more direct, more visceral, on John's musical maturity.

After a few workshop sessions at home, John brought Haygood's alto saxophone to band practice, proudly demonstrating to Miss Yokley his new proficiency on another horn. She approved; even to the extent of allowing him to play an unaccompanied solo on a currently popular song, as if he were performing for a class exercise. He had the entire 32-bar tune down, not just the saxophone solo, and his Hodges-influence phrasing earned him more than a scattering of applause when he concluded his version of "Tuxedo Junction."

He was known now as *the* musician in the band. Students sought him out at school, asking musical advice. Adults sometimes stopped him in the street to offer congratulations. Girls came up to him, giggling and asking for his autograph; he signed reluctantly, hoping they would pass over his squiggly, almost illegible penmanship.

And Floyd Phifer, his fellow clarinetist, seeing himself eclipsed, sometimes said, "Hey, Coltrane, you really think you're the best, don't you?"

John shrugged, looking away shyly.

He did not know then, but would learn much later, that Phifer, if not particularly prophetic, was still basically correct in his comments.

As Betty Leach recalls, the class of '43 did have a junior-senior prom but not as a dress-up affair. Not during wartime. Those who attended came in street clothes; nothing fancy or pretentious for anyone. John was there but not as a jitterbugger; he was playing in the dance band formed for this special occasion, using both clarinet and alto.

He was only sixteen; Franklin Brower and James Kinzer were both a year older, but all three graduated together.

They left High Point together, too, on June 11, 1943, with Philadelphia as their destination. Two of Brower's brothers, George and Governor, lived there, and they had passed the word back to Franklin that Philadelphia had plenty of jobs paying good money. Since the draft wouldn't hit them until they'd turned eighteen, there was sufficient time to put aside some savings before Uncle Sam could snatch them away.

So away they went, traveling by train.

> That sorrow which obsessed me during my youth was not caused by lack of amusement, because I could have had it; neither from lack of friends, because I could have found them. That sorrow was caused by an inward ailment which made me love solitude. It killed in me the inclination for games and amusement.
>
> KAHLIL GIBRAN

> The City of Brotherly Love (Philadelphia Motto)

> Philadelphia is as segregated as a typical southern city. There are two black ghettos, north and south. South Street is the dividing line, and anything below that was strictly black all the way to Snyder Avenue, about five miles. On the North Side, the ghetto stretched from Vine Street all the way up to Germantown. We musicians were about the only ones to break the barriers, because we could go to the white neighborhoods as entertainers. I don't recall any race riots when I lived there, but the same as down south it was well understood that we stayed in our own territory and they kept to theirs. But you know, such extreme racial separation, in some weird way, helps us black people to stick together and concentrate more on our own culture. In Philadelphia, most of us hung out with music, day and night.
>
> BOBBY TIMMONS

The blues.

This is where black music begins in America today; where it comes from, its genesis and the source of its creativity.

The traditional twelve-bar blues; three lines of four bars each, the first line repeated as the second, and the third line containing a terminal rhyme that completes the stanza. In poetic terms, it is iambic pentameter; in the raw reality of its thematic material, women and work are what the blues is all about.

Bent notes, glisses, quavers . . . anything to express the most basic emotions. Flatted third and seventh notes of the diatonic scale; later, bop would flat the fifth, forming a basic triad of blue notes.

Mostly in a minor key, but not always. Strike a minor note in a major context, or the major and minor together, it's still the blues. There are eight-bar and sixteen-bar blues, too; even a ten-measure blues with a four-bar intro, such as Miles Davis' "Blue in Green."

Urban blues; that's mostly what we hear today, in technical terms. Blues with the stuff of life ripped from those shimmering, sputtering notes, delineating real experiences more than beautiful dreams. Before that, classic blues; more folklore than fact, more oriented toward sheer entertainment, more rural and "down home" in inflection. Very popular as "race" music, among whites as well as blacks. As was Victoria Spivey, for example; her first record in 1926, "Black Snake Blues," sold more than 150,000 copies that year alone.

If not sung, the blues were played primarily on guitar, a predominately African instrument, its American version being the banjo. And going back to New Orleans, where jazz was synthesized from European quadrilles and African dances, black people got hold of the white man's brass, reed, and string instruments and adapted them to their own musical heritage. This is not surprising; African musicians were using their own instruments in those three categories many centuries before, crafted from their own indigenous materials.

The blues, of course, began in slavery.

The work song was, in a way, an American calypso. The white plantation owners applauded anything that got the slaves working and kept them at it for ten or twelve hours each day. And the blacks, lifting their voices in that most basic call-and-response pattern that was so much their heritage, usually slipped in some "signifying" statements as an acceptable outlet for their own "blues."

Shouts and field hollers, like laments, almost lullabies, if sung softly enough, if sometimes crooned to a child in its crib.

Then there were spirituals.

The only justification for slavery, from a religious viewpoint, was that the lesser-endowed culturally could be converted to Christianity. Yet the all-black churches were the only places in America where the slaves could share a few moments free from white domination. Church took their minds away, if only temporarily, from their sad physical situation, in effect offering them an eventual release from bondage if only after death.

Later black people created rhythm-and-blues, a more popular and dance-inclined music that was, in the true definition of the word, vulgar: of, by, and for the great masses of people. Back beats, triplet figures, honking and screaming horn men; especially saxophone players, "screaming" the blues with their instruments not their voices. And who would "adopt" their stuff but some English rock groups—the Beatles, Rolling Stones, Moody Blues, et al—and then make lucrative American tours, bringing their whitewashed version of black music back to its country of origin, to be worshiped wildly by mostly whites who didn't really know where it all came from, but viscerally understood that it was vaguely evil, strongly suggestive, sexy as all hell and "great to dance to."

The source of these sounds remains Africa.

Where the making of music is not necessarily an aesthetic or even a commercial endeavor but a built-in part of being born, growing up, living and dying. There, all memorable events are celebrated in song: the birth of a baby, a female puberty rite, the purchase of a mate, an abundant harvest. And on a note of political realism probably unknown anywhere else, the Banun of Cameroon have a song to commemorate an occasion when a government minister was hanged.

African musical concepts bear little relationship to formalistic European harmonic theory. They are more like Indian music; pentatonic scales (sometimes diatonic, too), rich melodic invention, intervals smaller than semitones (quarter tones and less predominate), and polyrhythmic percussion improvisations that call for a master drummer who must learn dozens of difficult rhythms before being allowed to "lead" the band.

But instruments are primarily for accompaniment; it is the voice that counts most in African music, not so much the solo but the choir, as befits a communally oriented culture. The choir sings by using parallel melodic lines a third, fourth, fifth, or octave above or below the basic line. They sometimes sing "around" the beat, displacing accents to set up cross rhythms provided by the drummers, who are often playing in time signatures of three against four and even more complex breakdowns of the basic meters.

African music is like its languages, structured for the human voice. The choir leader—or leaders; sometimes there are two or three—"talks" to the chorus, not so much concerned with scales or keys but with the sound and feeling of the words and how they match up with the melodic lines. He leads; they follow, in an A and B form, or call-and-response pattern familiar to anyone who has ever listened to the Basie band even on a bad night. It is the same relationship as is found in many spirituals. For example, a study by M. Kolinski showed that thirty-six spirituals were identical with West African songs, and the opening rhythms of all but two were parallel with the still-sung music of Ghana and Dahomey.

Behind the singers, the master drummer kicks the rhythm, setting up a time-line that provides a frame of reference for the other musicians. From this, the other musicians can determine their mutual relationship. Africans are taught from childhood to acquire this inherent metronomic sense, and to attend the Ballet Africains on one of its many U.S. tours is to see the primal relationship between song and dance in African culture.

The drummers "talk" to the people, as well as supply the basic beat for the singers and dancers. African percussion is pitched to approximate the sound of the human voice and to harmonize with the inflections of language. If you have seen the Nigerian musician Olatunji, then you know the sound of the talking drum and the way in which a crooked stick, like a shepherd's staff, is used to rattle off intricate rhythms in a highly "vocal" style. There are other kinds of talking drums, too, especially those with a "male" voice (bass) on one drumhead and a "female" (treble) on the other.

Technically speaking, these are the four categories of African instrumentation:

Idiophones: rattling bodies—xylophones, bells, drums.

Membranophones: vibrating membranes—trumpets, drums.
Aerophones: vibrating air columns—flutes, oboes.
Chordophones: vibrating strings—guitars, violins.

These are directly related to European music as percussion, brass, woodwinds, and strings, respectively.

But Africans have some subtleties that we Westerners don't often attempt. For example: using the body itself as a percussion instrument by slapping the chest, knocking on the headbone, and "clicking" the voice, the latter made famous by Miriam Makeba of the Xosa tribe in South Africa.

And so the blues came from Africa to America, where the blues were still colored black.

> Make your Negroes pleasant and cheerful, make them dance to the beat of the drum.
>
> LONDON SLAVE MERCHANT

John Coltrane, Franklin Brower, and James Kinzer all had birthdays within thirty days of each other. However, since John was one year younger, it was his buddies who would become eighteen that following fall of 1943 and thus be subject to instant military induction.

There was nothing in High Point for any of them, so the move to Philadelphia had been made. Upon arrival, Franklin found a room in the same house as his brother George. That was previously arranged, but left John and James without a place. The solution: Franklin got in touch with his aunt, Mae Hillman, who lived on North Twelfth Street, and she told him there was an apartment available on the third floor of her four-story building. John and James took it and moved right in.

Brower got a job as a civilian working with the U. S. Signal Corps office, Coltrane became a laborer in a sugar-refining factory, and Kinzer went into the grocery business as a clerk. None of these positions were anything special. But all three were earning income and marking time, waiting for World War II to end so that they could decide their futures for themselves.

In November 1943 James was called for induction, accepted, and shipped out. Franklin was called too, but not taken due to a hyperthyroid condition he was unaware of, for it had never caused him any pain. He certainly didn't protest the decision. Since he'd received a scholarship from William Penn, he enrolled at Temple University in Philadelphia, graduating in 1947 with a degree in journalism. He then became a reporter for the Philadelphia *Afro-American* newspaper; a few years later, he would write the first article on John Coltrane as a musician.

For the moment, though, Franklin and John stayed in Philadelphia, Brower studying, Coltrane working. Cousin Mary showed up in June 1944, after her high school graduation; since Kinzer was still in service, she moved in with John. Mrs. Coltrane, still employed in Atlantic City, stopped by to visit once or twice a month, and though she and her son were not to live together again for several more years, her presence, even when not physically in Philadelphia, was as palpably real as if she had been there baking him sweet potato pies or reminding him to read his Bible every night before he went to bed.

For John Coltrane's mother was, and would remain, the most commanding woman in his life. Judging by the frequent visits he would make to her when he was later living in New York, he would continue the closeness, the almost confessional nature of their relationship until the day he died.

> He was easily the best student in my class. I wrote out complex chord progressions and special exercises in chromatic scales, and he was one of the few who brought his homework back practically the next day and played it on sight. It was amazing the way he absorbed everything I gave him. He was always asking for more.
>
> MIKE GUERRA

A few months after Coltrane arrived in Philadelphia, he was accepted as a student at the Ornstein School of Music. One of the better musical institutions in the city, it was located on Nineteenth and Spruce streets. Its founder was Leo Ornstein, a pianist who had once studied under Paderewski.

John's mother had bought him a used alto saxophone as an early birthday present, and the horn was in sufficiently good shape for Mike Guerra to teach him saxophone technique at Ornstein. Guerra, a dapper man of five-four, with wavy black hair and expressive gesticulations, was fifty-six at the time and had more than twenty years of playing and teaching behind him. A converted clarinetist, he had started playing the alto and tenor saxophones in pit bands, backing musicals at the Schubert theaters in Philadelphia. His friends called him "The Reluctant Saxophonist," for it had required considerable persuasion to switch him to saxophone from his beloved clarinet. But saxophone sections had taken the place of clarinets, so if you were a woodwind player, it was simply a matter of switch or starve.

Coltrane studied with Guerra for about a year while continuing to work full-time in the sugar refinery. In that same class was Philadelphian Bill Barron, then getting his tenor sax technique together. Barron was as tall as his Carolina classmate, five-eleven, but more husky, with larger bone structure and a deep bass voice well qualified to read radio commercials (had he done so, he probably would have made more money but not had as much fun). From even a short distance away, he bore a startling resemblance to drummer Max Roach.

When they met, he said, "You're John Coltrane? From North Carolina?"

"Yes," John replied, puzzled.

"I toured the South with the Carolina Cottonpickers. Did you ever hear of them?"

He had not; they were a territory band based in Indianapolis, playing dance and club dates in the Midwest and the South. Bill had joined them in Philadelphia when a tenor chair became vacant. The band's style was blues-based, similar to that of Kansas City's Jay McShann's, the nest that Bird flew out of.

Coltrane, in his quiet but curiously persistent way, asked Barron about the band. He seemed especially interested in the band's book pertaining to tenor saxophone, as if he might have had a premonition that he would eventually take up the big horn himself.

They became friends; Bill stopped by John's apartment and John visited Bill at his parents' home. They'd talk mostly about music, discussing the different sounds of alto versus tenor sax, in particular that register where the ranges of the two horns intersect and overlap.

But their conversations were cut short, like John's with Kinzer, due to the intervention of the draft. In the summer of 1944, Bill Barron was taken into the Army.

> John used to sit in an overstuffed chair in our living room with one leg dangling over the arm and his alto resting on the cushion. I'd play some piano chords and he'd take right off. Then we'd switch and John would play piano. He must have picked up piano by himself. Even then, I could tell that he knew harmony, and knew it well.
>
> BENNY GOLSON

> The saxophone is an instrument distinct in itself and must be taught as such, with as high a degree of seriousness as any other concert instrument.
>
> FRED HEMKE

Antoine Joseph (Adolphe) Sax was born in Dinant, Belgium, on November 6, 1814, just seven months after Napoleon's abdication. His father, Charles Joseph, was an instrument maker who spent most of his adult life trying to perfect the bass clarinet. Adolphe followed his father into the trade, doing his bit for the bass clarinet as well. Adolphe Sax thus refined that particular instrument for classical and band music; Eric Dolphy, a close companion of Coltrane's, would accomplish the same for jazz 150 years after Sax's birth.

Sax the younger graduated from the Brussels Conservatory, majoring in clarinet and flute, with clarinet remaining his favorite instrument throughout his life. Supposedly, he had no thought of immortalizing his name by inventing a new brand of horn, merely being interested in improving the tonal qualities of the clarinet. He moved to Paris in 1842, where his experimentation brought about two horn families that didn't last very long: saxhorn, replaced by the bugle, and saxo-tromba, an impractical upright horn that simply couldn't hold its own with marching bands.

Undiscouraged, he kept tinkering and thinking until he invented the saxophone, which he patented on June 22, 1846. He then secured a monopoly on his instrument; but apparently in common with many other artists and craftsmen he was better at non-business affairs, for he went bankrupt in 1852. However, he soon bounced back, exhibiting at the Paris Industrial Exhibition of 1855 and winning a Gold Medal. When the instrument pitch was reformed in 1859, every band in France had to buy new wind instruments. They bought saxophones, making Adolphe Sax a musical monopolist.

Until he failed for the second time and was financially reduced to the point of having to sell his complete collection of musical instruments at auction in December 1877. He died in poverty on February 4, 1894, and no saxophones were played at his funeral.

Yet Sax created not one instrument but an entire family of saxophones that were structured in relation to the range of the human voice. Most people who know of the saxophone have probably been exposed to either alto or tenor, or both; and others, if in the vicinity of a big band, have seen and heard the baritone. With the contemporary interest in the soprano saxophone, thanks to John Coltrane and Sidney Bechet before him, those four horns are now fairly familiar. There is also a bass sax, a cumbersome monster that such bandleaders as Stan Kenton and the late Johnny Richards have used in their reed sections to bring them into a tuba-level range.

However, there are really seven different saxophones, all transposing instruments; if you can play one, you can play them all. The alto and baritone are pitched in E♭, with tenor and soprano as B♭ instruments, as also is the bass sax. But there are still two more members of the saxophone family, though rarely used except for special effects; the E♭ sopranino and the B♭ contrabass, the latter requiring not only an excellent embouchure but weightlifter muscles just to hoist it into place.

All saxophones come equipped with six key buttons and one octave key, with the range of the entire family reading B♭ to F, bottom to top. Each overblows an octave, enabling the saxophone to reproduce a natural scale an octave and a fifth higher. Its component parts break down into bell, mouthpiece, ligature, and reed, plus a neck strap for every one except the soprano.

Since 1920, the approximate date of its legitimate musical usage in America, the saxophone has been redesigned four times, primarily to improve its pitch. According to Selmer, the last change took place in 1954 when the first Model Mark VI was introduced—the horn John Coltrane was probably playing when he joined Miles Davis the following year.

As musical instruments go, the saxophone is comparatively young, little more than a century old. The earliest recorded knowledge of the instrument's presence in America was in the Will Marion Cook Orchestra of 1905. It wasn't really heard from until after World War I, and then mainly in a vaudeville context. For example, there were the Six Brown Brothers, a saxophone sextet who came on stage in clown suits and introduced such memorable compositions as "Chasin' the Chickens" and "That Moaning Saxophone Rag." A fellow named Rudy Wiedoeft played C-melody sax, an easy-operating horn with a range between alto and tenor, around 1919, and was billed as the "Kreisler of the Saxophone." It would take Coleman Hawkins until 1939, with his monumental recording of "Body and Soul," to make the saxophone a solo instrument in its own right, replacing the trumpet as the reigning horn in jazz and pop music.

As for classical music, the great colorist Hector Berlioz used the instrument in his *Hymne Sacre,* first performed in 1844 but now lost. Probably the best-known classical saxophone solo is the one Maurice Ravel introduced for soprano in the score of his *Bolero.* There is also Jacques Ibert's *Concertino da Camera for Alto Saxophone and Eleven Instruments.* And Sergei Prokofiev's *Lieutenant Kije* spotlighted such a whining, wheezing overlegitimized tone quality from the tenor solo that it was almost enough to drive Freddie Martin out of the music business.

A scholarly tome entitled *Compositions for Saxophone* lists more than 2,000 other saxophone scores, mostly of a classical or marching band nature, but also including the works of some surprisingly contemporary composers not normally associated with jazz. Such as Elliot Carter's *Prelude, Fanfare and Polka;* the well-known *The Creation of the World,* by Darius Milhaud; Heitor Villa-Lobos and his *Quartet;* and Alan Hovhaness' *After Water* and *The World Beneath the Sea.* Of the work of more jazz-oriented composers, these names stand out: David Amram's *Trio;* the *Exploration* of Teo Macero; and Michel Legrand and his *Porcelain Saxophone.*

That, in capsule form, is the story of the saxophone, as the story of John Coltrane continues, the two very much connected with each other.

Sonny Rollins would practice on the bridge, I'd go in the park, but Coltrane would do it in his room.

HANK MOBLEY

At night, after work, in 1943, John Coltrane sits in his apartment in Philadelphia.

He is alone in the bedroom, for it is practice time. He has eaten, he is relaxed, and ready to begin the methodical preparation for the creation of some notes, perhaps a few chords, that will be played as precisely as notated in the saxophone exercise book.

First, the reed.

He is using a ※2½ Rico, a fine beginner's reed. The cane it is made from is a deep yellow color, with a dark heart in the middle. He takes this reed and trims just the slightest shavings from a point about one-third from the edge, holding the reed up to the light afterward, to make sure that he has trimmed it evenly.

Then he fastens it to the ligature, turning the twin screws so that the reed is firmly held against the mouthpiece but not so tightly as to pinch or break it. The mouthpiece is twisted into the neck of his horn, which is slipped into the bell at a 90° angle and then affixed in place, making the saxophone whole again.

His mouthpiece is also for new players, ※4 requiring a minimum of blowing power so that his lungs will not be strained too early. Later, he will progress to a more open mouthpiece and a harder reed. But what he is using now will suffice for his break-in period.

He puts the horn aside and picks up his exercise book. He chooses a simple scalar exercise, one from which he can develop his fluency, practicing each note in succession until it sounds exactly right. He places the book on top of his dresser, using a paperweight to hold it open at the proper page.

Next, he slips on his neck strap. Now, the fondly polished and carefully cleaned alto saxophone is about to become an extension of his thoughts, personality, feelings, dreams. He walks over to the dresser, the horn angled slightly to his right side but otherwise held parallel to his lean, supple body. His right thumb is hooked into the thumb rest, and his fingers caress the buttons.

All is in readiness, everything is in place.

He starts to breathe.

As he feels the air flowing from his diaphragm, his lower lips and upper teeth bite down on the mouthpiece. His embouchure is similar to that for clarinet, though not quite as tight but requiring more power to get that much larger column of air inside the alto. He needs that extra thrust to make the reed vibrate and cause the shimmering legato sound that he so admires in Johnny Hodges' playing to come forth from his horn.

The notes pour out.

He can hear them as he plays. His fingers are pressing the buttons properly, though one or two of them sometimes stick. But that cannot be helped with a secondhand horn. He knows his fingers are in fine shape, but he feels strangely about the pressure in his mouth, the grip like a wrench clasped around a pipe that his mouth must make on the mouthpiece to keep the sounds coming out beautiful and true.

He squeaks.

Sighing, he releases the saxophone from his grip and checks the reed. It looks all right, but one never knows.

Removing the horn from its strap, he disassembles the mouthpiece again and goes to work with the reed cutter. Perhaps that will do it for now. This is the third reed he's tried this week; they don't last long, which is why he buys them by the box.

Again, the horn is together, locked into his mouth and gripped by his hands.

His ears tell him, as the notes leave the saxophone and rise and fall in the lonely confines of his room, that his sound is getting better, getting closer to the liquid luminosity of his idol.

Practice makes perfect, so they say.

But John Coltrane does not really care what *they* say.

All he knows is that he has never experienced such a total involvement, such a feeling of freedom, from anything else he has ever done in his still-short life that is now happening to him when he puts his saxophone in his mouth and holds it like a woman in his hands.

Even if the music he is creating is, so far, for his ears only.

In 1945, John Coltrane was called into the U. S. Navy, a service perhaps managed more by logic than perversity, for when they discovered that he was an aspiring musician they assigned him to the Navy band.

He was shipped to Hawaii, where he played clarinet in the marching and dance bands and still practiced saxophone on the side. When he was released in June 1946, he'd logged thousands of hours on clarinet, an instrument he still liked but did not love as much as the stronger-sounding saxophone.

And it was saxophone he would again be playing after he returned to Philadelphia and started his first musical employment (his union card would come later; those matters usually took time) with a cocktail combo, consisting of organ, drums . . . and saxophone.

I really got to know John when he came to Wildwood, New Jersey, in the summer. It's a seaside resort where I had a summer gig. On weekends, John and a bunch of young Philadelphia musicians would bring Charlie Parker records with them, discuss the music with myself and the other working musicians there, then sit in with us after hours.

BILL BARRON

I knew an alto player in high school named Cunningham—we always called ourselves by our last names, it's an old custom with black people—who told me, "There's a new guy in town, name of John Coltrane. He plays alto, and you should check him out because he's something else." I play tenor, so I said I would, then forgot about it until Cunningham brought Coltrane over to my house one day. John had his alto, and he played with a fat, exquisite sound that I'd never heard before. It was even bigger and broader than Johnny Hodges'. He played "On the Sunny Side of the Street," a tune Hodges played quite often. He played it so beautifully that the next time he came back, my mother asked him to play the same song again.

BENNY GOLSON

John Coltrane had never heard much real black music until he moved to Philadelphia. After he returned from his Navy hitch, to live again in the heart of the North Side ghetto, he was hearing and playing more rhythm-and-blues than anything else.

The war was over; it was time to cash in the Savings Bonds and live a little, if not a lot. Charlie Parker and Dizzy Gillespie were making the word "bop" a black national anthem, but most whites —and probably many blacks as well—were still thinking about jazz for dancing first and listening to later. To them, that meant the raw, honking, gutsy sound of R&B; and if you were to become a superior musician, you had to play with others to learn the music as well as to practice by yourself. Thus, if the only sounds around that would provide you with room and board were those of rhythm-and-blues—especially if you were black—then that's what you'd be playing, period.

John worked with whomever and whenever he could. In the bands of King Kolax and Joe Webb. With organists the caliber of Shirley Scott and Jimmy Smith. Backing singers such as Big Maybelle, who liked his sound so much she always asked for him to back her up whenever she was in town.

He also resumed his studies with Mike Guerra at Ornstein.

James Kinzer was back from service, too. He returned to the apartment on Twelfth Street with John and became involved in a co-operative grocery store, a business he would later make his life's work. Franklin Brower was still at Temple, and he'd stop by on occasion to talk with his fellow High Pointers. Also, Bill Barron and Benny Golson were becoming close friends with Coltrane, the three of them playing just for pleasure, if not for income, whenever and wherever they could.

Their base of operations was a small club near John's apartment.

The neighborhood was studded with these corner bars, featuring three- or four-piece bands who played mostly for food money and primarily to work out their musical ideas in public and with their peers. They were listening to Jimmy Oliver, a tough-toned tenor man who was nicknamed "Little Bad Man" and with good reason; his fingering was almost as fast as a submachinegun on automatic fire, and John was thinking about increasing his ability to play fast.

He was still Coltrane, not yet Trane. But in Philly nicknames were more important than real names, so someone started calling John "The Swinging One" and Bill became "The Weird One." Benny was "The Professor" and looked like one, with his precise diction, pressed suits, dainty mustache, and glasses with two-tone frames.

Coltrane continued his faithful practicing. Once, Barron noticed John practicing silently, moving the keys but not blowing into the mouthpiece. As Bill explains, "This was something psychologists went to much trouble to discover, and John grasped it intuitively. It's working with kinetics, the muscle movements that are so much a part of learning how much finger and hand co-ordination you can develop."

One evening, Benny Golson took John Coltrane to hear Charlie Parker.

Well, not exactly; Benny and John really went to the Academy of Music on Broad and Locust to catch Dizzy Gillespie, whose music they were more familiar with than that of Bird, though the latter was then playing with Gillespie. They were sitting in the cheapest seats, in the next-to-the-last row in the top balcony, when, as Golson recalls, "This short, squat guy in a pin-stripe suit stepped on stage. The band took the break and he started playing alto while coming out of a crouch. John just sat there, taking it all in. All over the hall, people were standing up and shouting, clapping their hands and stamping their feet. Imagine being a saxophonist and never having heard this kind of music before."

After the show, the two young saxophonists went backstage to get Charlie Parker's autograph. There was a long line of signature seekers, and Benny joined in at once. But John waited in a corner, his eyes intently taking everything in, staring at Parker as if trying to absorb some of his saxophone knowledge by ESP.

Finally, Bird signed for the last in line, then looked around and caught sight of Coltrane, who raised his head to stare directly at the older man. Their eyes met for a brief instant; then John glanced down at the floor again and didn't say anything until Parker said, expansively, "Well, young man, you are not a chicken, so I'm not going to eat you, and you are not a saxophone, so I'm not going to play you. Exactly what is it you want?"

There was, of course, an implicit put-on in Bird's phrasing. Yet the essence of his little speech was that he was curious about this shy-seeming fellow sticking around this long and not saying anything, as if he was simply pleased to be in the presence of the master saxophonist and would be just as happy to stand around and say nothing as long as he could be near Bird.

Parker felt this and was touched; he put his arm around John's shoulder and said, "Do you play, my fine young fellow?"

Golson, who had been patiently waiting for his friend, took this moment to interject, "He plays alto"—pause—"and I think he plays it very well."

"And who might you be, his older brother?"

Benny knew enough of Bird's reputation to separate the serious from the flippant, so he told Bird exactly what they were there for.

At this, Parker gave out one of his throaty guffaws and said, "Well, the next time I visit Philadelphia I would like to hear you play." He glanced at his watch. "But I must go now; Dizzy is having me over for a barbecue." He chuckled. "As his guest, you understand, not the main course." Turning to Coltrane, he said, "And just what name do you go under, my man?"

At last, John spoke, and said, "John Coltrane."

Bird asked him to repeat it; then, to spell it. John did. Then Charlie Parker gave out another of his great guffaws and, as he was leaving, he looked back at Benny and John, winked at Coltrane, and said, "I like your name, my man. It reminds me of a quality brand of English muffins."

When it comes to getting summer
I get me such a pretty tan
You can hear those women holler
Where can I find that clean-headed man?

EDDIE "CLEANHEAD" VINSON

Eddie "Cleanhead" Vinson—called Mr. Clean decades before the detergent—comes from Houston, Texas. He played alto saxophone with Cootie Williams, among others, before taking his own band on the road in 1947, with John Coltrane sitting in the tenor chair.

A slick dresser and a suave gentleman, Cleanhead lost most of his hair at the tender age of twenty. "Too much conking," he told Malcolm X (then called Detroit Red, who henceforth let his own hair grow natural). Disliking both toupees and hats, Mr. Clean upstaged Yul Brynner by a generation and got his head shaved all the way.

His saxophone style is an intriguing blend of blues and bop, the latter directly attributed to the Charlie Parker influence. For in 1939, in Shreveport, Louisiana, while touring with the Milt Larkins band, Cleanhead first heard Bird, who was playing there with Jay McShann. At the usual after-hours jam session, Vinson was wiping out everyone in sight until, as he recalls, "This young kid walked on the stand with his alto in his mouth and started to blow the wildest things I ever heard in my life. He cut me good—he cut me up." Bird was then nineteen. Vinson continues, "I put my arm around that boy and told him, man, you're not gonna get out of my sight until you show me how you make your horn go like that."

Bird did just that; all night long, and all the next morning.

Some years later, in 1947, Vinson passed through Philadelphia to hire musicians for his new band. He was sounding much like Bird and searching for another saxophonist who could play like Parker, too. He caught Coltrane rehearsing at the musicians' union hall with Red Garland, a transplanted Texan from Dallas whose block-chord style was known for its thick, complex textures and unerring accompaniment. Vinson liked the Coltrane sound, but there was a problem, for his band had room for only one altoist and that was the man who ran it.

"Hey, would you like to play tenor with my band?" he asked John, who hesitated. Not that he disliked tenor; he was now listening to the light, legato phrasing of Lester Young with great interest. Still, he was an *alto* player, that was his horn. He hesitated some more, until Cleanhead said, "Look, Johnny, I'll buy you a tenor and you can jam on alto after hours, 'cause there's always places where you can do that. Now, what do you say?"

"Take it," said Red Garland, who had already been hired for the band. Then, informing Coltrane about his job as pianist for Vinson, Garland added, "If you take the gig, we can both travel with Cleanhead."

So John Coltrane signed on with Eddie Vinson.

The band toured cross-country, especially through the South and Southwest. There, the predominately black audiences, who could pick up the latest sounds by radio but didn't always have the opportunity to catch their musical heroes in person, would support live music such as that provided by Vinson's band with their patronage—and their pocketbooks.

John Coltrane's situation with the Vinson group was almost parallel with that of Charlie Parker's and the Earl Hines band just a few years before. Then, the only open chair was also for tenor, so Hines had bought one for Bird, who joined the band and played the big horn. As for John, though he didn't really like handling the extra weight and size of the tenor saxophone—it also required a larger column of air, and that meant more energy expended than was necessary for playing alto—he began to think more and more about the instrument after leaving the band. When back in Philadelphia, he started borrowing Golson's tenor and practicing with it, thus giving the big horn nearly equal time with his alto.

For now, though, he was still working with Cleanhead, who had developed an entertaining routine to keep their chops together and grab the audience's attention. Eddie would play a long, loping blues line on alto, with John filling in on tenor behind him; then they would exchange horns, each flipping his sax to the other and immediately duplicating what had just been played, only this time on the other's horn. Sometimes they'd break off in mid-phrase, one taking up where the other left off. They rarely muffed it, and it became an excellent exercise in co-ordination for both of them.

The band's basic book was essentially rhythm-and-blues, but a few Charlie Parker tunes were also featured and on occasion the musicians would slow down the tempo long enough to play a ballad. But no matter what the band was playing, Coltrane, when not sight-reading, watched his boss attentively, picking up whatever saxophone tips he could. Vinson was a superb technician with an agile style; he had a way of bending and sustaining notes that John really liked. Later, he would notice a similar technique with Miles after he joined the Davis band.

Cleanhead was learning, too, as he listened to Coltrane developing the initial stages of his advanced harmonic style. John was always taking notes and studying the arrangements, asking his employer why this particular chord resolved into another and what their interrelationships were. Eddie, a relaxed taskmaster, explained patiently; then John would sometimes startle him by moving into another chord progression entirely, but still sounding properly in tune.

They often played "Tune Up," a fast blues containing some quirky changes. It was a Vinson composition, and Coltrane became so entranced with the song that he later adapted it for his own quartet, altering the chord progression ever so slightly and calling his version "Countdown."

John liked the music and tolerated the traveling, though checking in and out of a different hotel and town each evening can get tiresome, if not lonesome, for almost anyone. This was especially true for John, who had never really been away from home before, except for his Navy service. And living in Philadelphia didn't really count, since two hometown buddies were also there. In addition, Cousin Mary was right in his apartment and his mother was visiting him regularly.

While on the road, he missed them all.

And he was lonely. So he ate candy bars and drank Cokes—but he drank more bourbon than anything else. He was smoking, too; cigarets had been with him since high school, and now he had a two-pack-a-day habit. He drank not only to relieve the tension of constant traveling but also to get himself high, to reach a greater and more sustained high than the music could provide. Of course, this is perverse; music, like any art, is the greatest high in itself, but John was young and still maturing, and would not learn such an essential truth until many more years of experience had taught him that most basic lesson of all.

His traveling life, then, was mostly music and talk. And, with the easy availability of liquor and ladies for the transient pleasure of the traveling musician, booze and sex.

Not to forget food; more precisely, pie.

There were, of course, many places in the South and Southwest where sweet potato pie could be procured, that is, if one had the time to check these places out. John usually didn't; but once, in a small town in Georgia, he lucked out from a fellow musician's tip and bought not one but three large pies. That afternoon, he devoured them in his room, by himself, one after the other. And he paid for his greediness with pain, not in the stomach but in the mouth.

He got a toothache.

His teeth had always given him trouble. It was a case of poor root canals and too many sweets, causing a chain of cavities to spread throughout his mouth. He loathed dentists and with good reason; with his teeth in such a shape, sometimes merely breathing was enough to set off lightning bolts of pain inside his sensitive mouth. And whenever he had, however reluctantly, visited a dentist, even the sight of a drill heading for his teeth had scared him so silly that it usually required two or more assistants, if not the dentist himself, to restrain him in the chair and keep him from leaping out the nearest window and legging his way home.

Besides, if you have bad teeth and play a reed instrument, the ensuing vibrations caused by blowing your horn can be, and often are, excruciatingly painful.

That same night of the toothache, John just played the first set; he only got through that hour by not switching horns with his boss and by keeping his eyes tightly closed. At intermission, Cleanhead, noticing the difference in his young ward's playing and appearance, asked John what was wrong. When advised about the teeth trouble, Eddie sent his young saxophonist back to the hotel with a bottle of his own bourbon and a strict admonition to see the dentist first thing in the morning.

But Coltrane, awake throughout most of the night with the pain he tried to ward off by continuous drinking, naturally overslept. And, when he had finally worked up enough courage to visit the man in the white coat with the drill, his reward was the loss of two rear teeth and his seat on the band bus, which had moved on to the next date without him. He hitched a ride to the terminal and caught another bus, finally rejoining the band one job and one city later. His boss was relieved to see him; he was more concerned that his young musician might have come to some harm than about the empty saxophone chair from the previous engagement.

For as Eddie Vinson said about John Coltrane, in the older man's warmest avuncular manner, "He was a fine young man, and I loved him like a son."

> Coltrane used to talk about Johnny Hodges all the time until after we saw Charlie Parker at the Academy of Music. Not long after, John pulled a disappearing act, as he sometimes did, and I didn't see him for almost two weeks. Whenever he did this, he'd usually be into something new when he showed up again. This time, he dropped by my house with his alto, and when he started playing I heard more Charlie Parker than Johnny Hodges coming out of his horn. Hodges was dead; but Bird lived.
>
> BENNY GOLSON

> When I went with Eddie Vinson on tenor, a wider area of listening opened up for me. On alto, Bird had been my whole influence, but on tenor I found there was no one man whose ideas were so dominant as Charlie's were on alto. Therefore, I drew from all the men I heard during this period on tenor, especially Lester Young and his melodic phrasing. I found out about Coleman Hawkins later and became fascinated by his arpeggios and the way he played. I got a copy of "Body and Soul" and listened real hard. Even though I dug Pres, as I grew musically, I appreciated Hawk more and more.
>
> JOHN COLTRANE

John Coltrane left Eddie Vinson in mid-1948, but before he departed the band played an extended engagement in California during late 1947. There, Coltrane met Charlie Parker again; Bird had just been released from Camarillo where he'd been confined during a nervous breakdown.

Bassist Red Callender had a house near the ocean in one of Los Angeles' beachfront suburbs, where Bird would often drop by after his release and relax with the sounds of the surf. Pianist Erroll Garner was then staying with Callender, and they often played duets; Parker would sometimes join in, trying to get his music and his mind back together.

John heard about these impromptu sessions, so one Sunday afternoon he hitched a ride to Red's place. Drummer Harold West was visiting that afternoon, and when Coltrane arrived he found four musicians playing an abstract, lovely blues that he had never heard before. The melody's changes startled him, with the implied melancholy lurking just below the sunny surface of the tune. John was strangely fascinated by the baroque sadness he heard in Bird's playing. He waited patiently to sit in, fingering his alto, until Bird, who recognized him from their Philadelphia encounter, stopped playing, winked at John, and said, "Well, I'm tired; I think it's time for someone else to play, don't you?"

John played.

His well-trained ears caught some of the changes; the remainder he simply improvised, playing the ones that seemed most logical. Cleanhead had taught him some tricks about intonation, and Coltrane had certainly been listening to Parker's records long enough that his basic conception was strongly influenced by Bird. Yet he still retained a definite personal identification, for Bird was a melodic improviser and John inclined more toward harmonic progression. If you can imagine Bird's melodic lines grafted over Hawkins' sweeping arpeggios, then that was what John sounded like at that time.

After John had played, Bird said, "You'd really like me to show you that tune, wouldn't you?"

John nodded.

Bird smiled; and Bird showed him.

It was called "Relaxin' at Camarillo."

When John Coltrane returned to Philadelphia after leaving Eddie Vinson, he played that same song for Benny Golson and Bill Barron, who both thought it was the most advanced music they'd ever heard.

Then, a trumpeter in Philadelphia named Mel Melvin formed a band, which Coltrane and Barron joined. The Heath brothers were the nucleus; Al on drums, bassist Percy (later with the Modern Jazz Quartet), and Jimmy's alto saxophone. Later that same year, 1948, the Heath brothers formed their own band, taking Coltrane with them as the second altoist. Jimmy, still playing alto himself, fronted the band; he was called "Little Bird" because his sound was even more Parker-influenced than John's. Jimmy and John often played alto duets, rephrasing Bird's riffs back and forth. Jimmy was the better technician then; later, of course, John, with his then-obsessive practice regimen, would surpass him.

During this period Coltrane also met Cal Massey, the Brooklyn-born trumpeter and composer who later became such a close friend that he would read John's poem from *A Love Supreme* at John's funeral. Massey's father was from Philadelphia, and one day when eighteen-year-old Cal was visiting the city in search of his father, the young musician was walking down a side street when he heard the explosive sounds of a big band playing from somebody's garage. At the same time, he heard an alto player whose sound was so personal and penetrating that it stopped him in his tracks. It was the Heath brothers' band; so Massey, entering the garage and discovering this, asked to sit in, since he'd brought his trumpet with him. Jimmy said, "Sure, we're short a trumpet," and since Cal was an excellent sight reader, he ended up getting the gig. During the break, he asked about the alto player he'd heard; Jimmy told him, "That was John Coltrane," and thus Massey and Coltrane began their friendship.

Again, during that same year, trumpeter Howard McGhee came through Philadelphia looking for musicians to join the big band he was then fronting at the Apollo Theater in Harlem. Maggie, as many musicians called him, had just returned to New York from California but knew that the Quaker City was an excellent environment in which to recruit promising young musicians. He heard the Heath band, which was in reality more a rehearsal band than an income-producing entity, and was able to hire both Coltrane and Jimmy Heath for his two alto saxophone chairs.

The McGhee band continued on a theater tour to Chicago after leaving the Apollo. When they returned to New York, Maggie broke up the big band and cut down to a sextet, keeping Jimmy but letting John go. As he explains, "I thought Jimmy was the stronger player."

And John was out of a job.

He then played casuals around Philadelphia, one-time gigs for

$10 a night, sometimes less. Like many other musicians, he sat in with some, rehearsed with others when and where the music moved him. He worked some bars where he couldn't even hear himself play over the barrage of voices engaged in loud conversation, with glasses and bottles clattering against the bar and tables at a decibel level equivalent to that of a bowling alley. During intermission, the jukebox was playing with enough volume to pass his threshold of pain. There were times when he couldn't even think about the music for the next set until he'd taken a walk outside just to clear his head before that same scene started all over again.

He played those places, though. Not because a musician, like anyone else, must eat. But a musician must also create, and, to create, he must play and keep on playing.

I saw John with Dizzy Gillespie at the Earle Theater on Eleventh and Market, a movie theater that featured stage shows. I wrote the first article about him as a musician after that concert, and it appeared in the November 5, 1949, edition of the *Afro-American*, I compared his career to that of Dizzy, because they both got their start in Philadelphia.

FRANKLIN BROWER

Dizzy Gillespie's band played for a dance at the Armory in Winston-Salem, and I saw John with the band there in the summer of 1950. He invited all the musicians over to his mother's house afterwards. I recall the musicians called John "Country Boy," because he didn't like to wear shoes. He'd take them off while sitting behind his music stand, and put them on again whenever he had to step out in front and play a solo.

BETTY LEACH

I saw the Gillespie band in Milwaukee in 1950, playing at a local ballroom. John Coltrane and Jimmy Heath were the two altoists, but what they did offstage caught my attention more. During intermission, they were standing in a corner, playing Charlie Parker solos note for note. One would play a line, and the other would counter with a complementary line. What they were really doing, I guess, was playing Bird duets with each other.

BUNKY GREEN

Texas-born tenor saxophonist Jesse Powell, a genial man of gargantuan size from Houston, returned from a European tour in mid-1949 and was asked to join the Dizzy Gillespie big band the following fall. He had once worked in Philadelphia and knew of the Heath brothers' band. When Gillespie asked him about possible section mates, Powell suggested Jimmy Heath on alto. Heath brought Coltrane with him to the audition and asked Gillespie to listen to both of them. Dizzy did, and Jimmy and John both joined the band.

This was the Gillespie before the uptilted 45°-angle trumpet, but still the Dizzy of the chipmunk cheeks, bop glasses and beret, the exuberant comic who sometimes conducted the band by shaking his rump and closed the set with the comment, "And now, ladies and gentlemen, I would like to turn you over . . ." as he then walked offstage.

Gillespie was an excellent leader, though. He knew how to inspire his musicians and how to handle the audience; he could also deal decisively with the backstage brokers and the smiling simpletons in the booking agencies. However, since he was not an economist, he still persisted in fronting a sixteen-man band, despite the fact that the very form of music he cofounded with Charlie Parker, bop, had hastened the decline of the large orchestral ensemble for dancing and accentuated the popularity of the small combo that played strictly for listening.

Nevertheless, a big band Gillespie's new group was, and it lasted less than two years. The band was of major importance in Coltrane's life in several ways, but one in particular may have caused him to effect a radical change in his life style.

Yusef Lateef, a tenor saxophonist who was sufficiently influenced by Eastern philosophy, music, and religion to become, as his name implies, an orthodox Moslem, was briefly in the band, and he and

John met. Yusef aroused a latent interest of John's in religion and philosophy. He took an instant liking to John and suggested that the young saxophonist read Kahlil Gibran, the Koran, and Krishnamurti. He insisted that such literature had changed his life for the better and broadened his musical abilities as well. A most persuasive figure, Lateef was a big, bald man, sometimes called the "Gentle Giant," and Coltrane promised to take his advice. Yusef then gave John some of his personal collection of Orientalia to browse through during those long bus rides that he knew were in the offing.

Before John went on the road with Dizzy, Bill Barron gave him a book on yoga, which Barron was then investigating. Coltrane, though appreciative of their interest in his spiritual and religious welfare, seemed slightly puzzled at the time. For to a Carolina Christian—even one who was rarely attending church any more—such Eastern texts and practices seemed truly occult, as well as foreign to his ingrained beliefs.

Gillespie himself was involved in many arcane matters of the mind, since he was as perpetually curious a person as Coltrane. Dizzy was often suggesting a talk with this fellow or a perusal of that pamphlet. Big Bad Jesse, who often exchanged comic asides with his leader, would sit in on these sessions of intellectual esoterica between Dizzy and John and counter, at the most appropriate moment, with his own practical advice, "Come on, John, let's go get drunk."

They would, with Johnnie Walker Black Label. And, while drinking, it would seem only natural to puff a cigaret or two, between sips. And if Coltrane coughed from the tobacco's effects on his throat, then a quick slug of scotch would make everything right again.

But other times—in fact, most times—John was quiet and withdrawn, practicing in his hotel room or in the back of the bus as the band was traveling. Changing his reed, adjusting his mouthpiece, altering his fingering; he was constantly searching for some new sound that he still hadn't heard on his horn, only in his head.

Jesse Powell, wondering why his section mate was spending so much time, both on and off the stand, with his horn, asked, "Why?"

"It's not where I want it," John replied, continuing his adjustments and experimentations.

"Listen, your alto sounds fine to me."

"It might to you, but you're not me."

"Well, you're not Bird, either."

Powell had intended to expand on the latter comment, adding that even Bird, genius that he was, had his uncreative moments too, the times when there was simply nothing new coming out of his horn. But Coltrane didn't give him a chance to amplify further. Jesse's statement had jolted John, reminding him again that his entire approach to alto saxophone at that time was based on Charlie Parker, as his earlier influence had been Johnny Hodges. John cut Jesse off and wouldn't speak to him for the rest of the week. Yet they continued sitting next to each other in the reed section, playing the richly orchestrated saxophone ensembles and listening to their leader running those cascades of high notes and grand flourishes that he was famous for.

Jimmy Heath also sat next to Coltrane in the sax section. Jimmy took the majority of the alto solos, as John was generally playing lead. However, Monk's "'Round Midnight" was one of John's featured solos; he would later become extremely involved in Monk's music as a member of his quartet in 1957. John also played on "A Night in Tunisia," which spotlighted Dizzy's stratospheric closing coda; "Manteca," that Afro-Cuban composition featuring the band as vocal chorus chanting "I'll never go back to Georgia"; and "Cubana Be, Cubana Bop," as its title indicates, a fusion of North American and Caribbean motifs.

Then Majeed would break everybody up, on stand and off, if Dizzy wasn't already doing so.

Hernifan Majeed, his Moslem name; his Christian name was Charles Greenlee. Later, he would marry Cousin Mary; still later, she would divorce him. But at the moment, he was one of three trombonists in the Gillespie band, playing with a bravura style that caught the audience's attention almost as often as the leader's trumpet tricks.

Once, the band bus stopped at a gas station outside Mexico, Missouri, where the hospitality was neither southern nor Mexican but nonexistent. The musicians were hungry, but the proprietor of the cafe at the station had four blunt words for them:

"We don't serve niggers."

Undaunted, Majeed flashed his driver's license, pointed out his Islamic name imprinted thereon, and added that he was "a Moslem, not a Negro, but I don't eat pork so gimme anything except that."

The proprietor stared, openmouthed, as Majeed took the license from its plastic case and thrust it under the former's eyes. After examining the license carefully, the white man returned it and instructed the waitress to take care of the black customer.

"But you told me we don't serve colored . . ." she protested.

"He ain't colored; he's *Moslem* . . . so serve him."

She did.

And Majeed, after stuffing himself, returned to the bus to rejoin the rest of the band.

As for Coltrane, he'd often sit with Heath on the bus, sometimes Powell (after the latter and he had made up). John and Jimmy remained as tight as before. John was also becoming tight with Jesse. Coltrane had developed an admiration for the Hawkins-like sound that Powell got on tenor, and kept asking him, "Jesse, how do you get that big beautiful sound?"

"I practice behind the door."

John looked at Jesse with his huge eyes, slowly raising his eyebrows until Jesse explained, "I have the bell of my horn pointed at the door, and I'm standing behind it while I play. That way, the sound bounces around my head and I can hear what I'm playing when I play it."

It was not that Coltrane wanted a huge, enveloping sound for himself; just a penetrating, brilliant intonation, like the sonorous speaking voice that he knew he would never have. So he worked on that sound, taking such tips from Powell, as just mentioned and learning from anyone else in the reed section that he could. But his teeth were still troubling him; there were times when the pain became so intense that he'd drink, and heavily, to alleviate the agony and to prolong as much as possible the inevitable next visit to the dentist.

That helped; but only for a short while.

In the meantime, worsening economic conditions during 1950 didn't help at all with the band payroll, which included a salary of $125 per week or more for the musicians. The expenses remained constant while the bookings decreased; in fact, sometimes the transportation costs, especially if the band was traveling more than five hundred miles between engagements, spurted upward so rapidly that Gillespie once remarked that "it would be cheaper to buy you guys bicycles."

During Thanksgiving week, the band began a six-week job at New York's Bop City at Broadway and Forty-ninth Street. The band did well, as far as audience attraction was concerned—much better than their concert in Little Rock, Arkansas, where only two dozen people had shown up in a hall seating five thousand—but not well enough. Times were so bad for big bands that even Count Basie cut his orchestra to a six-man combo in order to survive. (Two years later, though, he went back to the big band format and has kept his band together even to this day.)

But that was Basie, not Gillespie. For, on Christmas Eve 1950, Dizzy told his musicians that after they had finished the week, on New Year's Day, "Fellas, this is *it!*"

Except for John and Jimmy.

Gillespie dropped down to a septet, keeping both saxophonists but switching John to tenor as Vinson had done. John had sometimes doubled on tenor in the big band when one of the other hornmen couldn't make the gig, and Dizzy had liked John's work on tenor as much as on alto. And John, perhaps recalling Jesse's comment about Bird and himself, was thinking about changing saxophones. Thus, the switch from alto to tenor was fine with him.

Jimmy Heath only stayed with the small band for a few weeks. So, for the first few months of 1951, it was Coltrane on tenor, Gillespie's trumpet, the rhythm section—and that was all.

> Coltrane was so far out in his ideas and techniques that every time I heard him practicing, I'd stop and listen.
>
> MATTHEW RASTELLI

> Every time John came back to Philadelphia, he'd ask me for mouthpieces. The teachers he studied with referred him to me. I'd show him mouthpieces from 5-star to 7-star—wide lays that required considerable breath control and lung

power. Once, he ordered a number 10. It's difficult to get a mouthpiece that gives you equal facility in both upper and lower registers, but he kept trying anyway.

GEORGE SARKIS

I taught John Coltrane advanced musical techniques. I started him in theory, then moved him along. He asked me about bitonalities and polytonalities, combining more than one key signature. I suggested tetrachord techniques and pentatonic as well as diatonic scales, and he was soon playing arpeggios on all of them. I taught him from my thesaurus of scales that I've compiled through the years, using notes from foreign scales and mixing them with Western scales until everything was just right. He also studied semitonal scales, modal scales, pedal point clusters, and harmony derived from melodic lines, with no chord structure involved.

DENNIS SANDOLE

When John Coltrane returned to Philadelphia in early 1951, after leaving Dizzy Gillespie, his mother had moved in with Cousin Mary, and James Kinzer was still there. This was too little space and too many people in the one apartment. It was time to make a change.

They all moved.

From the decaying black ghetto with its crumbling brownstone-style buildings and garbage-littered streets, they relocated to an area on Philadelphia's Northwest Side called Strawberry Mansions. It had been primarily a Jewish neighborhood until the late 1940s, when a few black families made their appearance on the block. Then, Jewish or not, the whites for the most part had disappeared, certainly by the time the Coltrane family and Kinzer moved there.

Their new home was a three-story brick house on North Thirty-third Street overlooking Fairmount Park, an inner-city oasis that offered grass and trees in contrast to the crowded city streets. They owned this house, too; John had secured a GI loan and

Mrs. Coltrane had saved her money from her years of domestic labor. For less than $10,000 and 10 per cent down, they became homeowners instead of tenants, furnishing eight rooms with comfortable southern-style furniture. John and James each had a room on the second floor, where the latter would remain for nearly two years before finding other quarters. Mrs. Coltrane and Cousin Mary had their accommodations on the third floor.

Coltrane had decided to stay in town for at least a full year; he wanted to attend music school and obtain the formal training he felt he lacked. He had learned a lot while playing with Gillespie, but how much time was there to practice, much less study, while on the road? Besides, he was making a permanent switch to tenor saxophone. On tenor, he could be his own man at last. There were many talented tenor players around, such as Lester Young, Coleman Hawkins, Dexter Gordon, and Stan Getz, all of whom he had been hearing since he first started thinking seriously about the big horn.

Coltrane was especially interested in the latter two saxophonists. Gordon was a powerful swing player, capable of rousing even sagging rhythm sections into pulsating energy units, while Getz's tenor tone was among the smoothest and most flowing.

Granoff School of Music was Coltrane's choice.

The recommendations of former students Dizzy Gillespie and Percy Heath, and an audition John breezed through, were sufficient to make him a member of the student body. The school was then more than a generation old, founded in 1918 by Isadore Granoff, a Russian *émigré* violinist who'd played at the Paris *première* of Stravinsky's *Le Sacre du Printemps* in 1913.

Dennis Sandole, a soft-spoken, meticulous man not much older than Coltrane himself, was John's theory teacher, while Matthew Rastelli, a foppish, equally demanding taskmaster, gave John his saxophone lessons. Coltrane now owned a tenor saxophone, and it was tenor only that he was practicing, studying, and playing.

Rastelli was once a student of Mike Guerra's, with whom Coltrane had previously studied. But Sandole was a completely new influence in his life; he had been recommended by a vocalist acquaintance of Coltrane's named Larry Nesbitt, who had brought John to Sandole's voice class. John was impressed with the way Dennis went out of his way to answer his questions, giving extremely detailed and logical replies, which the saxophonist then double-checked and discovered to be correct.

Coltrane spent most of his weekdays at school, taking evening and weekend playing jobs whenever possible. When not studying or playing, he was practicing or reading books recommended by Gillespie and his bandsmen. Reading was a natural consequence of his ever-increasing desire to know more, not just of the musical world but of the reason for his being put on this planet in the first place. A certain inclination toward philosophical speculation, perhaps an outgrowth of his introspective tendencies, possibly from his religious upbringing, and a questing for something beyond the realm of his five senses, seemed to be driving him toward a kind of fulfillment. He was exploring music books and other books, and learning from and loving both.

It would seem logical that given Rastelli's background and the fact that Coltrane was studying saxophone with him, John would have become close with this teacher. Not so, though; there was a brusqueness about Rastelli that could be off-putting, while Sandole was almost fatherly in his enthusiasm for each and every one of his students. To such a person as Sandole, Coltrane would normally gravitate as a matter of personal as well as musical preference.

Dennis was, like John himself at that particular period, a self-taught musician whose instrument was guitar and whose musical allegiance was to Duke Ellington. He had also been a Hollywood studio musician. Therefore he could read anything placed before him, and had taught himself enough piano to enable him to compose as well as teach.

"Listen to classical music, John," he advised, for he knew that Coltrane had not been as exposed to European music as he should have been, except for those necessary ingredients of his formal studies. "Listen to the way the great composers write for any number of instruments, from a solo violin to a hundred-piece symphony. Then distill all that music and translate it into the instrument you love so much—the saxophone."

Coltrane sheepishly accepted the advice. He turned, for example, to Debussy and Ravel. But it was Bartók whom Sandole recommended more than any contemporary composer except Stravinsky. He said, "In Bartók's string quartets, you can hear an entire symphony orchestra."

It was this kind of gentle prodding and avuncular good advice that made John receptive to other kinds of music. He reported back occasionally at his teacher's request. Once, he told Sandole that listening to *La Mer* gave him the feeling of swimming in a sea of instruments, each musical wave carrying him higher as he floated toward the shore.

"Beautiful," Sandole said. "But do you know what those strings were doing?"

Coltrane shook his head, puzzled; he wasn't quite sure what his teacher had in mind.

"They were playing extended tonalities in upper partials, making exquisite use of the overtone series. Just as you're doing on tenor, when you extend every seventh note chord up to its thirteenth. They start high and go higher. And that's what you're doing, too."

"Yes," John nodded. "Now I know what you mean." He shrugged, his eyes smiling, as he added, "I guess I'm just a castoff alto player, always wanting to go higher."

Sandole was silent for several seconds.

Coltrane waited, his own silence echoing in his teacher's ears, until the latter said, "No, John, I don't really hear you on alto. I know you're playing tenor higher than most, or at least trying to extend the upper range of the horn, and that's very good. But I really hear you on another horn."

He paused, then added, prophetically, "Soprano, John. I'd like you to think about soprano saxophone." Another pause. "Think about it a lot."

I remember that John had such a strong inner ear. When I talked with him about chord progressions, he'd finger the notes on his horn and say, "That was this chord, and this is the one following it."

BILL BARRON

Coltrane and I used to drink wine together, whenever he came through Chicago. I was playing piano with Gene Ammons, and I switched to tenor about that time, around 1951. John and I would often practice together. I knew about his bad teeth, so I got my dentist to put a cap over his right front tooth. It was so badly chipped I'm surprised he could ever play. The pain must have been incredibly intense.

EDDIE HARRIS

During those rhythm-and-blues days of the 1950s, currently being lionized, a custom prevailed that was exquisite in its quaintness, congenial in its straightforwardness, and entertaining in the extreme. Club owners and bartenders favored it as a proven crowd-pleaser and a sure way to bolster sagging business. Customers applauded it as the best example of dramatic vaudeville since Fred Allen or the most elegant terpsichorean fantasy since Fred Astaire.

If the musicians' opinion had been solicited—it wasn't; they were usually the last to be informed about basic working conditions—they would have said, "Jive." Or any of several similar four-letter words. But they were not asked, and this practice became in many cases a prerequisite of their employment.

No one knows the exact origin of this custom, but it may have resulted from a fusion of Lionel Hampton's tenor-saxophonist-playing-while-lying-on-back and Bill Haley's Comets dancing-like-drunks-while-playing-loud-and-fast.

It was called: Walking the Bar.

It was primarily performed in those clubs with bandstands built behind the bar, or with sufficient space on top of the bar itself so that the musicians walking the bar wouldn't step into the customers' drinks or onto their hands. The musicians were required to tramp from one end of the bar to the other. The more bizarre the body English used, the wilder and weirder the gesticulations and gyrations they could demonstrate, the more unmusical and nauseous the sounds they could coax from their horns, the greater the goon show they could put on for the patrons—that was Walking the Bar with *style*.

Pianist Ray Bryant remembers watching John Coltrane walking

the bar in such Philadelphia clubs as Cafe Society, Joe Pitt's Musical Bar, and the Zanzibar. Bill Barron recalls Coltrane once asking him during intermission at a club where both were playing, "What do I have to do to please people?" when the club owner, standing nearby, said, "Honk more than you play, you're not honking enough."

John Coltrane walked the bar.

To him, as to any other sensitive and creative musician, it was like walking the plank, and the sharks were the club owners, their teeth chomping down on the musicians' dignity and the customers' pocketbooks with one sharp slash.

Take the Snake Bar, for example; a joint located at Columbia and Ridge, no better and no worse than its predecessors and/or competitors. Like its namesake, the bar coiled along the length of the place itself, expanding here, contracting there.

There Coltrane is, dressed in suit and tie, his tenor saxophone strapped to his neck and positioned between his fingers. He walks slowly, almost shuffling, weaving his horn from side to side, bending, almost crouching, then coming up again as if for air, the smoke thick, the whiskey aroma filtering into his lungs and fueling the tenor sax.

He blows into the horn; a series of upper-register squawks spill out. Honking and squealing, walking and shaking; it goes on and on. Walking the Bar.

Walking in the door one night came Benny Golson and a few friends; not to gawk at John Coltrane but simply to hear how he was sounding. Just friends, dropping by to catch a few sets by a fellow musician and to say hello.

They arrived just as John was going into a right-angle crouch, his head almost between his legs, his horn sputtering out a flattened, frustrated note of near-defeat.

Benny said, "Oh *no!*"

John said nothing.

But he saw Benny, and the next note died in his diaphragm.

As if rehearsed, or simply an intuitive, visceral reaction, John quickly stood erect, placed the saxophone's neck over his shoulder, and walked the bar again.

Walked to the end of the bar, the end closest to the door.

Walked right off the bar—some say he jumped—and right out the door.

> All escapes are the same, there is no superior or inferior escape. God and drink are on the same level as long as they are escapes from what we are.
>
> JIDDU KRISHNAMURTI

John Coltrane drank and continued to drink.

This is not surprising; while playing in bars and clubs with all that alcoholic release available, friendly bartenders were only too anxious to "put it on your tab, man, we'll take it out of your pay . . . later."

So Coltrane drank to forget the music that he was forced to play in order to earn a living so that he could afford to study and practice the sounds that he could only hear in his head.

"Hey, buddy, I like the way you play. Let's have a drink and talk about music, huh?"

The instant camaraderie of a customer who buys two half-dollar drinks and thinks that the price of admission entitles him to tell his troubles to the musicians on *their* time.

"Say, baby, you've got class. If you're real nice to me and play my favorite song during the last set, I just might let you take me home."

She just might; she does it all the time, a different musician each night, never recalling his music and only occasionally remembering his name for the purpose of impressing her girl friends with whom she scored and how prestigious it was, especially for herself.

Fringe benefits of the glamorous life a musician leads.

John Coltrane recognized the folly of much of it several years later. Riverside Records' Orrin Keepnews was standing at Birdland's bar with John Coltrane during intermission. Keepnews offered to buy Coltrane a drink; John said, "Just a Coke."

Making conversation, Keepnews apologized for his late conversion to Coltrane's music and said, "I'm sorry I hadn't known you sooner."

And John Coltrane replied, "You shouldn't be. I wish I hadn't known me sooner, either."

I recall being at Minton's Playhouse in Harlem around 1950 when Earl Bostic came to town and sat in. Coltrane was with me, and we heard Bostic play in any key, any tempo, playing almost an octave above the range of the alto saxophone. We talked with him, and he told us how each brand of saxophone should sound. He said, "On the Martin you finger it this way, the Buescher is that way, and like so on the Selmer."

BENNY GOLSON

If Coltrane played with Bostic, I know he learned a lot. Nobody knew more about the saxophone than Bostic, I mean technically, and that includes Bird. Bostic could take any make of saxophone and tell you its faults and its best points. Working with Earl Bostic is like attending a university of the saxophone.

ART BLAKEY

Everyone in the Bostic band got along with everyone else. We were a peaceful bunch of fellows. All Earl ever cared about was that each musician could sight read on the spot. We had more than 150 tunes in the book, and if you couldn't read them the first time around, you were out of a job.

JOE KNIGHT

Earl Bostic is now deceased. But when he was still alive and quite young, he moved from his native Tulsa, Oklahoma, to New Orleans in search of the advanced musical knowledge that the Crescent City of that lively era could offer him. There, he graduated from Xavier University, played in various territory bands, and finally put his own unit together in the late 1940s. He made his most famous musical breakthrough in the early 1950s, when his rhythm-and-blues version of "Flamingo" caught on and put enough cash in his pocket to enable him to keep his band working on a full-time basis.

Bostic was a dapper dresser, a man of medium height whose horn-rimmed glasses framed a saucer-round face of *joie de vivre*. He had studied and practiced his saxophone technique so extensively and for so many years that he was, in effect, overtrained. That is, he had sacrificed style for technique, and his "sound" could be stated in one word—strident.

The band was primarily a showcase for Bostic's alto. The other guys got their eight-bar breaks, but it was the leader who took the extended solos.

Coltrane joined the Bostic band in early 1952, for the same reasons he'd taken the job with Vinson; to learn more about his chosen horn, to work with a master saxophonist, and most elementary of all—because Bostic had offered him a good job.

He became friendly with pianist Joe Knight, a self-taught musician with philosophical inclinations, who urged Coltrane to read Plato and Aristotle in preference to Gibran and the Koran. Musically, Knight backed him with well-chosen chords whenever Coltrane would take one of his occasional solos. The pianist's style was somewhere between Bud Powell and Earl Hines, with occasional hints of the block-chord patterns of Red Garland. John and Joe were the most "modern" musicians in that nine-piece unit. John would often listen to Joe's tasty comping behind the soloists, almost as much as he paid strict attention to the leader's saxophone technique.

Coltrane would often arrive early at rehearsals with Knight, and they would work out their own explorations of Bostic's music. John was becoming more interested in harmony, and Joe urged him to study as much piano as possible. He reminded John that "the tempered scale and the piano only date from the eighteenth century, and that's really where European harmony comes from."

After hours, the two of them jammed with other band members or with whoever else was in town. Bostic didn't jam much; he squired the ladies instead, driving them around in his eight-passenger Cadillac. To black people at that time—and vestigially so today—a Caddy was the tops in motor vehicle status symbols, the most prestigious and "in" car anyone could wheel around to let others know that one had indeed "arrived."

"That was a drinking man's band," Knight recalls, "and Coltrane and I were just two of the 'pint-a-night' guys who'd knock off that much J. W. Dant at two dollars the bottle."

They could afford to; most of the musicians earned about $175 a week, and at that time $100 a month rented a near-luxury apartment in New York.

The musicians traveled in Bostic's Cadillac, with their leader at the wheel, followed by a Chevrolet pickup truck carrying their instruments. Bostic always drove; he loved the power that emerged with just a flick of his wrist or the tiniest pressure of his toe. Once, he drove all the way from Los Angeles to Midlands, Texas, more than a thousand miles and close to seventeen hours, without allowing anyone else to sub for him as chief chauffeur.

Coltrane was always asking Bostic questions about saxophone technique. His leader spent as much time as possible showing the younger saxophonist, for example, certain fingerings that would better facilitate the playing of his ideas. The saxophone keys are structured for normal fingers, and Coltrane's were unusually long. Earl demonstrated how to "bend" the fingers to fit the curvature of the horn and, as he did, commented, "John, the saxophone's not made of plastic. It won't change its shape, so you'll have to change yours."

In his boyish eagerness to learn, Coltrane usually sat next to his boss in the car, asking Bostic questions and taking down the information in a notebook. This did not bother the leader except when the road was of such a nature that 100 per cent alertness was necessary. Then, Earl might raise both hands from the wheel while zooming along at seventy and offer to write down whatever information John desired, saying, "Pass me your notebook and I'll jot down the changes just before we go over that thousand-foot cliff a few hundred yards ahead."

Thus chastised, Coltrane would back off and briefly move his mind to other matters, such as chess. Joe Knight and trumpeter Gene Redd had started reading chess books and playing a game a day during an extended engagement in San Francisco. They managed to interest John in the game, and Joe recalls that he kept talking to John about "the relationship between chess and music, both being based on mathematics." Knight had a portable board with peg-bottomed chessmen, easy to carry and use. Soon it was Knight and Coltrane rather than Redd on the chess circuit. Joe won most games, but John improved with practice and was winning nearly half the matches by the third week of their California visit.

The band was then playing at the Blackhawk when the two of them met the English girl whom they had noticed was sitting at a front row table almost every evening.

She was a tall, auburn-haired girl with a Mayfair accent and an Evelyn Waugh sense of humor. In addition, she was a chess nut as well as a music lover. When she discovered there were three chess players in the Bostic band, she challenged them all to simultaneous matches. The musicians declined at first, but she kept asking, and finally one evening—actually, about four in the morning, after the band had played its last set—she persuaded Coltrane, Knight, and Redd to bring her to their hotel. They did; but the uptight white night manager took one long look at the three black men with the white girl and said, with unctuous officiality, "No."

Not "No, sir" or "No, gentlemen." The way the man spoke, without using that most obvious word to describe his distaste for this racially mixed gathering, was all the more meaningfully conveyed to those present. John had heard the unsaid word before but rarely directed toward himself. However, in Philadelphia, if he ventured into the wrong place in the right neighborhood, he knew he'd be called by that name quickly enough, with the word just as nastily dispensed.

Joe Knight says, "If you want to understand Coltrane, read Schopenhauer's definition of genius."

> Genius is simply the completest objectivity; that is, the objective tendency of the mind. Genius is the power of leaving one's own interests, wishes and aims entirely out of sight, of entirely renouncing one's own personality for a time, so as to remain pure knowing subject, clear vision of the world. Genius holds up to us the magic glass in which all that is essential and

significant appears to us collected and placed in the clearest light, and what is accidental and foreign is left out. The pleasure which he receives from all beauty, the consolation which art affords, the enthusiasm of the artist, enable him to forget the cares of life and repay him for the suffering that increases in proportion to the clearness of consciousness, and for his desert loneliness among a different race of men.

ARTHUR SCHOPENHAUER

There are few musicians who are touched with genius. But more than a few musicians, unfortunately, become touched with, and addicted to, drugs.

I think narcotics addiction got started in the 1920s, maybe in the speakeasies where a lot of black musicians played. The gangsters put it into the ghetto; I mean the white gangsters, making money off black people they don't give a goddam about. You never heard about narcotics as a problem until it got into the white suburbs and middle-class kids started shooting up.

BOBBY TIMMONS

To me, the reason musicians got into drugs so heavily was that, as artists and performers, they wanted to get closer to each other, to communicate as intimately as possible, and at that time shooting up seemed the best way to do this. It became such a habit with so many of them that it was almost expected for any new man in the band to show his sense of brotherhood by sticking that needle into his arm, just like his buddies would.

GEORGE FREEMAN

At some still unknown point in time and space, after leaving Earl Bostic but before joining Johnny Hodges, John Coltrane was introduced to drugs, specifically heroin, by "good friends."

Who these good friends were, no one seems to know; or at least no one wants to talk about it.

But in Philadelphia, and probably in 1953, John Coltrane became a junkie.

Not necessarily a six-bag-a-day man. But he did become addicted, and there is no such thing as being a little addicted, anymore than one can be a little pregnant; you either are, or you aren't.

Philadelphia, the Quaker City, was founded by William Penn in 1682. And the Quakers believed that a person needed no spiritual intermediary but could receive the proper religious guidance through what they called the "inward light" supplied by the Holy Spirit.

Through heroin, John Coltrane received his own version of an inward light.

The darkest light he'd ever been blinded with.

> I think Coltrane always had the desire to be a leader and have his own band. He didn't say much about it, but you could sense it in the way he'd watch Hodges cueing the sections, calling the soloists and selecting the tunes. The way his eyes would light up, as if absorbing everything in the room while Hodges was soloing out front, you instinctively knew he was wishing it was himself out there.
>
> JOHN WILLIAMS

The late Johnny Hodges was the alto saxophonist's alto saxophonist, the major stylist before Bird. He'd been around since the 1930s, primarily with Duke Ellington, where his name and fame were almost synonymous with that of the now-deceased Duke. His style was the antithesis of that of Charlie Parker; limpid where Bird was liquid, with a leisurely legato phrasing that used one note to stretch out the melodic lines of a song, while Bird, in that same space, would string together four notes or more.

Hodges was a Bostonian, though not so much proper as punctilious; be on time for his gig or don't bother to show up. A short, compact man who seemed perfectly formed for the double-breasted suits of his day, he had the nickname of Rabbit. However, a more appropriate one would have been Mole, since Hodges would sit quietly in Ellington's saxophone section, his eyes tightly closed as if afraid of the light, until he heard the leader's piano cueing him into his solo. Then he'd suddenly, startlingly stand up and deliver a gorgeous solo of such glowing beauty that the audience would utter a collective gasp of appreciation. Afterward, he'd resume his place in the section, returning to his deceptive somnambulistic state.

But Hodges became restless and decided in 1953 that he'd rather have his own band than remain with the Duke. He gave notice and left Ellington, carrying away with him such sidemen as Lawrence Brown on trombone, trumpeter Harold "Shorty" Baker, Sonny Greer on drums, and, for a few recording dates, baritone saxophonist Harry Carney. The band's book was about 90 per cent Ellingtonia, and sounded exactly like what it was; a small band plucked directly from the Duke's big band.

Coltrane was in the tenor chair. He and Hodges were the only permanent saxophonists in the band. Ironically, John, whose influences had ranged from Shaw to Hodges to Bird to Pres to Hawk to Gordon to Getz, was now back home, in a sense, playing with Hodges. For it was the Rabbit who had been Coltrane's very first saxophone idol back in High Point.

There were some striking parallels between the two saxophonists, despite the differences in their physical appearance and musical style. Their music was their life. Also, Johnny's eyes glowed with the same luminosity of absorbing his surroundings that John's did.

But Johnny was clean; and John was not.

Coltrane's addiction didn't show much and rarely affected his music, but there were times when he was nodding out while waiting for his solos. Other band members noticed it, and sometimes one of them would wake him with a well-placed nudge. Hodges, generally looking straight ahead at the audience, was the last to see it but among the first to sense it. However, his philosophy was, What you do is your business, as long as you don't mess up the music.

John asked Johnny many questions about the saxophone, but,

at this stage in his career, he was learning more by simply listening to Hodges play. He also checked out the band's charts, paying particular attention to the bass parts. He asked bassist John Williams to demonstrate how his playing supplied the harmonic and rhythmic foundations for the band, and to show him how the bass could play melodic lines, too. Later, Coltrane would pay particular attention to his own group's bass players, going through several until he found the proper player for him, Jimmy Garrison, who'd stay in the background and supply the basic harmonic and rhythmic foundation.

More than anything else, Coltrane learned intonation from Hodges, listening to his employer linger over each note, caressing each one as if he loved them all like women and could not choose among them. While watching Johnny play "Warm Valley," for example, John would follow Hodges' fingering with his eyes and then emulate this on his own horn, fingering his tenor silently but not blowing a breath into the mouthpiece.

Coltrane's ballad feature was "Smoke Gets in Your Eyes." He stayed close to the melody but extended some of the lines while substituting others, shifting the chords around until he had practically reharmonized the song. It was this continuous fascination with harmony that would capture and contain his attention for the remaining years of his musical life.

The rest of the band's book was of equal, if not greater, quality. Ellington, Kern, and Berlin, to name just three composers. Especially the Duke's songs; deceptively simple on first hearing, demandingly complex upon repeated playing. And Coltrane was earning $250 a week for playing them.

He remained with the Hodges band until September 1954. During the summer of that year, the band was expanded for an extended tour with vocalists Billy Eckstine and Ruth Brown. One of the added musicians was Benny Golson, who had recently spent two years of formal music study at Howard University but had left school and returned to Philadelphia, believing that he could learn more by active playing and practicing and studying by himself. John was, of course, overjoyed to see Benny again. They sat next to each other in the sax section and on the bus, and also roomed together while on the road.

Despite all these attractions, John Coltrane's stay with the band ended as indicated above; Johnny Hodges simple had to let him go. "Coltrane would be sitting in his chair, holding his horn but not moving his fingers, the sax still in his mouth but not playing," John Williams recalls. "It was obvious that he was using drugs, and when this got to be a habit, Hodges talked to him and asked him to watch it. John agreed with him, realizing that Johnny was right. But the next night, or the night after that, it would happen all over again, just as before."

Johnny Hodges loved John Coltrane as much as, if not more than, John Coltrane loved Johnny Hodges. But Johnny knew he couldn't have a junkie in his band if his habit was going to get in the way of the music. So, John was out. That's the way it had to be.

I saw John playing with Bull Moose Jackson. I'm sure that job was strictly due to economics. If you need a job and you're a musician and the only gig you can get is with a rhythm-and-blues band, you'll probably take it.

Bill Barron

Coltrane once told me about a band he worked with called Daisy Mae and the Hepcats. This was the kind of band you'd find in Las Vegas lounges ten years later. Daisy Mae would shimmy out front in a sparkling dress while her husband, the guitar player, was boogieing behind her. John said the guitarist had discovered the lost chord, because it sounded as if he'd found the one chord that fitted everything—a chromatic crunch.

Bill Evans

John and I worked a date in Cleveland in 1954 backing Big Maybelle. The club owner wanted John to walk the bar, but John just looked down and patted his stomach, saying, "Sorry, I've got ulcers." We cracked up and the club owner got hostile, until our guitarist, Junior Walker, offered to walk the bar because he had an extra long cord from his guitar to the amp. He did it while John played some wailing blues behind Big Maybelle. She was so pleased she told the audience, "John Coltrane is my favorite musician, and you'd better believe it, because that's the truth!"

STEVE DAVIS

There was a place called Pat's around the corner from the Coltrane home in Philadelphia, where John and other musicians often hung out after a night's work and stuffed themselves with submarine sandwiches called hoagies locally. If they had no gig, they'd go there anyway, since food is a common antidote for frustration. Among the musicians usually present was the late pianist Bobby Timmons, who introduced John Coltrane to the pleasures of the hoagie.

Coltrane was becoming fat but not necessarily from frustration. He was now ingesting as much heroin as alcohol. When that dangerous combination slowed him down, making him feel sluggish, he'd think that he needed more food to recover his strength, so he'd eat more, and more often. He had been weighing about 160 for most of his adult life, and when another twenty pounds were added, they showed. His mother had let out all of his clothes, and that showed, too.

Hoagies are made with a two-foot chunk of Italian bread, slit down the side and stuffed with tomatoes, cheese, onions, salami, peppers, mayonnaise, ham, ketchup, and mustard.

More than once John would take one between his fingers, poise it in front of his mouth, and bite down. But, before he could even taste this super sandwich . . . the pain began.

It was his teeth, of course; they were still not right. But a dentist costs money, he loathed dentists anyway, he wasn't working very much, and he wondered where he was going musically and why he ever got started on drugs and what about his drinking and what was going to happen to him next.

John often had stomach problems, the way he was mixing drugs and drinking. We recorded together on a Gene Ammons date, and I recall that all the musicians were assembled at the Prestige office, waiting to be taken to Rudy van Gelder's studio to record. John wasn't feeling well, and he was asking everybody what to take for his stomach. One cat suggested Brioschi, somebody else told him to take Alka-Seltzer, and another said, "Try some bitters." Then John asked me for advice, and I said, jokingly, "This is an important recording session, so you ought to take *all* of them." As I remember, he took none of our suggestions. He ate some fruit Naima had given him instead.

PEPPER ADAMS

I met John Coltrane in June 1954 at Steve Davis' house. I thought John was a very nice person, but a little on the country side. He was wearing a short-sleeve shirt with no undershirt, and he wasn't wearing socks. Steve's wife was joking with him, asking him, "What are you doing here without your undershirt and socks?" Then, when I was introduced to him, his name sounded so strange that I said, "Coltrane? What kind of name is that? How do you spell it?"

NAIMA COLTRANE

As Shakespeare had his Dark Lady of the Sonnets, so would Coltrane have his Dark Lady of the Song. Naima, whose Christian name was Juanita, was born in Philadelphia in a small house on Darien Street on January 2, 1926. She is the sister of Earl Grubbs, and was graduated from high school in 1943, taking a job as seamstress in a fabrics factory. At the time she met John Coltrane she was involved with astrology, and she was pleased that John's sign, Virgo, was compatible with her sign of Capricorn. She was also a Moslem; her daughter Antonia, sometimes called Syeeda, was then nearly five years old and fatherless, for Naima had never been married.

She was then living with her brother and his wife, Lucy, in a three-story house on West Thompson Street that Earl Grubbs had bought in October 1950. She and Toni had rooms on the third floor. When Naima wasn't working, she was listening to the latest sounds. She liked musicians and their music; if Dizzy Gillespie or Miles Davis was in town, she'd be there.

She had never heard John play when they met. But she could feel musical and extramusical vibrations from his presence. She recalls that he had an "offhanded way of talking." When he first noticed her, he said, commenting on her wide leather belt studded with artificial jewels, "I don't like that belt; it's just not you. I think you should get another one in a plain color, without all this junk cluttering it up."

His eyes were glowing with a subtle smile as they looked into hers. She was five-seven, with a sweet round face that was more handsome than pretty, and with a basic earthy quality that he found attractive. She was just folks; he called her "back yard," telling her he could be comfortable with her any time, any place, for she was backstage rather than in front of the footlights.

In short, she was real. And with Coltrane's drinking and drug fantasies becoming more fantastic each day, Naima offered him the kind of reality he was brought up with and still wished to retain or return to.

He also told her, "You know, I don't talk much." Then he proceeded to prove it by taking her home and, as she recalls, "talking my ears off until the sun came up the next morning."

They would often talk about music, among other shared interests.

In her childhood home, Naima had heard all kinds of music; she was exposed to Bartók as well as blues. In school, she had attended concerts. Once, a symphony orchestra played for her class, and afterward the conductor explained what they had just played. She thought that was strange. To her, it was not necessary to understand the music; merely to appreciate it was enough.

"You either like it or you don't," she told John.

"I'd like you to hear me play," he told Naima.

It was not until the next month that she did, at a club where he was backing up a name singer. He was allowed a few solos, and she heard his sound. She recalls that his music reminded her "of clouds, because clouds cover the earth like a blanket."

That night, his music made the hairs rise on her neck.

Another month passed, and John told Naima that he was going

to marry her. It was a manner that was strictly matter-of-fact; they were sharing a hoagie at Pat's when he mentioned it, using about as much emotional inflection as he might in asking for a glass of water.

"How do you know *that?*" she protested. "You haven't even *asked* me!"

"Then I'll ask you now," he replied, and quietly proposed to her.

They were married on October 3, 1955, the same momentous month that he first recorded with Miles Davis, whose quintet he had joined the preceding spring.

Naima and John had no religious conflicts. She retained her Moslem beliefs and he, though now no more than a nominal Christian, was becoming more involved in his philosophical readings. As he would later explain, "I believe in all religions." And as Naima would clarify, "I never thought of John as a non-Moslem, because to me he was always a very spiritual person."

After the wedding, they all moved in, Naima and Toni and John, with John's mother on North Thirty-third Street.

> One thing I remember, watching Coltrane backstage; he was fingering his horn without playing it, as if he was going over in his mind what he was going to play next. It's like a drummer with a practice pad, his own way of thinking through his music before he actually plays it.
>
> BILLY TAYLOR

Billy Taylor appears ageless; he seems to possess the same boyish, youthful appearance that he had in his twenties. Whether you saw him as music director on the David Frost TV show a few years ago or as house pianist at Birdland two decades before that, he still appears much the same today. He was a protégé of Art Tatum, and his piano style still reflects the master's influence: fast two-handed runs, unexpected arabesques, and the ability to thoroughly cover the piano's seven-plus octave range in all keys.

Coltrane, though still residing in Philadelphia, came into New York for occasional jobs during 1954–55. One of them was the regular Monday night jam session at Birdland. Taylor recalls him as playing mostly bop phrases but with "something extra, a strange turn of phrase, an odd substitution of chords that, the more you thought about it, seemed just right for his style." Taylor's job was, of course, to accompany the dozens of different musicians who'd show up for the session. But with John, Billy played differently, challenging him with unusual musical detours that encouraged the saxophonist to extend his ideas further.

Coltrane knew that Taylor had studied with Tatum. He often asked the pianist about Tatum's technique, with as much interest as if he were a piano player himself. This was probably a prelude to John's later practice sessions with a piano book.

During intermission, the two of them often took a coffee break at a place around the corner. A typical Coltrane question to Taylor might be, "Billy, how did you do that? What chord progressions did you use to make that kind of run?" Then the pianist wrote his ideas down on manuscript paper, giving full details about the musical progressions so that the saxophonist could study the specifics by himself.

Coltrane also asked Taylor about many of the older musicians, some famous and others not, who had been active during the postwar period. It almost seemed as if John wished he'd been old enough to know them personally as well as he knew their music. As it he'd been born too late to participate in that glorious bop revolution, and wondered when the next ousting of the musical establishment would take place, not then knowing that he himself would be the leader of a forthcoming musical *coup d'état*.

In turn, Billy questioned John about the latter's days with rhythm-and-blues bands. He wondered whether the saxophonist's drug addiction might have been caused, if not aggravated, by his being forced, at least for the moment, to play this kind of music for sheer economic survival. But what Billy actually asked John was, did he really learn anything from playing with Bull Moose Jackson, King Kolax, and of course the fabulous Daisy Mae and the Hepcats?

Coltrane sighed; he tried to shrug off the question, seemingly embarrassed to be reminded of what he was still doing in Philadelphia (and occasionally on the road). Finally, he admitted, "It gets to people. It's a direct emotional communication, and the audience gets involved."

And he refused to say any more.

> I heard John Coltrane on tenor before I ever saw him with Miles Davis, and I followed his career all the way until his death. The one word I would always use to describe his music is "vigorous." I heard bop and beyond; I also caught a stomping tenor sound, probably from his background in rhythm-and-blues. I perceived a serious meditative gift in his music, something I had previously associated with only one musician, Charlie Parker, who was a melodic genius. Though Coltrane's meditative gift was primarily harmonic rather than melodic, I still associate that gift with genius.
>
> BARRY ULANOV

Now it is time to call him Trane.

Just before he joined Miles Davis in 1955, someone, as apparently unknown as the person who'd put him on drugs, gave him the nickname of Trane, and it stuck. With the exception of Benny Golson, Bill Barron, and a few other close friends who would always think of him as John, Coltrane was "Trane" to most musicians and fans from then on. As Charlie Parker was originally called Yardbird, then later shortened to Bird.

The metaphorical allusions are perfectly suited to both musicians. Bird *was* a high flyer, a man ripped loose from his roots through a combination of artistic genius and a complete lack of personal discipline. He was as restless as he was rootless, a spirit so free from constraints that like his medium, the air, he could never be contained and therefore could not connect with those he was trying to communicate with. Bird was on a stubborn, self-destructive course that could only result in one grand finale—an early death.

Trane, on the other hand, for all the wildness and exploring in his music, was a man always in control of himself. He was a person of deep roots who was ever conscious of his heritage, a self-contained and self-disciplined man who, as his name implied, built up his power and strength by degrees, gradually increasing his ground speed as he roared along his tracks, the twin disciplines of his music and his mind, arriving at his eventual destination perhaps not as quickly as Bird but in substantially better shape.

Since Freud has postulated that motion is the first pleasure principle, any form of transportation is naturally a representation of kinetic energy at work. And John Coltrane was certainly a musician always in motion; music was always moving him, especially in his mind.

> Coltrane and I first met in 1950 in New York, where we worked together for a few memorable gigs with Miles Davis. I really had to listen carefully to him. I often wondered, what was he doing, where was he going? I didn't think it would be proper to ask, but I listened harder, and eventually I began to better understand his music. Later, we became good friends. Good enough friends for me to borrow money from him, and Coltrane and Monk were the only two people I would ever ask for a loan.
>
> SONNY ROLLINS

Sonny Rollins is three years younger, two inches taller, and one life removed from John Coltrane. However, their paths intersected when they both worked with Miles (twice: Sonny in 1954 and 1957, Trane from 1955 to 1956 and 1957 to 1960). Coincidentally, both started on alto saxophone and switched to tenor.

Their musical influences, though, were different; Rollins is out of Pres and Bird, a melodic improviser par excellence, while Hawk and Dex moved Coltrane more into areas of advanced harmonics. Rollins is the more "traditional" of the two, sounding very "tenorish" on his horn, with a breadth and strength that would only be matched, and later exceeded, by Coltrane's penetration, brilliance, and melancholy.

But their personal rapport was immediate, for Sonny possesses in abundance those traits that attracted Trane: individualistic persona, searching mind, and philosophical tendencies. Trane would later list Sonny among his four most-admired musicians. He would also do for Rollins what he did only for those he loved, personally or musically—write a song dedicated to them. Thus, "Like Sonny" (recorded in the *Coltrane Jazz* album).

Rollins may have repaid the favor in his own esoteric way. Trane joined Miles in spring 1955 as a full-time member of the quintet. Sonny was the previous tenor saxophonist, but he shortly went into one of his "retirements" and Miles definitely needed a saxophonist who would be available at all times. It is entirely possible that Rollins, knowing of Coltrane's increasing frustration due to lack of musical recognition, may have "moved over" so that Coltrane would have the opportunity he'd long been waiting for.

Drummer Philly Joe Jones certainly helped Trane. As the name implies, he's from Philadelphia; he uses that nickname to differentiate himself from ex-Basie drummer Jo Jones. He is also no relation to either Jones drummer, Jo or Elvin. Philly Joe and Trane had worked together in Philadelphia, so when Miles hired the drummer he recommended Trane for the tenor chair.

Ironically enough, both Coltrane and Jones became the two musicians Davis was most often requested to get rid of. As Miles recalls, "People used to tell me Trane couldn't play and Philly Joe played too loud. But I know what I want, and if I didn't think they knew what they were doing, they wouldn't be there."

Red Garland was the pianist, and he put in some good words for the saxophonist, while bassist Paul Chambers also knew Coltrane well enough to suggest him to Davis. So it's almost an understatement to say that John Coltrane came well recommended.

He was also well recommended—and well remembered—by Bird's third wife, Doris, who was living in Chicago when the Davis band played a date at the Sutherland Lounge. Many still thought of Trane as a superstraight guy; few knew of his subtle, offbeat sense of humor, and Doris Parker's first encounter with John Coltrane illustrates this well.

She had bought some groceries for Paul Chambers, who had a room with kitchenette at the Sutherland Hotel, and was carrying two heavy bags toward the hotel when a man stopped her in the street and asked her if she would like some help. She hesitated, but the man seemed genuinely friendly, so she let him carry the groceries and walk along with her to Chambers' room.

Mrs. Parker thought there was something vaguely familiar about this man, but she couldn't place him and didn't want to ask him anything directly. When Paul answered the door, he stared at Doris' companion and said, "Do you know him?" The man stared back at Chambers, set the sacks down, and walked away.

As Paul was carrying the groceries inside, Doris asked, "Paul, who was that man? Do you know him, or don't you?"

He winked at her. "Don't you know him?"

She hesitated. "Was that . . . was it really . . ."

He answered, "John Coltrane."

Paul Chambers and I are both from Detroit, and Paul got me a gig in November 1955 to record for a new record label in Boston. It was called Transition, and John Coltrane was on the date with us. Unfortunately—or fortunately, depending on whether you're a critic or a musician—the album was never released, but a single blues track was put out as a sampler. The reviews of that track were so bad they never issued the album. I recall that the *Down Beat* critic liked everybody except Coltrane and myself—I play baritone, and I'd certainly call that a case of sax discrimination—and he said of Trane, "He sounds hysterical . . . and Oriental." The next time I saw John, I said, "Hello there, you hysterical Oriental." And he smiled . . . inscrutably.

PEPPER ADAMS

Other musicians were not so kind, but some could be as candid and honest with John Coltrane as he tried to be with them. For example:

I'm going to be honest with you, Coltrane. I don't know what you're doing. Do you really know what you're doing?

TONY RULLI

Tony Rulli sells Selmer horns. He's based in New York now, but during the late 1950s and early 1960s he was working out of the Selmer headquarters and factory in Elkhart, Indiana. He also plays tenor sax himself and understands saxophone techniques as well as any teacher. But when he caught Miles Davis at the Sutherland during that fall 1955 engagement, he was not so much in attendance to see Coltrane as to sell Davis a Selmer trumpet.

He doesn't recall whether he ever did or not. What he does remember is that Coltrane was playing a Selmer saxophone; thinking he must be having problems with it from the way he sounded, Rulli invited him to the factory to have his horn inspected. It was there that Rulli asked Coltrane what he was doing.

And Trane told him.

More than that; Trane showed him. He took out some manuscript paper and sketched out a series of chord progressions, melodic lines, and rhythmic figures. While he was doing this, he was also speaking, explaining everything to Rulli in great detail as the saxophone salesman sat there with his mouth—and mind—opening wider by the minute.

When John Coltrane was finished, Tony Rulli looked at him and said, slowly and with great admiration, "Now I know why I didn't know what you were doing, because I just didn't understand what you were doing. Now that I understand what you were doing, I know what you're doing."

Long pause.

"At least . . . I *think* I understand."

Welcome to New York, Brother . . . It's a City Full of Fun.

LEON THOMAS

When I first me John Coltrane, he was standing in front of the Cafe Bohemia on Barrow Street. This was in spring 1956, when Miles Davis was playing there. I went outside during intermission, and there was Coltrane eating a piece of pie. I remember his eyes, huge but not staring, friendly and almost bemused. We looked at each other for the longest time, until I said hello and told him how much I liked his music. I'd played with Charles Mingus, and I mentioned this to Coltrane, who said he was quite an admirer of Mingus' music. He also said that one of the things he was trying to do was to take music beyond the 32-bar song form, to constantly develop and improvise on an idea or a simple line, as Indian musicians do with a raga. We talked about the French horn, which I play. We talked about many instruments and the way their individual intonations could best be utilized. I think this was the most serious musical discussion during the shortest amount of time I've ever had in my life.

DAVID AMRAM

I saw Coltrane at the Bohemia in late 1956, and this was one of the times Sonny Rollins and Trane both played with Miles. I knew Sonny's style, but Trane really surprised me. I'd always thought of Rollins as a great tenor virtuoso, but Coltrane more than held his own. He followed Sonny's melodic solos with some of the strangest, most convoluted harmonies and chord progressions I'd ever heard. During intermission, I went up to talk to him and he said, "You're Paul Jeffery? I've heard about you. Come out in the alley." We did, and Trane handed me his horn and said, "I'd like to hear you play." I was so scared I could barely finger the keys, but I managed to play a few passable runs. Then he gave me his address and said to stop by whenever I was in the neighborhood.

PAUL JEFFREY

The John Coltrane family moved into New York in June 1956 on a temporary basis, staying with Paul Chambers in his Brooklyn apartment while looking for a permanent place. They had decided that a New York residency was both logical and necessary, for not only did Davis and other musicians make their homes there, but the largest number of record companies, clubs, and press outlets were available in New York City. While Philadelphia was comfortably close enough when Trane was just another struggling musician, now that he was beginning to make his name with Miles it would be best to move where the musical action was.

The Miles Davis Quintet was then recording for Prestige. Trane persuaded Miles to include a Benny Golson tune, "Stablemates," in one of Davis' albums as a favor to Golson. The tune became a jazz classic; it also helped Benny become better known as a composer and Trane as a soloist. Miles benefited, too, for the extra exposure he received as the leader on the date was instrumental in getting him out of his Prestige contract—a move he wanted desperately to make—and into a more rewarding record company relationship, both artistically and financially.

George Avakian of Columbia Records wanted Miles.

Avakian was a producer in charge of jazz and pop albums. He had heard Davis at the Newport Jazz Festival in 1954, when Miles played Monk's exquisite ballad "'Round Midnight" and got most of the critics talking about his "comeback." Avakian was sufficiently impressed to talk Columbia into signing the trumpeter for a $4,000 advance. This was quite a windfall for Miles, considering that he was only working an occasional Monday night at Birdland, despite the fact that he was recording frequently.

With Davis, of course, came Coltrane.

Avakian recalls, "I met Coltrane with Miles at the Cafe Bohemia late in 1955. He reminded me of a large cherub, though a rather expressionless one. He was not easy to start a conversation with, but I sensed the depths of the man and I felt he was highly intelligent. Our family is Armenian, and when I mentioned my interest in Eastern cultures, John really opened up. He told me about books he'd read and things he'd learned that were well in advance of my personal knowledge at that time. While we talked, I couldn't help noticing his eyes. They had an arresting quality, and whenever he looked at me, or anyone else, he really looked deeply."

He listened to several sets that evening. What most impressed him were the jagged, explosive harmonies Coltrane was investigating. Avakian heard Coltrane screaming, as if shouting for attention and crying for release. He remembers how intently and intensely he watched the saxophonist while he was playing. To George, John "seemed to grow taller in height, larger in size, with each note that he played, each chord he seemed to be pushing to its outer limits."

Then, Miles Davis recorded the album *'Round about Midnight.*

The title tune was by Thelonious Monk, as mentioned previously; why the "about" was added, no one seems to know. "Midnight" and the five other songs comprising the album were recorded in three separate sessions, from late 1955 through early 1956. Monk's tune, the album's opening selection, with Miles playing a muted solo and followed by Trane in double time, bursting with energy and spraying out a profusion of notes spaced so closely together that they almost overlapped one another, was considered *the* classic cut. But the connoisseurs paid particular attention to "Bye Bye Blackbird," an archaic pop tune that Miles often used for some quite contemporary improvisations. As did Trane, whose "Blackbird" solo was a geyser of arpeggios and bent notes, sounding as if they were coming from the bottom of some deep, clear well of creativity. With the Davis band, Coltrane was finding his voice, refining his sound, and revealing his conceptions for fellow musicians and fans alike.

One musician who later became a fan, altoist Jerry Dodgion, was then living in San Francisco. When he first heard Trane, he thought that the latter "was still struggling with his horn." However, Dodgion gave Trane a full hearing when Miles Davis played the Blackhawk, and in common with many of the other customers, he was mesmerized with more than Miles that evening.

Wanting to hear more, he followed the musicians to an after-hours place called The Streets of Paris, expecting to catch some more Coltrane sounds.

He didn't.

Trane just sat quietly in the back, drinking and smoking, nodding and listening to the other musicians playing. When Jerry introduced himself and said, "Come on up and play," John replied, "Not right now, I'd rather listen."

That's what he did; for three nights straight.

Coltrane and I were working at the Showboat in Philadelphia, and one night during intermission some guy came up to us and said, "I'd like to see you both upstairs in the men's room." I thought he was a faggot; I just said, "So what?" Trane didn't say anything. Then the guy flashed a badge and said, "Don't make a scene, I'm a narcotics officer." We all went to the men's room, and he had us take off our shirts. He claimed some lady had told him we were on drugs. I showed him my arms and said, "Aren't they beautiful?" Then he looked at Coltrane's arms and asked, "What about those marks?" Trane looked sheepish, and said, "Those are birthmarks; I've had them as long as I can remember." I almost cracked up, but Trane looked so boyishly innocent that the narcotics cop believed him, and he ended up letting both of us go.

JIMMY COBB

The Miles Davis Quintet of 1955–56 was a most unusual environment for John Coltrane, not so much musically but personally.

For a prime example, there is the leader himself.

Davis, like Coltrane, was and is a continually growing musician whose musical style and conception would change as often as his wardrobe, and usually for the better. Taciturn to the point of diffidence, most of the time, and on other occasions abrasive to the extreme of arousing personal hostility, Miles remains a man and musician with a mystique comparable to no one and a persona that one must accept or reject strictly on the trumpeter's terms. He is the spoiled son of a black bourgeois family who strides off stage after the completion of his solo on each and every song; he is also the kind of leader who gives his men maximum space for their own musical statements and pays them well above scale for that particular privilege. Controversial, paradoxical, unpredictable, and unclassifiable; that was and is Miles, and, if you like him or leave him, he couldn't care less either way.

Of the five men in his band, he was also the only musician who was "clean."

He'd kicked his own drug habit prior to his successful Newport appearance in 1954. However, his musicians, to a man, were still shooting up, at least in part due to the pervasive influence of Philly Joe Jones, who was to drugs what W. C. Fields was to booze. The constant presence of the big "H" didn't seem to unduly affect the music, though; only the musicians, internally, where it wasn't noticed.

Was the fact of their getting high helping, or hindering, the music? And why get high if the music was a great enough high by itself?

And why did John Coltrane and Miles Davis so abruptly part company in November 1956, triggering Trane's return to Philadelphia and his move back to his mother's house?

> After I joined Miles in 1955, I found that he doesn't talk much and will rarely discuss his music. He's completely unpredictable; sometimes he'd walk off stage after just playing a few notes, not even completing one chorus. If I asked him something about his music, I never knew how he was going to take it.
>
> JOHN COLTRANE

> Miles is more paradoxical than any musician I ever knew, even Coltrane. I heard that he gave Trane an ultimatum to stop drinking and taking drugs or get out of the band. I think that for some unknown reason, Coltrane was really bored with the music and in effect engineered his own discharge. I also think Miles let him go in the hope that Trane would straighten himself out and come back after he was clean.
>
> MICHAEL HARPER

If Coltrane was not clean, the following scene could easily give rise to an innumerable amount of replays:

> In 1957 I was on a record date with Coltrane, and he was definitely high on junk, of that I'm sure. We were sitting near the rhythm section while the leader was taking a long piano solo. It was almost time for Coltrane's solo, and as I

turned to look at him I noticed that he was nodding out, holding his horn in his lap. Before I could do anything, the leader happened to look up from the piano, saw Trane's condition, and screamed, "Coltrane . . . *Coltrane!*" What happened next was so amazing I'll never forget it as long as I live. Trane was suddenly on his feet, playing in perfect cadence and following the piano solo as if nothing had happened. He played a pretty good solo, and when he was finished he sat down again and went back to nodding out.

RAY COPELAND

In the early spring of 1957, John Coltrane took three giant steps: he stopped smoking, drinking, and taking drugs.

The family was staying at Mrs. Coltrane's home in Philadelphia. John wasn't working much; instead, he was generously partaking of cigarets, liquor, and drugs during this frustrating absence and abstinence from his beloved music. But, as Naima recalls, he woke up one morning and said to her, "Naima, I'm through."

His words chilled her; she wondered whether he meant something else, until his next statement, "I've decided to stop smoking, drinking, and taking drugs." Pause. "But I need your help, I can't do this all by myself." Longer pause. "Will you help me, Naima? Will you back me up all the way?"

She said, with fervor, "You *know* I will."

He got up and dressed; he went into his mother's room and had the same conversation with her. Mrs. Coltrane, who had personally absorbed much of the excruciating pain of these preoccupations of her only son during the past several years—especially the heroin habit—was as overwhelmed as she was overjoyed. She said, "John, let's do it now, let's not wait another minute."

Coltrane nodded in agreement. He had finally realized that he couldn't concentrate on making music and making his system sick at the same time; one simply interfered too much with the other. And it was for musical more than personal reasons that he was kicking everything; not because he loved his family less but his music more. His saxophone was still his major love object; nothing gave him greater satisfaction.

With God's grace, he believed, and his own determination, all things were possible. His readings in religion and philosophy had convinced him that he should now cleanse himself of physical and psychological impurities and dedicate his music to God, in whom he believed with increasing involvement each passing day.

Then he excused himself, first to the bathroom to clean up, and next to retire to his room. Like a prisoner, but a self-sentenced one, he would subsist on water alone. He would fast, not sweat, it out; and he would not walk again among his family until he was clean. From time to time either Naima or John's mother would knock on his door, asking him if he was all right. He would either say "Yes" or "May I have some more water?"

He only left his bedroom for the bathroom; he went nowhere else in the apartment while he was going through his ordeal. The two women in his life prayed for him. When Toni, home from school, inquired after her father, she was simply told that he was sick and resting by himself. Then, they allowed her to see John for just a few minutes, and that was all.

Naima does not remember how long this period lasted; perhaps three or four days, but not more than a week. And when it was over, that was it; no more poison in Coltrane's system.

Except for tobacco.

Like his sweet tooth, he still retained a lingering taste for tobacco and could only quit that habit for brief periods. From cigarets he switched to cigars, then to a meerschaum pipe (perhaps due to the influence of producer Bob Thiele, who smoked one). Finally, during his last years of life, he managed to banish the weed entirely, becoming a vegetarian as well. He reached an almost total abstinence from all the stimulations of the world; the important exceptions were music and God, but to him one was equally a part of the other, and both were now an integral part of his psyche.

As he wrote when he recorded *A Love Supreme:*

"During the year 1957, I experienced, by the grace of God, a spiritual awakening which was to lead me to a richer, fuller, more productive life. At that time, in gratitude, I humbly asked to be given the means and privilege to make others happy through music. I feel this has been granted through His grace. ALL PRAISE TO GOD."

> Working with Monk brought me close to a musical architect of the highest order. I felt I learned from him in every way—sensually, theoretically, technically. I would talk to Monk about musical problems, and he would show me the answers by playing them on the piano. He gave me complete freedom in my playing, and no one ever did that before.
>
> JOHN COLTRANE

> I once saw John with Monk, and I think he learned an incredible amount of harmonic background from him. Monk opened him up to the point where he was able to compose complex tunes like, "Giant Steps." I learned a lot myself just listening to Monk play. His concept of space alone was one of the most important things he taught Coltrane; when to lay out and let somebody else fill up that space, or just leave the space open. I think John was already going in that direction, but working with Monk helped him reach his goal that much faster.
>
> McCOY TYNER

Thelonious Sphere Monk is one of the most reclusive people one could meet, yet paradoxically, or perhaps perversely, he is listed in the Manhattan telephone directory. However, he is not especially fond of receiving phone calls, and if he answers at all it's usually to say "Monk's not here" and then hang up.

He comes from Coltrane's home state—his birthplace is Rocky Mount—but was brought to New York as a child, remaining with his mother when his father returned to stay in North Carolina due to illness. By the time he reached his teens he was a good enough pianist to get jobs playing Harlem rent parties. At sixteen he quit school to go on the road with a faith healer, and at nineteen he was house pianist at Minton's.

As a self-taught musician, he claims few influences; but one he does acknowledge, and surprisingly so to many of his listeners, is Fats Waller. And with some striking parallels to the fellow Carolina boy he'd work with during 1957, Monk also lived with his mother for a long, extended period, moving his wife, Nellie, right into the same West Sixties apartment with her after he got married. In addition, like Coltrane's, his music can be difficult to dig, and he can be quiet (and sometimes what he calls "disconnected") to the point of catatonia.

Much respected by musicians, Monk's music is oblique and astringent; his advanced harmonics are sometimes broken down into quarter tones or even smaller musical measurements. Yet his drawing power is so strong that when the Five Spot booked him on an open contract, weekend customers lined up for blocks, and even during the week the house was rarely less than full. Monk brought Trane with him for that gig, which began in spring 1957 and carried on well into the following fall, when, for reasons no one will reveal, the job was terminated almost as abruptly as it had begun. A strangely similar situation to Trane's sudden departure from Miles the preceding year.

Monk, of course, knew of Coltrane's work with Davis. Once, while backstage at the Bohemia to say hello, Monk saw Miles slap Trane in the face and then punch him in the stomach, probably in a dispute about something Trane had, or hadn't, played. Coltrane, gentle to the point of passivity, let it pass. But Monk didn't; he said to Trane, "As much saxophone as you play, you don't have to take that. Why don't you come to work for me?"

Thus the genesis of the Thelonious Monk Quartet, which also included Wilbur Ware on bass and Shadow Wilson on drums.

The music was mostly by Monk, with a few standard songs added for variety and because the leader liked their changes. His own music, however, was marked by the eccentric sentiments of its composer: "Well, You Needn't"; "Criss Cross"; "Off Minor"; "Epistrophy"; "Blue Monk"; "Crepuscule With Nellie." Each tune sounds as if the title had been phonetically applied to the harmonies at hand. They weren't Broadway show tunes or Bavarian drinking songs, but the music got right to the guts, made the toes tap. It was so naturally swinging that some of the customers got up to dance in the aisles.

Monk was one of them.

He'd do his dance too, choreographed by and for nobody but himself. After his solo, Monk would "stroll," that is, not play, but rise from the piano, bending and whirling, making pivots and foot stomps that accented his music right on the beat, as if he was leading the band with his body. Body English; he'd spin and shuffle, his wispy beard bouncing in time to the beat, his grinning eyes staring down his long nose, his fur hat stuck tightly to his skull. Sometimes he'd wave his hands, as if playing the role of symphony conductor.

Meanwhile, Trane was struggling with Monk's music, especially since Monk was not at the piano to feed him the accompanying chords. The saxophonist had to fend for himself while soloing, searching his way carefully among the extremely small intervals that were so much a part of the music. Of course, that was one of the ways that Trane really learned the leader's music; on stand, at least, he had no other choice.

Behind him, bassist Wilbur Ware, a graying, restless sprite, was playing melodic fills, weaving his lines in and around the music, setting up whoever was soloing and assisting him with just the right choice of notes. Meanwhile, drummer Shadow Wilson, handsomely mustached, a tight smile creased on his thin lips, was kicking the band with a savage subtlety, a loose propulsion he'd picked up when he had played with Count Basie.

The Thelonious Monk Quartet, wailing while they worked.

Naima often stopped by the Five Spot with a tape recorder, transcribing as many complete sets as possible. Then, upon returning, after the evening's engagement was over, to the hotel they had moved into in June 1957, while Trane was working with Monk, they'd play back the music for criticism and study. Naima would often fall asleep, but he'd continue listening until he'd heard and analyzed every note of not only his own performance but also Monk's and that of the rhythm section and the entire band.

Once, listening to a long arpeggiated solo of his own on another introspective Monk ballad, "Ruby, My Dear," the saxophonist heard something that was not tenor or piano but another instrument.

He played that passage back. Again and again.

He still couldn't match the sounds on tape to what he imagined he'd heard previously in his head. Sighing, he woke up Naima and asked her to listen. She knew classical music better than he did. She listened, at his suggestion, for some European influence he thought had slipped into his solo but whose origin he could not place. After a few minutes of listening and thinking, she said, "It reminds me of *Daphnis and Chloe*. What you played was very similar to the opening passages."

He nodded, looking at her with those huge eyes, and by the way he looked she knew that he wanted to know the composer but didn't ask, afraid of displaying his ignorance. She told him, "Ravel."

Then he recalled his former teacher, Dennis Sandole, suggesting that he listen to the French impressionists, in particular Debussy and Ravel.

"What instrument am I hearing?" he asked her. "I don't mean any instrument in the band; I mean another instrument that my solo reminds me of."

He explained what he meant. She placed her fist on her jaw, assuming a thoughtful pose. "Well . . . it's mostly strings and woodwinds, as I recall. . . ." Then, after a pause of several seconds, she added, "Now that I think about it . . . there's a harp solo. . . ."

Silence, for several more seconds.

Then Coltrane recalled hearing a harp concerto in Philadelphia, in a recital at the Academy of Music, where a friend had once taken him. He had wondered how the instrument could sustain such glissandos and overtones, as if the harp was really a giant guitar with a hidden amplifier causing those gorgeous, shimmering sounds.

"Harp," he said, thoughtfully, reverently, as if uttering a sacred word.

Then he said, decisively, "Tomorrow we're going to get some harp records." Pause. "So I can hear what I'm doing when I don't know what I'm doing."

Joe and Iggy Termini had originally opened the Five Spot at 5 Cooper Square, in the neighborhood now called Manhattan's East Village, in 1956. Later, they opened another club, the Jazz Gallery, and almost as quickly closed it, moving the Five Spot to 2 St. Marks Place in 1962.

Both brothers had many occasions to observe both Trane and Monk during that long-running gig of 1957.

> Trane was getting a lot of attention. I heard many people talk to him, urging him to go out on his own. But I remember many times when he'd sit in the back between sets, testing reeds, a worried look on his face, as if he was perpetually dissatisfied.
>
> JOE TERMINI

> I remember Monk doing his dancing bit. But sometimes, after he was through dancing, he'd wander into the kitchen and start talking to the dishwasher about God knows what. Once in a while he'd fall asleep at the piano, and when it was time for him to come in again, he'd wake up and start playing, just liked that.
>
> IGGY TERMINI

Trane, as if embarking on an astral projection and stepping out of his body to analyze his own visual and visceral performance, said about Monk and himself: "I always wanted a large tone, big and solid. I'd work out on ninth chords, but soon found that they limited me. I started playing fourth chords, and soon I could create more volume than on ninths. Monk gave me complete freedom. He'd leave the stand for a drink or to do his dance, and I could just improvise by myself for fifteen or twenty minutes before he returned."

Antonia/Syeeda Coltrane was out of school when the Coltrane family moved to New York. They stayed in their hotel until October 1957, then moved into a three-and-one-half-room, rent-controlled apartment on Manhattan's West 103rd Street. Their new home was on the second floor of a six-story building, with a tavern on the corner. Coltrane sometimes said that he chose that particular loca-

Here's Bird and Diz together, and the guy looking on is John Coltrane at 24. The photo was taken at a club on New York's West Fifty-second Street (the fabled "Swing Street") during 1950. Coltrane shouldn't look so scared; it was Charlie Parker himself who taught Trane the correct changes to Bird's lovely blues, "Relaxin' at Camarillo."

Dizzy Gillespie broke up his big band at the end of 1950, but a few carefully chosen sidemen were asked to stay and play in his new combo during 1951. Left to right: Milt Jackson (piano and vibes), Jimmy Heath (alto sax), Percy Heath (bass), Specs Wright (drums), Dizzy Gillespie (trumpet), Coltrane (tenor sax), Fred Strong (conga). REPRINTED COURTESY OF "DOWN BEAT."

THE ENCYCLOPEDIA YEARBOOK OF JAZZ

J A Z Z   E N C Y C L O P E D I A   Q U E S T I O N N A I R E

****

PLEASE FILL IN VERY CLEARLY IN BLOCK LETTERS:

PROFESSIONAL NAME: JOHN COLTRANE   FULL LEGAL NAME: John William Coltrane

PERMANENT ADDRESS: 1511 N. 33rd ST. Phila. Pa. TELEPHONE: ST-4-9921

INSTRUMENTS PLAYED: Tenor Saxophone

EXACT BIRTHDATE: MONTH 9 DAY 23 YEAR 26 WHERE BORN: Hamlet N.C.

ANY PARENTS, BROTHERS, SISTERS OR OTHER RELATIVES MUSICALLY INCLINED? GIVE DETAILS. My Father, A Tailor, Enjoyed his spare time playing violin, ukelele & Clarinet.

WHERE AND WHEN DID YOU STUDY MUSIC? WHAT INSTRUMENTS FIRST? in high school. Eb Alto horn - Clarinet & Finally Alto Saxophone. Later at Granoff Studios & Ornstein school of Music.

HOW DID YOU GET INTO THE MUSIC BUSINESS? in Philadelphia with a Cocktail Trio. This Job was in 1945. I also Joined The musician's union at That same Time.

GIVE FULL DETAILS, WITH DATES, OF ALL BANDS OR COMBOS YOU HAVE WORKED WITH.

1947 - Eddie Vinson's Band Through mid 1948.
Dizzy Gillespie - 1949 - 1951
Earl Bostic - 1952 - 1953
Johnny Hodges - 1953 - 1954
Miles Davis - 1955 - present Date

HAVE YOU EVER WORKED OVERSEAS? IF SO, STATE WHAT TOWNS, COUNTRIES AND DATES

Only in The Naval Band in Hawaii
Dec. 1945 Through June 1946.

Coltrane's completed application for the Encyclopedia Yearbook of Jazz includes a list of his favorite saxophonists. The inclusion of Gordon and Rollins should elicit no surprises; but Coltrane's choice of Stitt, considering that the latter is a lineal descendant of Bird on

JAZZ ENCYCLOPEDIA QUESTIONNAIRE, PAGE TWO

WHERE AND WHEN DID YOU MAKE YOUR DEBUT ON RECORDS? In Detroit with Dizzy Gillespie in 1950.

GIVE FULL DETAILS OF ALL IMPORTANT RECORDINGS YOU HAVE MADE, STATING FOR WHAT COMPANIES, AND STATE WHICH YOU THINK IS YOUR OWN BEST SOLO PERFORMANCE ON RECORD. I have only made a few that I liked. These were a group made with Paul Chambers in los angeles for Alladin + a recent album with Miles Davis for Columbia.

ANY MOVIE, RADIO OR TV APPEARANCES?

A few TV dates with the Dizzy Gillespie + Miles Davis bands.

EVER WON ANY MAGAZINE AWARDS? IF SO, WHAT YEAR?
No

WHO ARE YOUR FAVORITE MUSICIANS ON YOUR INSTRUMENT? (IF AN ARRANGER, NAME YOUR FAVORITE ARRANGERS.)

Sonny Stitt, Dexter Gordon, Sonny Rollins, Stan Getz

GIVE ANY OTHER DETAILS ABOUT YOURSELF, YOUR BACKGROUND, YOUR AMBITIONS THAT YOU THINK WOULD BE OF INTEREST FOR INCLUSION IN "JAZZ ENCYCLOPEDIA".

I'm very happy to be in this music world + I have been lucky in being close to many creative musicians. It is a very great pleasure to play in a good, well knit group + I hope that I will be able to stay at it for a long time.

PLEASE RETURN THIS QUESTIONNAIRE PROMPTLY TO LEONARD FEATHER
340 RIVERSIDE DRIVE
NEW YORK 25, N. Y.

alto, is intriguing. And Trane's mention of Getz is especially revealing because of their being booked together on several occasions as if a "cutting contest" or saxophone "battle" were involved. COURTESY OF THE INSTITUTE OF JAZZ STUDIES, RUTGERS UNIVERSITY.

Miles Davis was the man with whom John Coltrane made his musical name, after joining the trumpeter in 1955. But some say that complaints from musical conservatives persuaded a reluctant Miles to ease Trane out in late 1956. Shortly after "disbanding," Davis reformed his quintet in early 1957 with Sonny Rollins, not John Coltrane, on tenor. REPRINTED COURTESY OF "DOWN BEAT."

Trane often practiced in the bedroom, alone. However, when musicians the caliber of Bobby Timmons and cousins-in-law Earl and Carl Grubbs were visiting from Philadelphia and playing in the living room, John Coltrane could not help but join in the jamming. This photo was taken at Naima and John Coltrane's apartment on West 103rd Street, New York, during Easter 1958. Left to right: B. Timmons (piano), E. Grubbs (alto sax), C. Grubbs (clarinet), Coltrane (tenor sax). COURTESY OF EARL AND CARL GRUBBS.

Classical pianist Zita Carno transcribed John Coltrane's eight-chorus solo, note for note, from the recorded version of his own composition, "Blue Train." When she met the saxophonist in person, she asked him to play that same solo again, reading from her transcription. He replied, "I can't; it's too difficult." Above: The first four choruses of "Blue Train." COURTESY OF THE "JAZZ REVIEW" (VOL. 2, NO. 10, NOVEMBER 1959) AND ZITA CARNO.

Try as he might, John Coltrane could never completely give up smoking. He switched from cigarets to cigars to pipes, all in vain. However, here he was certainly entitled to a few moments of meditation with his pipe, for this photo was taken while the saxophonist was recording some of his most turbulent and convoluted music ever, during June 1965: *Ascension*. COURTESY OF ABC/IMPULSE RECORDS.

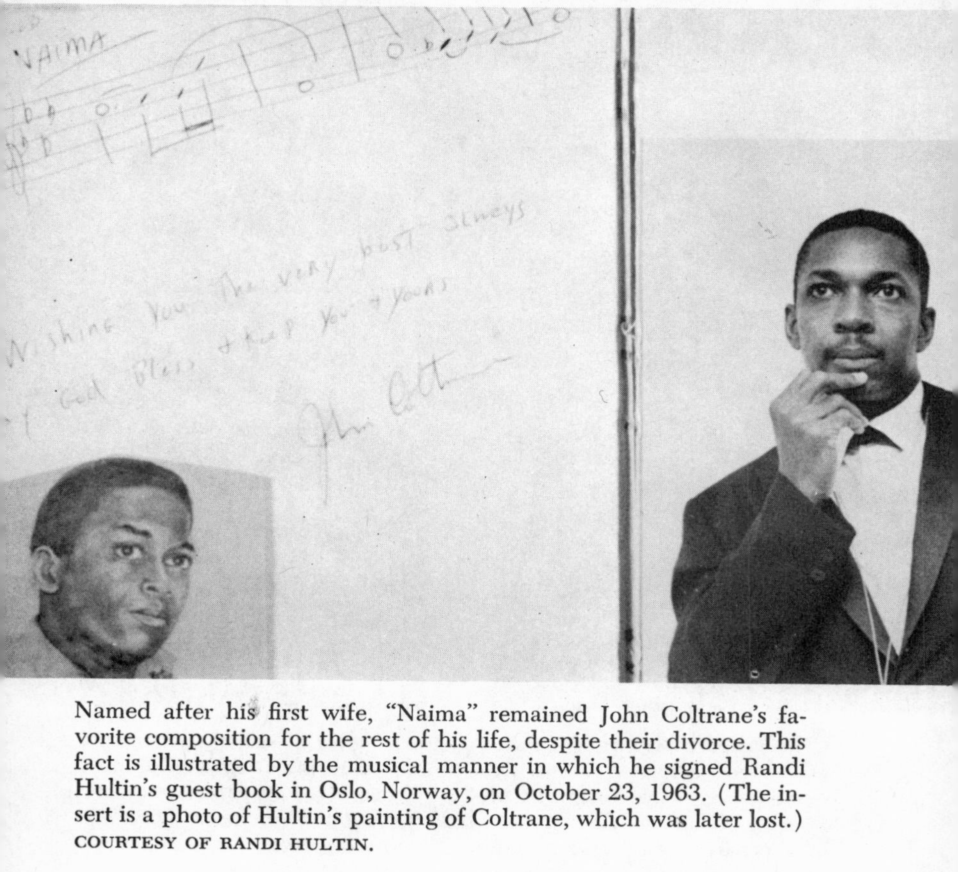

Named after his first wife, "Naima" remained John Coltrane's favorite composition for the rest of his life, despite their divorce. This fact is illustrated by the musical manner in which he signed Randi Hultin's guest book in Oslo, Norway, on October 23, 1963. (The insert is a photo of Hultin's painting of Coltrane, which was later lost.) COURTESY OF RANDI HULTIN.

The "classic" Coltrane Quartet, appearing as classically attired as the Modern Jazz Quartet or the Budapest String Quartet. Coltrane (tenor sax) (TOP LEFT); McCoy Tyner (piano) (TOP RIGHT); Jimmy Garrison (bass) (BOTTOM LEFT); Elvin Jones (drums) (BOTTOM RIGHT). PHOTOGRAPHER: RANDI HULTIN.

tion so that he'd have to pass the tavern every time he came home, thus testing himself daily and with a concrete reminder that he was through with liquor for good.

The Coltranes bought new furniture, in a contemporary style; not exactly plain but nothing fancy. And they bought an upright piano for Coltrane's composing, for he was now spending considerable time writing tunes to play or record later, under his own name.

Six nights a week, he put on a suit and tie, kissed his family good-by, walked out the door with saxophone case in hand, and took the subway to his job at the Five Spot. There, more than 150 people were jammed shoulder to shoulder in the small, smoky room, some crowded around small tables, others pushed alongside the bar, all absorbing Monk's music.

And Trane's music, too.

David Amram recalls, "Trane was getting into different harmonic textures, pouring out such a cascade of notes that he was attracting the audience's attention as much as Monk. A lot of musicians were there, digging Monk at first, then commenting more and more on Trane each time they'd come in. One thing I really noticed, though, was that Trane was always playing himself, even in the context of Monk's music."

The audience was quite mixed, from a few as young as fourteen to some in their seventies. One night a merchant seaman from Sweden dropped by, telling everyone within earshot that he'd shipped out just to be in New York while Monk and Trane were playing together.

Painters were there, too; especially those of the Abstract Expressionist school, such as Franz Kline and Willem de Kooning. Amram and de Kooning often talked about music—the painter liked New Orleans jazz in particular; he'd created a canvas of trumpeter Bunk Johnson once—and de Kooning proved more than receptive to Trane. He once told Amram, "Coltrane is so different; he's almost like an Einstein of music."

How strangely prophetic; John Coltrane would later say that there was one man he admired more than any other.

Albert Einstein.

I think there's a strong analogy between the abstract painters and avant-garde jazz musicians. They're both into colors and shapes and basically non-programmatic art. Almost all the painters I knew in the 1950s, and the 60s too, were interested in jazz. And in their painting, they were splashing or dripping colors on canvas, using random and chance techniques. Like the musicians, they placed extreme reliance on improvisation to get the results they wanted.

MALCOLM RAPHAEL

Monk was one of the first to show me how to make two or three notes at one time on tenor. It's done by false fingering and adjusting your lips, and if it's done right you get triads. He also got me into the habit of playing long solos on his pieces, playing the same piece for a long time to find new conceptions for solos. It got so I would go as far as possible on one phrase until I ran out of ideas. The harmonies got to be an obsession for me. Sometimes I'd think I was making music through the wrong end of a magnifying glass.

JOHN COLTRANE

I played drums on the *Monk's Music* album for Riverside, where Monk expanded his group to a septet, with both Coleman Hawkins and John Coltrane on tenor. Naturally, Monk wrote all the music, but Hawk was having trouble reading it, so he asked Monk to explain it to both Trane and himself. Monk said to Hawk, "You're the great Coleman Hawkins, right? You're the guy who invented the tenor saxophone, right?" Hawk agreed. Then Monk said to Trane, "You're the great John Coltrane, right?" Trane blushed, and mumbled, "Aw . . . I'm not so great." Then Monk said to both of them, "You both play saxophone, right?" They nodded. "Well, the music is on the horn. Between the two of you, you should be able to find it."

ART BLAKEY

Bob Weinstock is a phlegmatic, slow-moving man whose thick glasses give him an even blander expression than he would otherwise possess without them. However, the fact that he retired to Florida while only in his forties says something else about the way his mind works.

He founded Prestige Records in 1949, after running his own record shop and mail-order business and making his name known in the music world. Among his first recording artists were Lenny Tristano, the avant-garde pianist and composer, and alto saxophonist Lee Konitz, the possessor of a highly personal and introspective style, who to this day is still studying Coltrane's music and admires him more than anything else as a "straight-ahead" player. At that time, the Prestige office was located on Eighth Avenue near the old Madison Square Garden, and musicians would often stop by after a particularly bloody boxing match and talk business.

Others, perhaps bitter about not receiving as much money as they'd expected, called Prestige the "junkies' jazz label," meaning that a lot of musicians who were strung out and needed a quick fix would walk in and with permission record several tunes and walk out with cash in their pockets. One must remember, of course, that record company executives have to make a living, too.

Weinstock knew Coltrane from recording him as a member of Miles's quintet until Davis moved to Columbia, as well as from his appearances as a sideman with, among others, pianist Tadd Dameron (who later wrote "Soultrane" for him) and Sonny Rollins ("Tenor Madness" was their twosome, and some say that Trane took care of business better than Rollins on that date). Coltrane had also recorded frequently with Red Garland, who was one of Prestige's better sellers, and it was he who persuaded the company to sign Coltrane as an exclusive recording artist for two years, starting in 1957. He received union scale as a leader on these record dates, with probably an advance of only two or three hundred dollars. The designated two-year period may also have been a one-year contract plus a one-year option, too, but no one seems to know for sure.

Briefly, this is how the record business works:

A record company will make a contract with an artist; it may be for a single album, two or more albums a year, a one-year contract, a one-year contract with renewal options for an additional one or two years, or any other combination that seems most practical. An advance against royalties is paid to the artist. If he is a leader of his own group, or if he simply selects (or the company, on occasion, chooses) sidemen to work with him, the company pays them scale for their time. The company also pays for the technicians (engineer and his assistants) and the studio time. However, before the artist can collect a penny of record royalties—from four to 16 per cent of 90 per cent of album list prices, or from $.22 to $.85 on a $5.98 album—the above costs, plus packaging allowances, are deducted.

At first, the mix on Trane's albums was about half and half between standard songs and original material. But later albums showcased more of his own tunes (or those of fellow musicians whom he really respected, such as McCoy Tyner's "The Believer," Cal Massey's "Nakatini Serenade," or Dizzy Gillespie's "Birks Works"), with only an occasional standard thrown in for balance. Trane's original music, though, had to be published with Prestige's in-house music publishing company, Prestige Music. Such an agreement was a common record company hedge; under it, the company would automatically collect 50 per cent of mechanical royalties —royalties paid on records sold—leaving the musician/composer with only half the rewards of his creative labors. This was (and is) why many musicians, including Coltrane, set up their own music publishing firms, for the purpose of receiving *all* their record royalties. This would only happen, however, if their record companies agreed with this arrangement, and usually only under pressure, or if the musician was becoming a superstar and threatened to take his recording business elsewhere.

Prestige instantly capitalized on Coltrane's name as soon as he began selling records and developing an audience of his own. Any other record company would have done the same. As soon as Trane became moderately successful, the then out-of-print records (sometimes still listed in the catalogue) issued under another leader's name, with himself listed strictly as a sideman, were reissued under Coltrane's name, renumbered and given new cover art, liner notes, and new everything except the music itself. No musicians ever got paid for these reissues—except for normal royalties, which often take their own sweet time to show up by check in a musician's mailbox—for no new recording had actually taken place.

Tenor saxophonist Hank Mobley, who recorded several Prestige sessions with Coltrane, recalls, "The *Two Tenors* date was originally issued under pianist Elmo Hope's name, but it was influenced by the Gene Ammons-Sonny Stitt two-tenor combination. I suggested some of the tunes, and I think Trane played best on 'Avalon.' It was a ferocious, fast tempo, but he kept right up there without flagging and I really had to sweat to stay with him. I really began to understand his music better from that date on."

They also shared a three-tenor date on Blue Note under the leadership of Chicago tenorist Johnny Griffin. Mobley says, "Griffin is a speed merchant, a really *fast* tenor player. I remember I got into two false starts on 'The Way You Look Tonight,' because Johnny was setting such a fast tempo and still playing cool. Trane didn't have any trouble keeping up with him, and he was making Johnny work like a sprinter hustling for the finish line. Now I pride myself on being able to play fast, too, but *whoo-ee,* what a workout!"

There was also a four-tenor date with Mobley and Coltrane that included Al Cohn and Zoot Sims. Mobley puts it this way, "Prestige has a habit of not giving the musicians enough rehearsal time because blowing sessions, where you just walk in off the street and choose your tunes in the studio, are so much cheaper to record. So the four of us decided to improvise, picking some tunes we liked and setting up the order of the solos, and it worked out all right. I liked 'Tenor Conclave' the best, but 'How Deep Is the Ocean?' was probably the best vehicle for Trane, he really had the changes down and he swung beautifully."

Then came *Blue Train.* But for Blue Note, not Prestige.

Alfred Lion, a suave man with continental manners and an *aficionado's* interest in jazz, founded Blue Note in 1939; his friend Frank Wolff joined him as a partner in 1942. The first artist they recorded was New Orleans clarinetist Sidney Bechet, who later became a seminal influence on Coltrane's music but was then just becoming known as the first exponent of the rarely heard soprano saxophone. Later, the company got into more contemporary sounds when it recorded as leaders Coltrane companions Paul Chambers and trumpeter Lee Morgan, the latter only nineteen in 1957 and just off the road from a lengthy Middle East tour with Dizzy Gillespie's reactivated big band. (Morgan later died at the age of thirty-three under rather bizarre circumstances on February 19, 1972. While playing a date at Slugs' Saloon on the Lower East Side, he and his wife had an argument during intermission, and before he could get back on the bandstand again, she left the club, returned with a gun, and shot him.)

Lion knew of Coltrane's work, and he recalls the day they first met for "business" that led to the *Blue Train* recording:

"One warm spring day I was sitting in the old office on Broadway and Sixty-fourth Street. It was a Friday around one o'clock, and I was alone, the help was out to lunch and my partner was at the bank. Our pet Persian cat was sunning itself at the open window. Suddenly, as I looked up from my desk, the cat was gone. By some freak accident it had fallen out the window. When I looked down, I saw a woman getting into a cab with our cat. We never saw either the woman or our cat again."

Exit cat and catnapper.

Enter Coltrane.

Less than half an hour later, John stopped by to check on some new record releases. He asked for some Bechet albums, mentioning that he was now listening to Sidney on soprano. Lion recommended the albums that contained two particular songs: "Summertime" (Trane would later record that same tune on tenor for Atlantic) and a Bechet original, "Blue Horizon."

They discussed a possible Blue Note recording affiliation, and Lion offered to talk with Wolff about signing Coltrane.

No more was said about the matter until the following week, when the Blue Note partners read in a trade paper that Trane had signed with Prestige.

However, in August of that year, Lion caught Trane at the Five Spot with Monk. He told the saxophonist that he really wanted him to record as a leader but that his new contractual affiliation probably precluded this. Trane replied, "I'd still like to do a date with you. Let me talk with Prestige, and we'll see."

He got a release from Prestige to make one record for Blue Note. Selecting the musicians and the tunes himself, he assembled the group, a sextet, for a September 15, 1957, recording date.

The strange paradox of a perfectionist such as Coltrane is that he is often equally insecure; a common affliction of artists, especially when they don't always know where their next dollar is coming from. As if to demonstate this insecurity, the saxophonist used the actual medium of transportation, train, as the album title, not his nickname Trane. It was the last time he'd do so, for the title tune itself, with his exemplary eight-chorus solo, was sufficiently successful, both musically and financially, to give him the confidence to use his distinctive sobriquet from then on.

Zita Carno, a classical pianist and graduate of Manhattan School of music, was introduced to John Coltrane's music through trumpeter Donald Byrd, her schoolmate, in 1957. She became so involved and entranced that she wrote what is probably the most definitive analysis of his style, conception, improvisational and compositional ability ever put on paper. She published this article in an erudite magazine called the *Jazz Review,* and some of her comments from the November 1959 issue follow:

"His range is something to marvel at; a full three octaves upward from the lowest note obtainable on the horn (concert A-flat). What sets Coltrane apart from other tenor players is the equality of strength in all registers which he has obtained through long, hard practice. His sound is just as clear, full and unforced in the topmost notes as it is down at the bottom.

"That tone of his is a result of the particular combination of mouthpiece and reed he uses plus an extremely tight embouchure; it is powerful, resonant and sharply penetrating. Some say it's not a good tenor sound. Nonsense. A sound is good if it suits the player's style and conception, and so it is with Trane. And, as far as his intonation goes, those who say he doesn't play in tune are wrong, deceived by the sharp edge of his sound. He plays in tune—always.

"He has a terrific impact on the various rhythm sections he's played with; when he takes over, immediately the rhythm section tightens up and plays harder. He is driving them ahead, most noticeably on medium and up tempos.

"That powerful sound of his you hear consists of very long phrases played at such an extremely rapid tempo that the notes he plays cease to be mere notes and fuse into a continuous flow of pure sound. Sometimes they don't come out the way he wants; then they say he's playing 'just scales.' But, what scales—irregular, often arhythmic phrasing, variations of dynamics and that fantastic sense of timing. When they do work—most of the time—we hear a tremendous emotional impact, plus a fantastic residual harmonic effect that's so pronounced the piano wouldn't be missed if it wasn't playing. He has few equals in building up a solo, especially on a blues—not an easy thing to do for many.

"His solo on *Blue Train* reveals many facets of his style and conception, especially his harmonic conception, which is so advanced. He really knows what to do with the changes of his tunes—also apparent in his writing. He knows when to stick with basic changes and when to employ unusual extensions and alterations that some call 'blowing out of the changes.' Some of the devices he uses in building a solo like this include the trick of building up on a single note or a short phrase, then taking off from there. Another is his use of sequences (pet phrases). And, he has a way of starting his solos in the least expected places, never doing anything exactly the same way twice. He has a peculiarly individual way of altering the phrasing, involving an extremely subtle shifting of accentuation that results in previous often arhythmic phrasing.

"Now, with 'Blue Train,' the tune is a revealing sample of his writing, as direct and straightforward as his playing; it's a powerful blues line, brooding and mysterious like a chant, with more than just the meaning of the blues in it. His solo continues to build all the way to the last chorus, reaching a peak at the sixth chorus. This constant building-up is the most striking feature of his work, apparent since his days with Miles. And, he tends to stay in the high register of his horn. He slurs those long phrases all the way and still plays them so clearly—a beautiful example of his solid technique and unerring fingering."

"Blue Train": from Zita Carno's analysis of Coltrane's solo to a set of special lyrics, written by, and included with the courtesy of, New York artist and poet Chris Acemandese Hall:

Greetings everybody, 'cuse me . . .
But—I would—like to say just a word—
    about John Coltrane now
Speakin' of Trane now
But before I start you better meet some of his friends
On the drums—was Philly Joe Jones
and anybody who's hip to it know that
    Philly Joe Jones really
hit some mean licks he sho
is a cooker
and Paul really smoked—a bass on out
and my man Curtis Fuller—you know he really laid some
heavy stuff down on his trombone he's still
out there just a cookin' and a cookin' away
and Mr. Kenny Drew—now—he just dances all—up and
down—the keyboard everything he plays sounds
so pretty it's like sailin' through a dream
from somewhere else
Now that brings us on over to Lee Morgan
You know he was really somethin' else to be-hold—poor Lee
he—was such a hip cat—he played—some real
slick things—made his trumpet sing—year
like Clif-ford Brown showed him
But I heard some people talkin' 'bout this
wom-an—that he had—said she saved his hip soul now
and when he turned his back on her—she—she did it—well
Yes she blew
this young giant on away
People use to wonder where Coltrane was

comin' from now they're trying to figure out
where he's been but he has already been there and gone some
where else, he really went somewhere else
diggin' his soprano or tenor—I—can envision
spirits dancin', elephants prancin', really feel cosmic
vibrations from all over the whole entire solar universe
Hear African drums
taste the best of rums I didn't even have to smoke
on any pot,
I just laid with the music and floated on the
sounds waves sailin' through space like a shootin'
star I dug it I really dug it yes you know I really
had to dig what Coltrane was doing
with his tenor saxophone
always doing somethin' different—
creatin' new things all the time while
other musicians were a-wondering—what's hap'ning
Blow Coltrane go on and play them pretty things
make it hip sometimes it's new sometimes,
it's so blue that's when it git—
so close to you
Ohhh—it makes me feel alive and there's nothin'
like the feelin' of *A Love—Supreme* oh can you dig—
Yes—Trane's really a giant but like a lot of artists he
gave so much and received such a little taste it's
not worth talkin' 'bout . . . when will people even
be able to really dig a living source I wonder
Somewhere along the way he met up—with Elvin Jones
and McCoy Tyner they showed us some real new things
Of course that was after I heard Miles and Trane
they were playing—really cookin' "A-Round Midnight"—
they were cookin'
I ain't never heard—no other horn now

really playing all them hip kind of things
like Coltrane play
He dug on Monk and Bird Hodges and Rollins
were his kind of peo-ple and you really should know—it
But—of course he developed his own thing
reachin' new heights takin' the music
into a new African bag reminiscent of
African glory he did all of this in spite
of jealous colleagues and a system that always
dictates adversity—especially for our—black
pe-ople
while he
was tryin' to git—to his goal he had
Juanita to caress his weary soul
And it's so good to see a woman dig—
her man's work so she act-ually espoused on it
Carry on now Alice Coltrane
cook—Coltrane inspired us all now
maybe one day we can contribute somethin' too . . .
Sometimes I can hear the screams
of revolu-tion—or I can see—
the beauty of a pretty woman, or hear a baby cry—
Hear roaches crawl
a freedom call—see, Bojangles danc-ing
or—black lovers romanc-ing—
If you really git—into it—you can feel
the heat—of the sun—or the cold—of the
hawk floatin' through . . . a sound wave from way out beyond
And if you open up an ear you may even be able to feel . . .
the sound of a—
sound of a tear and you even smell the fund of,
the games of the mack—and you can—probe the
secrets of the . . . zodiac

I've been tellin' y'all . . . 'bout Coltrane and
I hope I said somethin' worth while—well now—
There is only one thing left to say now
and that is that Coltrane is

CHRIS ACEMANDESE HALL

John Coltrane is practicing.

He is in the bedroom of his apartment; the tape recorder is running and he is standing, feet slightly apart and toes pointing outward, posture erect, six pounds of tenor saxophone pulling at his neck. This is a 25 per cent increase in weight from the alto; for comparison, a Pentax camera weighs just a few ounces over two pounds, a Nikon four.

His horn is a Selmer Mark VI, equipped with a 5-star medium metal Otto Link mouthpiece and a #4 Rico reed. The soprano he'd later purchase would be the same model and reed, the mouthpiece would be a metal Selmer, size E.

The saxophone he is holding is the Paris model, though actually made in a small town, Mantes, about forty miles away. Special-formula brass is the material, and the work is handcrafted. The saxophone parts are cut out and smoothed on a lathe, then hand-hammered before being assembled and shipped to the Selmer factory in Elkhart, Indiana. There, the horn is then stripped down, buffed, and lacquered. The keys and pads are rejoined to the body again, and a mechanic tests each saxophone separately (the intonation adjustments were already made in France). The cost of the instrument at that time (1958) was close to $500, and to hear Trane's sound on his Selmer, it was well worth it.

He is practicing from a book by Sigurd Rascher, a German expatriate living in upstate New York and an exponent of the French school of saxophone technique: a limpid vibrato and an intonation as smooth (and sometimes as syrupy) as French cream. Nevertheless, Rascher is a technician who knows the horn well enough to devise 158 exercises with no key signatures, tempo markings, or bar lines to constrict the player. These exercises are written primarily in eighth notes, with a constant crescendo and diminuendo, a continuous rising and falling of scales; they are so complex that some of them resemble snowflake patterns as seen through a microscope.

Coltrane hears the sounds of the scales in his ear, feels his fingers flicking over the saxophone keys and his breath coming strong and full, almost choking the horn with a huge onrushing column of air. His embouchure is as tight as the mouthpiece and reed connections. But he still feels the occasional, sometimes frequent, stabbing pain in his increasingly disintegrating molars. More bridgework is now there, but still the pain continues, digging like a dentist's drill into his nerves. But he does not stop; nothing short of nuclear war can stop his incessant, compulsive practice sessions.

The exercise book lies on his bed as he reads the notes, playing them faster and faster until they begin to bunch against each other, each note crowding the next. The notes bounce off the walls and ceiling, seep into the carpeting, and are sucked into the whirring tape recorder in the corner.

Then he is finished. But not with practicing; only with the saxophone book.

He unstraps his tenor, placing it on the bed. He puts the saxophone book away, replacing it with another practice book, this one for piano. It is called the *Thesaurus of Scales and Melodic Patterns,* written by Nicolas Slonimsky, a piano and composition teacher who commands great respect from classical and other musicians.

Opening the book, Trane straps his horn to his body again and starts playing from, and by, the book.

He begins with tritone progressions, intervals of augmented fourths that contain three whole tones. He continues with a series of scales that call for interpolation of four or more notes, constructed from a complex series of sixteenth notes and an amazing number of accidentals, for almost every other note seems to have a sharp or flat preceding it, indicating an immediate change of tone, either up or down a half step. These exercises are excellent for developing the lower register, as the tenor saxophone range extends to the first space in the bass clef.

Again, only the tape recorder and himself are present.

A few years ago, in Detroit, Paul Chambers had introduced Coltrane to pianist Barry Harris, a man with a formidable reputation as teacher and theorist who includes such Detroit musicians as pianist Hugh Lawson, trumpeter Lonnie Hillyer, and altoist Charles McPherson among his more diligent students. Coltrane and Harris often played tenor-piano duets at the latter's house. It was Harris who told him about the Slonimsky book, and the pianist would also pass on, to anyone who would listen, his particular music theory, which placed a stronger emphasis on scales than chords as a method of fostering improvisation, including the interrelationship of common or complimentary notes between different scales and the ease of moving from one to another. He believed that the dominant rather than the tonic degree of the scale should do exactly what it says, dominate; he'd often hold court around the piano, playing exactly what he was talking about.

Trane continues his practicing.

The room is full of music now; so much music that it seems as if he is as engulfed in notes and chords as a fish swimming in deep water, so deep that the density of his music is putting pressure against every part of his body.

When he finishes with piano, he will switch to violin. A violin practice book, since the best classical music is written for the instruments that predominate in the symphony orchestra—the strings.

His practice method for violin exercises is the same as with piano music; he plays it straight from the pages, without transposing. This is an extra obstacle course for the musician, certainly designed to improve his dexterity but damned abrasive on his patience.

Coltrane closes this practice session with a harp book.

Hugh Lawson explains, "The harp has an extremely high range, more than six octaves, and you can hear some incredible chromatic runs when it's played properly. Saxophone music is not written high because the horn has a range of less than three octaves. But harp music is written for the very top notes on the treble clef, so I think Trane used this music for practicing to increase his range on tenor, to play as high as he could. It might have started him thinking about soprano, too, because he often said he was hearing things higher than he could play on tenor."

The music goes round and round inside John Coltrane's head, pouring forth from his horn as he continues his creative explorations, the only way any artist must if he is to be worthy of the name.

Alone.

I used to think John was reading all the stuff he was playing, so I thought I'd better get my reading together. Then, when

Earl and I were visiting him one weekend, we saw him practicing. He was playing some complicated chord progressions without any sheet music in sight.

CARL GRUBBS

Such intense dedication to any goal, be it making music or missionary work or many other kinds of obsessive endeavor, might be called extreme by some. And in connection with John Coltrane, it was.

I think Coltrane was an extremist, because whatever he did he did all the way, with no middle ground.

LOUIS HAYES

Trane once told me, "I can't do anything unless it's in the extreme."

HAROLD LOVETTE

Ernie Smith is an ex-adman who collects jazz films, any filmed or TV appearance that includes jazz musicians, from a few-second clip to a full feature. One of these is an eighteen-minute version of Miles Davis playing "So What," taken from a one-hour show called *The Sound of Miles Davis* that was made in 1957 as part of the Robert Herridge Presents series. It is the Miles Davis Sextet of that period, minus Cannonball Adderley but with Wynton Kelly on piano rather than Bill Evans. This is one of only three appearances Coltrane made on American TV. Later, in Europe, both with Miles and heading his own group, he'd get video time and space for fifty or more such shows.

The "So What" film clip is part of a two-hour presentation that Smith makes at various colleges and music festivals. The complete program includes Bessie Smith, Louis Armstrong, Billie Holiday, Lester Young, Charles Parker, and Thelonious Monk, among others. But it is John Coltrane who apparently moves those audiences most, for Smith says, "When Billie comes on, there's applause; when Trane appears, he's worshiped."

He continues, "In the Miles Davis segment, Miles solos first. People are digging him, but I can also detect a kind of expectancy, as if they're really waiting for Trane. Just before he comes on, there's an appreciative murmur from the audience. Then Coltrane follows Miles, and you can really feel the transformation, from enjoyment to ecstasy. They like Miles . . . but they love Trane."

> I recall John and I playing Bartók. I had some albums, especially the *Concerto for Orchestra*, and we played along with the music, sometimes playing the exact lines and other times improvising over them. He was particularly interested in the violin parts of the first and third movements.
>
> BIG NICK NICHOLAS

> Coltrane subdivided jazz rhythm. Rhythmically, Louis Armstrong thought in quarter notes; Charlie Parker thought in eighth notes. Coltrane's phrases and accents imply that he was thinking rhythmically in sixteenths.
>
> MARTIN WILLIAMS

Many were the fans, if few the critics, who believed that John Coltrane and Miles Davis had made memorable music together during 1955–56. Though altoist Cannonball Adderley was the band's saxophone player in late 1957, Davis still wanted Coltrane to return, especially after hearing him with Monk during that long engagement at the Five Spot.

So Miles called Trane one day and simply said, "I want you back."

And Trane replied, with equal simplicity, "All right."

> Miles was once interested in chords for their own sake, but now it seemed that he was moving in the opposite direction, using tunes with fewer chord changes and free-flowing melodic lines. This approach allowed the soloist the choice of playing chordally (vertically) or melodically (horizontally). I now found it easier to apply the harmonic ideas

that I had. I could stack up chords—say, on a C7, I sometimes superimposed an E♭7, up to an F♯7, down to an F. That way I could play three chords on one. But on the other hand, if I wanted to, I could play melodically. Miles's music gave me plenty of freedom.

JOHN COLTRANE

I wrote the first article in *Down Beat* about Coltrane, which appeared in the October 16, 1958, issue. I called his music "Sheets of Sound," because of the density of textures he was using. His multinote improvisations were so thick and complex they were almost flowing out of the horn by themselves. That really hit me, the continuous flow of ideas without stopping. It was almost superhuman, and the amount of energy he was using could have powered a space ship.

IRA GITLER

In 1958, John Coltrane and Miles Davis participated in a recording date that exposed the saxophonist to some of the most intricate voicings and textures he had ever encountered in "popular" music. The songs were complex, with unusual harmonic structures; the arrangements were difficult, with constantly shifting key signatures and tempos. The man responsible for the music was French composer-conductor Michel Legrand; the album was called *Legrand Jazz.*

I loved the way Miles Davis and John Coltrane played, but I was also a bit afraid. I wondered how they would react to my arrangements. Miles didn't say anything, but John asked me, "How do you want me to play my solo?" I was amazed. All I could say was, "John, play exactly the way you feel after you listen to what's happening around you." When it came time for him to solo, he integrated himself thoroughly into my arrangements without sacrificing one note of his own conception. I thought about that later, after I followed Coltrane's career through *Ascension* and *Meditations.* I began to draw parallels with his music and that of some classical composers I knew, Luciano Berio and Luigi

Nono. To me, both jazz and classical music have the same goal. There should be no lines of demarcation between them, for the end result should simply be—good music.

MICHEL LEGRAND

It was like old times when John Coltrane rejoined Miles Davis in November 1957. The original rhythm section of Red Garland, Paul Chambers, and Philly Joe Jones was still intact. With Cannonball Adderley on alto, the sextet recorded the *Milestones* album, which included such complex, convoluted tunes as Monk's "Straight, No Chaser"—easily Trane's best solo on the album—and alto saxophonist Jackie McLean's "Dr. Jackle" (murderously misspelled as *Dr. Jekyll*).

Trane was especially delighted to have Philly Joe spurring both him and the band from the drum chair. Jones was the most powerful percussionist since Max Roach, a strong, driving drummer whose snare accents and rim shots boosted the soloists just when and where they required stimulation. His steady ride on cymbals kept the rhythms flowing, and his speed and dexterity were easily the equal of Coltrane's on tenor. It was probably from working with Jones that Coltrane developed his habit of having a powerful drummer behind him at all times. Later, he'd go through several of them until he finally got Elvin Jones for his own band (and Rashied Ali after Elvin left). He would also work with African-style drummers, perhaps as an effort to get back to the very roots of his music. (Drummer Beaver Harris once said that, to him, the very first musical instrument was a man beating upon his chest.) Coltrane would also receive considerable encouragement from the Nigerian percussionist Olatunji, who was recording with an African drum choir for Columbia at that time.

Trane was, in short, hearing drums dancing around in his head, American and African.

Levada Countiss is a tall, elegant lady who looks more like an actress than a patroness of musicians. Perhaps this is why many of them call her Countess, though more than a few, Moms, which she prefers. She and her husband Elliott own a two-story brick house in an attractive neighborhood on Chicago's South Side, near Seventy-sixth Street. Whenever visiting musicians need either friendly conversation or a crash pad, they head for Moms' place like homing pigeons, where she puts them up and puts up with them, offering food, booze, and friendliness.

In February 1959, John Coltrane, saxophonist James Moody, and vocalist Eddie Jefferson were all staying with Moms. Late one evening, they were sitting around the kitchen table, talking music, and the name of Sidney Bechet came up so frequently that the seeds previously planted in Trane's brain popped up fully grown early the following morning. About 8 A.M. Coltrane pounded on Moody and Jefferson's door until they dragged themselves out of bed. He told them, "I've got to get to Elkhart. Can you drive me there this morning?"

Elkhart, Indiana—the Selmer saxophone factory.

Moody had a car, but it took him another hour to wake up enough to drive, and it took all of them another two hours to arrive at the factory. Tony Rulli was there, and he showed Coltrane at least a dozen soprano saxophones, for it was this horn that Coltrane had been thinking about since the previous evening's continuous references to Bechet. John proceeded to test each horn, one after the other; in some cases he checked certain sopranos two or three times, as if not trusting his ear the first time. Finally, after running complex chord changes, playing intricate scales, and asking about reeds and mouthpieces, he achieved satisfaction with one of the saxophones and took it with him.

As Rulli recalls, "Marcel Mule was making saxophone quartet recordings in France, using a soprano lead, and I'd suggested that John listen to them, which I think he did. I know other musicians were listening to them, and we'd also discussed Sidney Bechet's work many times. John was always telling me he was hearing things he had difficulty playing on tenor; they were so high and so far above the register of his horn. He was so intrigued after trying out all these sopranos that he had to get one for himself." Pause. "And you know what happened next."

The last time Trane played with Miles was on a tour of England in March 1960. All he had with him were his horns, an airlines bag, and a toilet kit. He didn't really want to make the gig, but Miles talked him into it. He sat next to me on the bus, looking like he was ready to split at any time. He spent most of the time looking out the window and playing Oriental-sounding scales on soprano.

JIMMY COBB

Jimmy Cobb was on drums, with Bill Evans as the pianist, when Miles Davis recorded *Kind of Blue* in March 1959. Evans compared the music to Japanese brush painting, and he should know; not only is his own piano style a similar combination of subtlety and strength but he also wrote the arrangements for all the tunes on the album. Though Miles is credited as composer, "Blue in Green" and "Flamenco Sketches" are, according to Evans, his songs.

The music was modal, with compositions of exquisite simplicity structured on one or a few scales. This was a seminal recording in the history of American music, offering the soloists unprecedented improvisational freedom and minimal chordal restrictions, with the subtlety of chamber music and the swing of jazz. It was music of beauty and brilliance, and offered the most arresting and advanced Coltrane solos on record so far.

Teo Macero, who had succeeded George Avakian at Columbia, was the producer. He was one of the few working musicians so employed; he'd played tenor with Mingus and others and had a Master's degree from Juilliard. His father had once owned a speakeasy, so he'd been around musicians for most of his life. Therefore, his collaboration with Miles on *Kind of Blue* involved minimal fuss and maximum freedom.

As Macero recalls, "All I remember about Coltrane, besides his music, was that he was a very sweet guy. He'd smile like a little boy when Miles would play something he liked."

Coltrane could superimpose a world of passing chords, substitute chords, and harmonic extensions upon a harmonic structure that was already complex. And at times he seemed prepared to gush out every possible note, find his way step by step through every complex chord, careen through every scale, and go beyond even that profusion by groping for impossible notes and sounds on a tenor saxophone that seemed ready to shatter under the strain.

MARTIN WILLIAMS

We were playing at the Sutherland in Chicago once, where Trane was just finishing one of his thirty-minute solos. I was feeling so tired of playing so long that a drumstick flew out of my hand and whipped by Trane's head, just missing him. When we finished the set, I told him, "I'm sorry, man, it just slipped out of my hand." He said, "I thought you finally threw something at me for playing so long."

JIMMY COBB

The aforementioned Zita Carno is a gregarious and dynamic lady who comes on with the impact of a Coltrane solo, and one does not soon forget her after the first meeting. Nor did Coltrane himself, to whom she sent, as a prank, an exact transcription of his eight-chorus solo on *Blue Train*, which she had taken down, note for note, by ear, talent and perseverance. She did not sign her name when she sent it, merely mentioning, "Does this look familiar?"

Ten days later, she called him after obtaining his number from a mutual friend and confessed her authorship. "What kind of ear have you got?" he said, and invited her to meet him at his apartment. She did; he played the record of *Blue Train* while she pointed out exactly which note went where.

When the record was finished, she asked him if he would play that same solo for her, on tenor, reading it right off the manuscript paper.

Trane looked at her transcription again, then back to her. He said, with a sad smile, "I can't; it's too difficult."

Carl and I used to catch John at the Showboat here in Philadelphia, when he was playing with Miles. We were still teenagers, so we'd darken our mustaches to look older, and we'd get in most of the time. John would come over to our table and talk with us, and everybody else would wonder who we were and why he was talking with us. He used to do that a lot. He always took time to talk with us and show us things about his music and help us to get our music down right.

EARL GRUBBS

My boys were playing in South Philadelphia one time and John stopped by to hear them. He sat in the corner by himself, but he was soon noticed and people turned around to look at him. He just wanted to hear what Earl and Carl had learned since he'd last talked with them. At intermission John came on the bandstand and talked with them, right in front of the audience.

LUCY GRUBBS

Earl and Carl Grubbs, the sons of Naima's brother, Earl Grubbs, and his wife, Lucy, are Naima Coltrane's nephews and therefore the nephews-in-law of John Coltrane. Earl plays tenor and soprano saxophones, Carl alto and clarinet, and both play good enough piano to compose their own songs. One of their compositions, "The Visit," was inspired jointly by Trane's calling on them in Philadelphia and their visiting him in New York. The frequency of these get-togethers also inspired the Grubbs brothers to name their band—themselves plus a rhythm section—"The Visitors."

However, they weren't the only visitors to the Coltrane apartment. Charles Davis, a former altoist who'd switched to baritone, was there, kidding Zita Carno about her perfect pitch and calling her the "flatted fifth lady," in honor of bop's most basic breakthrough. Charles Greenlee, Majeed, came by with Cousin Mary. Majeed offered some needed comic relief to the superseriousness of Wayne Shorter's tenor duets with John Coltrane. The trombonist once broke them both up with, "Why don't you guys stand against opposite walls, see who can hear the other playing first from across the room, and the winner gets the 'Up 'Gainst the Wall' award?"

Later, Trane wrote a tune titled "Up 'Gainst the Wall." Whether it was inspired by Majeed, he wouldn't say.

Zita, however, would always say what was on her mind. She once insisted that Trane's latest musical experiments reminded her of Hindemith, especially the violin parts in the second movement of his *Concerto for Horn and Orchestra.* Coltrane disagreed, saying, "That can't be, Zita; I've never heard him."

"Then Hindemith has heard you, Trane, because Zita's right. You do sound a lot alike," Paul Jeffrey commented. Jeffrey, who'd later play with Monk, would then discover that there was infinitely more Monk than Hindemith in Coltrane's music at that time; exactly how much, Jeffrey would see for himself as he dug into the intricacies of Monk's own music.

Trane then countered with, "Paul, let's go into the bedroom and read the books." This could lead to a mean scene; it meant that sight-reading time was here, and Jeffrey knew the Rascher practice book was tough because he had a copy, too. But he had no choice, being so challenged, so into the bedroom they went. There was unison playing first, note for note, then harmonic improvising on the chords, and more tricky chord changes until John said, "Paul, take a break, and when you come back bring your clarinet." Jeffrey was once a contest-winning clarinetist, and Coltrane still took his out now and then, so that meant clarinet duets were coming up.

The Grubbs brothers recall that their uncle-in-law was still having teeth trouble. Coltrane was then working on a double embouchure, using both lips on the mouthpiece for additional stability. He had also placed a patch on his mouthpiece to ease the vibrations against his teeth. At the time, Earl and Carl didn't understand the reason for the patch; while John and Paul were playing their clarinet duets, the Grubbs brothers removed the patch, thinking that Trane could play better without it. When John discovered what they had done, he reprimanded them by saying, "The patch is for my teeth, not yours."

Finally, both John and Zita took over the spinet piano in the living room, playing intricate duets with each other while the others watched.

John called me Toni, and sometimes Bony because I was so skinny when I was a little girl. He used to take me everywhere when he was home. In the summer to Coney Island, where I'd ride the Cyclone roller coaster while he watched, and in winter we'd go to Vincent Price horror movies and he'd grin while I got scared out of my skin. And when he'd get home after a long road tour, he'd have a pocket full of pennies he'd give me to put in my bank.

ANTONIA COLTRANE

John Coltrane did more than that for Toni. He immortalized her Moslem name by writing "Syeeda's Song Flute" and recording the song in the *Giant Steps* album. The tune was inspired by Toni's sometimes unsuccessful attempts to make music with her tonette, a child's kazoolike instrument.

When she graduated from high school in 1967, Trane was then married to another woman. But he did not forget Naima's daughter. She was his daughter too, and her graduation present told her all she needed to know about how John Coltrane still felt toward a now-grown Antonia Syeeda Coltrane.

A *real* flute.

Nesuhi and Ahmet Ertegun are the sons of a former Turkish ambassador to America. They are two self-confessed jazz lovers who founded Atlantic Records in 1948, after having first shaken up the staid Washington diplomatic community by holding interracial jam sessions on Sunday afternoons at the Turkish Embassy. They started Atlantic with $10,000 borrowed from a friendly dentist. In 1967, they sold the company to Warner Communications for $22 million, proving that, under carefully delineated circumstances, jazz does pay.

Their first artist was singer Ruth Brown, for they also had a strong affinity for the blues. But they are probably best known for signing and retaining the Modern Jazz Quartet during its entire recording existence, with the exception of a few early discs on Prestige and a few later ones from the Beatles' ill-fated Apple label.

Ahmet is the taller, balding brother with a goatee; Nesuhi, the short, graying fellow who waves his arms like a railroad signalman. Their offices and recording studio were then located on West Fifty-sixth Street, between Broadway and Eighth Avenue. In 1963, two years after Trane left, they moved to 1841 Broadway.

It was Nesuhi Ertegun who first became aware of John Coltrane.

Nesuhi heard the saxophonist with Miles at the Cafe Bohemia in 1956. As he recalls, "Coltrane was already way ahead of any records he'd previously made. His music seemed so different from what the rest of the band was playing. The construction of his solos, his advanced harmonics, the strange way the notes succeeded each other and the speed with which they were played—I found all these things most intriguing, but not all that comprehensible at one sitting."

Davis, a long-time friend of the Ertegun brothers, introduced Coltrane to Ertegun, who like so many others was immediately impressed with the saxophonist's sincerity, gentleness, and humility. Their ensuing friendship became a business relationship in April 1959, when Coltrane signed a two-year contract with Atlantic after the expiration of his Prestige pact. One year, plus a one-year option; that was the way the Atlantic contract was set up. And for a medium four-figure advance; not the greatest, but better than before, plus the personal interest shown him by the Ertegun brothers.

Harold Lovette thought it was a good deal, too.

A graduate of Columbia Law School and called "Counselor" by many musicians, due to his legal background, Lovette was then Miles Davis' manager. He had known Coltrane since he'd first joined Davis and was an astute enough talent scout to succeed in becoming the saxophonist's manager, assisting him in negotiating the Atlantic contract. After Trane formed his own band, Lovette signed him with the Shaw Agency, with whom Davis had been associated since 1955. There, Larry Myers and Jack Whittemore handled him with careful attention and great personal care.

How strangely coincidental that this agency, founded by Billy Shaw, was the same one that had long booked Charlie Parker.

> John Coltrane was very particular about the technical aspects of recording. He knew exactly what he and his group should sound like. Whenever he heard something he didn't like, he'd catch it immediately. We were very careful to give him just the sound he wanted.
>
> NESUHI ERTEGUN

"Giant Steps," the title piece in Coltrane's first album as a leader, sets up a difficult and ingenious series of sophisticated changes over an E-flat pedal tone with a B-flat in the bridge, allowing the soloist to take either course.

MARTIN WILLIAMS

Giant Steps was the album that also included "Naima," Trane's ballad tribute to his wife, which would become, with the title tune, the most widely-played of all Coltrane compositions by other musicians. The album also contained the gutsy blues "Cousin Mary," obviously nostalgically titled; "Syeeda's Song Flute," dedicated to daughter Antonia, as previously mentioned; and Coltrane's version of Eddie Vinson's blues, chord-changed from "Tune Up" to "Countdown." This was the record that really launched Trane's career as a leader, although he was still an integral part of the Davis group when the album was recorded. But he knew that he'd soon go out on his own; it was only a matter of the proper moment and the right musicians.

He had, moreover, taken an additional step in preparing himself for a leadership role by forming his own music publishing company with Lovette's legal assistance. All the songs on the *Giant Steps* album were published in the name of Jowcol, Coltrane's company, with Broadcast Music, Inc., assigned to monitor his air plays under their representation contract.

Nesuhi Ertegun recalls that Atlantic was one of the first companies to record with eight-track machines; the others were still using two tracks. When Coltrane recorded, it was with no more than two takes of each tune, no rehearsal time required. As Ertegun puts it, "John and the musicians walked in without any sheet music. I was worried until they started playing, and then I could hear that they must have rehearsed on their own time. I noticed there was less back and-forth conversation than with any other group I ever recorded. John rarely talked at all. He simply signaled to the musicians what he wanted, and he seemed to know exactly what he wanted at all times. After they had finished recording, the musicians just put on their coats, packed up their instruments, and left."

Giant Steps attracted the attention of many record reviewers, not all favorably. As a sideman, there was only so much controversy Coltrane could cause; as a leader and therefore "up front," he was getting criticism from every possible source. The heat certain critics, and some influential members of the audience, would put on Trane for the rest of his career would be substantial.

Excerpts from two reviews of this album will illustrate the point.

From Whitney Balliett in *The New Yorker:*

"That ugliness, like life, can be beautiful is the surprising discovery one makes after attempting to meet the challenge offered by Coltrane."

He goes on, "Coltrane's tone is harsh, flat, querulous, and at times almost vindictive. . . . His tone is bleaker than need be, many of his notes are useless, and his rhythmic methods are frequently just clothes flung all over a room. . . . But, despite his blatancy, Trane is an inventive, impassioned improviser who above all traps the listener with the unexpected."

Charles Hanna said, in the Minneapolis *Sunday Tribune*, "Coltrane's had something important to say for a long time, but only recently has he found a suitable way of expressing himself. . . . He plays a chord five different ways, milking every possible sound from its structure. He avoids the dangers of a clinical sound with use of a good rhythmic sense and a deeply emotional tone. . . . Coltrane has found his way."

When the Coltranes moved into the St. Albans section of Queens, in New York, the first thing John did after getting the family settled on December 23, 1959, was to wish them Merry Christmas, give Naima and Toni their presents, and go on the road for a date in Chicago with Miles Davis. Christmas in Chicago was then Miles's custom.

Their new home was a two-story brick house with a small front yard, a smaller back yard, three bedrooms, and a bath upstairs, and a living room, dining room, large kitchen, and small alcove downstairs. There was also a full basement; here, besides his usual practicing and tape recording, John worked out on a punching bag and lifted weights, something the Grubbs brothers were also doing.

After Coltrane returned from the Chicago engagement, he found the house filled with simple but contemporary furniture, including a new piano—and the cupboard stuffed with sweet potato pies. He couldn't resist; down went the diet instead of his weight. Later, McCoy Tyner, Zita Carno, and John Coltrane developed an all-consuming affinity for the specialty of the house at a pizza place just a few blocks away—onion pizza, at $2.25 a pie. Then the saxophonist got into the habit of popping Butter Rum Life Savers into his mouth; another futile attempt to appease his addictive sweet tooth.

Trane's weight was seesawing up and down, but sometimes going as high as thirty pounds too much. Upon advice from friends, he started eating health foods: tiger's milk, raw vegetables, organically grown fruits, kosher meat, and all kinds of beans. He frequented health food stores as often as he'd stop in at Sam Goody's to check the latest records. John's eating habits and Naima's general observance of Moslem dietary rules once prompted Toni to protest, "Mommy, can't you give me a hot dog or hamburger? I'm *so tired* of this health food stuff!"

Then there was, as with dentists, Coltrane's apparently unsuccessful efforts to reach agreement on the proper results of a collaboration with barbers. More than once, and in particular while on the road, he had gotten clipped unmercifully in barber shops. Not financially, but aesthetically. He liked his hair trimmed close, and more than one barber interpreted this preference as permission to chop off large chunks of hair or shave him nearly bald. After one savagely depressing experience, when the barber had nicked a choice cut of bleeding flesh from his left ear, he gave up on the barbering business and bought a set of clippers and shears. From then on, he cut his own hair, either at home or while traveling.

Paul Jeffrey often dropped over to the new Coltrane home. He and John would get out the books, go down to the basement, plug in the tape recorder, and go at it.

Earl and Carl Grubbs came into town every few months, bringing their horns and their music with them. Coltrane would comment, but never criticize or correct them; if they had a technical problem and didn't know how to solve it, he'd carefully and patiently, as Monk had done with him, explain the situation to them and offer further suggestions.

Once, Earl noticed a Ravi Shankar album in the Coltrane record collection and asked about it. John played them a morning raga and wrote out some pentatonic scales for them to study. He'd been listening to Indian music recently, probably due to Yusef Lateef's influence; Lateef had been deeply involved in Eastern music for years, and Coltrane could hear it clearly in his playing. This spare, abstract Indian music, with its overwhelming emphasis on melody and rhythm to the exclusion of harmony, would, oddly enough, seize him with such fervor that he started corresponding with Shankar in 1961, culminating in their first personal meeting in 1965.

Besides playing and writing music, John Coltrane seemed to spend much of his time with books, mostly non-musical ones. He didn't hang around bookstores, but he'd been influenced through the years by many articulate people who had persuaded him to join several book clubs and make some careful selections. He was particularly fond of books about religion and philosophy. Sonny Rollins had suggested *Autobiography of a Yogi;* Bill Evans had recommended Krishnamurti's *Commentaries on Living.* Edgar Cayce, Kahlil Gibran, Egyptology, Scientology, Plato, Aristotle; hundreds of books were stacked on the shelves, scattered around the rooms, and strewn beside the bed where his tenor and soprano often rested, for he was also fond of playing as well as reading before bedtime, as if serenading his wife to sleep.

When and where he found the time to read, Naima doesn't really know. The TV was often on, though more for Toni than anyone else. These sounds were strictly background for John, who'd often talk over them with Zita about space travel and the possibility of life on other planets. They discussed Einstein, too; John was fascinated by such matters as gravitational and electromagnetic attraction and read everything he could about relativity . . . with some strangely prophetic results.

He also loved driving. His means of transportation at that time was a 1958 Plymouth sedan, followed by a 1960 Mercury station wagon, and only Chrysler wagons after that. The first year of his quartet's existence, the musicians traveled cross country in the Mercury, his version of a band bus for four.

Zita Carno recalls, "I'd stop over to have coffee with John, then we'd drive to the club if he was playing in New York. He was a fanatic about getting to work on time. If he was late, he'd run red lights by the dozen and scare me half to death. I was always surprised that he was never stopped by a cop or run into by another car. At least, when I was with him."

Naima and Toni remember many pleasant and leisurely Sunday drives. But some were not so. For a latent impulsiveness would sometimes surface; John might walk in around suppertime, taste the food and say, "I'm not in the mood for this, let's eat out." Then he'd bundle his family into the car, and off they'd drive until he found a restaurant that suited him. Often it was Indian, for he was experimenting with that country's cuisine as well as its music and over-all culture.

Once Naima said, sighing, "I had to separate the musician from the man in order for me to live with him."

Sometimes she had to separate the musician from the musician, a more demanding task. For example, there was the day he brought home a harp, placed it in a corner of the living room, and asked her to see what she could do with it.

What she really wanted to do with it was to get rid of it; she'd fooled around with piano on occasion, but *harp?* She refused to take harp lessons, and that was that.

Once in a while Zita would bring over a classical harpist who would play a few symphonic excerpts for them. John would sit there, his eyes soaking up the scene, his head nodding dreamily. When the musician was finished, John would turn to Naima and say, with a sly smile, "Don't you wish you could play like that?"

He also made a habit of checking out the TV schedule to see if a Marx Brothers movie was scheduled. If so, he'd arrange to be home and watch the show until it was time for Harpo to play. Then, up went the volume, down went John on the floor and into an approximation of the Lotus position—he was studying yoga, too—while concentrating his primary attention on the film. When Harpo's stellar solo was finished, John would look longingly at the harp in the corner, then at his spouse and say, "You know, Harpo can *really* play."

"Well, *I* can't play, and you know that," she'd say. Then, opening her mouth, she'd gnash her teeth in mock anger, adding, "But I can still talk, and I've got my own teeth to prove it."

John laughed softly, for her comment had hit home. He had finally found a dentist, at Naima's urging, who told him the truth—that his teeth were like rotted trees and the sooner they were removed, the better. He'd made the decision, painful as the process was, that replacements were indeed required. And now he had the result of his wise decision in his mouth; a complete set of brand-new bridgework.

Some evenings, depending on the weather, it would be time for the telescope, another Coltrane interest.

"Neet, let's check out the stars; it looks like a clear night," he'd say, calling her by his favorite nickname, short for Juanita. Then, weather permitting, they set up the telescope he'd purchased while working in San Francisco. He'd bought it because of Naima and her interest in astrology; he wanted her to "read my stars and tell me something about myself I don't know." The telescope, now positioned in the back yard, was a refracting model with equatorial mounting, counterweight and finder, a four-lens orthoscopic piece about four feet long. Swinging on its tripod, it could sweep the skies, pick out any heavenly body, and hold it steady, pulling the stars and planets down to human size.

"Take a look," he'd say, offering her the first look. She would locate the positions of selected stars, updating his horoscope for the following day. If the omens were not good, he'd vow to stay in bed and practice his horn until better days were forthcoming.

Then he'd take his turn, and aim the scope not at the stars, but the planets; one planet in particular.

Mars, the Red Planet. He was so fascinated by its color and imagery that he later retitled a song he'd written for his previous employer, "Miles' Mode," in homage of his favorite planet.

Strange; in mythology, Mars is the planet that represents the god of war. And John Coltrane was a man of peace.

Naima once created a personal horoscope for her husband, but it is no longer available. Therefore, for those who are so inclined, John Coltrane's astrological profile has been analyzed by New York astrologer and author Edith Niles, as follows:

John William Coltrane was born September 23, 1926, at 5:30 P.M., as the sun was just leaving the sign of Virgo.

The Virgo male is hard-working, precise, and productive; the number of his compositions shows how true to type he was. Virgo is also in his house of partnership, so he would be drawn to work with people of similar characteristics, who would give equally of themselves in regard to performing his music.

According to palmistry, his long, sculptured fingers show the ability to handle work of an analytical nature.

Notice that his sun progressed into Libra immediately after his birth, remaining there for the rest of his life. He apparently took on the qualities of that sign which made him artistic, creative, and with a love of harmony. Especially the latter, personally and musically; Libra always seeks the ideal in a relationship and is usually disappointed. The frequent changing of his musical colleagues, the bands he worked with and those who worked in his band, reflects the Libra search for perfection and balance—a perfection he was rarely able to find and then not for long.

Pisces was rising at his birth, giving him social and musical ability and a compassionate understanding of others. However, this ascendant may also have contributed toward his being used by others and thus drained of energy and resources. This would constitute a major conflict in his life-desire, to give to others and still retain enough time and energy for his own creative work.

Note that upon his birth Uranus was rising. This planet rules the progressive sign of Aquarius, the space age planet, and since his midheaven ruler, Jupiter, which deals with career, is in the sign of Aquarius, he would be concerned with radical, revolutionary ideas in his work. The pioneering moon in Aries shows a man concerned with new and startling innovations. Notice also that Uranus can mean a person who attracts attention and publicity. And with Jupiter in the Twelfth House, which often deals with matters after death, this indicates that Coltrane may have achieved his greatest recognition posthumously.

His North Node of the Moon is located on the cusp of the Fifth House, the house of creativity, and a changing moon in the Second House of practical affairs shows a person constantly seeking change. This need for change would affect his relationships with women, for the love planet Venus in Virgo would make him particular in his choice of ladies.

With the glamorous planet Neptune in Leo ruling his rising sign Pisces, he is definitely someone who can succeed with the public. It also makes him prone toward the romantic and mystical. Since this planet is in the Sixth House of work and service, Coltrane would use his great magnetism to create art for mankind.

His early death, possibly brought on by his experiences with drugs and liquor, was foreshadowed by Pluto in the Fifth House, a sign of self-indulgence, and Jupiter, which rules the liver in the Twelfth House of Death. Since his grand trine was composed of the malefic planets Saturn, Uranus, and Pluto, he probably considered death a welcome release.

> We're now entering the Aquarian Age and musicians, who are quite sensitive to these things, are picking up these vibrations and getting attuned with the spiritual concepts of life through their music. I think we can thank John Coltrane for leading the way.
>
> HORACE SILVER

> Trane transfers the human voice to tenor and expresses in that way all emotions and expressions of the human being: he laughs, screams, whispers, cries, dances, groans, caresses, begs, demands, converses, tells a story.
>
> BJORN FREMER

Ornette Coleman told his own kind of story when he came to New York in the fall of 1959, and his strange tale of notoriety can be summed up in two words:

Freak Show.

The establishment, those in positions of power in any area of endeavor, will do it every time; they'll pick out the weirdest and wildest member of the avant-garde and promote him or her like a new brand of dog food, regardless of that person's artistic quality or lack of it. Just to publicly demonstrate how open-minded and big-hearted they really are. Of course, as far as the rest of the scuffling young artists still struggling for a few minutes of recognition goes, the establishment really couldn't care less.

Thus, alto saxophonist Coleman became the musical establishment's current Freak-in-Residence. His white plastic saxophone, the rococo clothing he and his sidemen wore, his constant use of the word "love" in describing his music . . . all these offbeat affectations could not fail to endear him to many of the "elite." John Lewis, pianist and leader of the Modern Jazz Quartet, introduced Coleman to Leonard Bernstein as "the new Bird." Further puffery was passed on by Bernstein when he then presented the saxophonist to the entire assembled membership of the New York Philharmonic and proclaimed the Texas-born musician as "a genius of jazz." Nesuhi Ertegun signed Coleman to an Atlantic recording contract, and soon four album releases made his music available to anyone who could afford a record player.

This was of course in marked contrast to John Coltrane, who was still working with Miles Davis and either being ignored or put down by almost every critic or "establishment" figure within earshot.

To give Coleman credit, he is an unusual innovator whose melodic and compositional gifts are self-evident. But he is rarely at home in any other music besides his own and does not possess nearly the technique and training that Trane developed through years of self-disciplined study and practice. However, he did become acquainted with Trane; the two saxophonists often discussed music during the early 1960s, but there is little evidence that either influenced the other's musical direction.

If anything, Coleman's influence on others came more from the media than from his music. Within less than a year after he arrived in New York, there were at least a dozen articles published about him. Not only in the music magazines but also in those of general circulation, so that many readers not involved in music knew who Ornette Coleman was if not what he was doing.

Meanwhile John Coltrane, who had played with, ironically enough, more members of the jazz establishment (Gillespie, Hodges, Davis, to name a few) than Ornette Coleman (none), was still relatively unrecognized outside of hard-core jazz circles. In addition, due no doubt to his lack of personal charisma and interest in self-publicity, he did not even receive the courtesy of so much as *one* in-depth article about him in any of the mass media. A few reviews, perhaps; and that was all.

In April 1960, Coltrane formed the basic musical unit that, with few exceptions, he would work with for the remainder of his career—the John Coltrane Quartet.

It was not the "classic" quartet, the one with pianist McCoy Tyner, bassist Jimmy Garrison, and drummer Elvin Jones. Not yet; none of those three were in his first group, though Tyner, for example, had been his first choice as pianist. Coltrane had known Tyner since the latter was seventeen; they had both played with Cal Massey's band and had worked on other jobs together in Philadelphia. But the pianist was now a member of Benny Golson's band, the Jazztet, fulfilling a previous commitment.

In any case, Coltrane had made up his mind to move *now*. His timing was right; Sonny Rollins was in retirement again, had been for a year and wouldn't play in public for another twelve-month period. Was Rollins again "making room" for Coltrane, helping the latter's career by being off the scene so that the public's—and critics'—attention could be concentrated on Coltrane as *the* new tenor player to watch?

Rollins has never said.

Coltrane still needed a piano player—at least until McCoy Tyner became available—and he finally selected a twenty-two-year-old Harvard graduate named Steve Kuhn, who was playing in trumpeter Kenny Dorham's band. Kuhn was a talented musician who knew Bach as well as Trane's blues. And, he was the only pianist of all those auditioned who could play the proper changes not only on standard songs but also on Coltrane originals.

The piano chair was thus filled, and the bass slot was already set for Philadelphian Steve Davis, who had worked with Trane in the house band at the Showboat and at whose home the saxophonist had met Naima. However, the drummer was still unchosen, though Coltrane knew of Elvin Jones's work from previous trips to Detroit, where Pontiac-born Jones had worked until moving to New York in 1955. But Jones was then doing time at Rikers Island for a drug bust. He was not only unavailable, but

Coltrane also hesitated to bring him into the band for that reason. He finally found a drummer through Steve Kuhn, who recommended Pete LaRoca. The latter's real name was Sims, but he'd worked with Latin bands for several years and picked up a Spanish pseudonym in the process. LaRoca was then with Slide Hampton but accepted Coltrane's offer immediately, joining the band in time for an eight-week Jazz Gallery engagement.

The Jazz Gallery, the Termini brothers' new club, was not more than a half-mile away from the Five Spot, their present club. They had booked Coltrane, as previously promised, as soon as he'd told them he had a band.

But that present band lasted only six weeks, then Steve Kuhn left.

"I didn't feel right playing in the group. I didn't think I was contributing as much as I should have," Kuhn recalls. "I was getting bored with my playing, so I was ready to quit anyway."

On the other hand he still felt badly about being asked to leave, despite John's diplomatic handling of the matter. One evening, after the last set, John put his arm around Steve's shoulders, took him aside and said, in the exact phrasing he would use on several future occasions when either personal or musical matters were not working out to his satisfaction, "Steve, I'm going to make a change." When Kuhn inquired why, Coltrane said, "There's some things I want to hear that you're not doing."

Later, after giving the situation a more objective analysis, Kuhn said, "The trouble was that I was getting out there too much, trying to match Trane solo for solo. He didn't want that. He wanted a piano player who'd comp behind him, give him more backup than anything else."

That, McCoy Tyner would accomplish with perfection.

He became Kuhn's replacement; he managed to secure his release from the Jazztet and finished out the remaining two weeks of the Jazz Gallery job.

Steve Davis, as well as John Coltrane, was pleased to be playing with McCoy Tyner again. They had both grown up in the same Philadelphia neighborhood, studied at one time with the same teacher, and married two sisters, thus making them brothers-in-law of a sort. All four were Moslems; Davis' wife was named Kadija and Tyner's, Aisha. Oddly enough, neither musician used his Arabic name in public, so few were aware of their religious affiliation.

Like their leader, both Davis and Tyner were quiet and unassuming. Davis was short and slim, Tyner taller and broader; both had small mustaches, as did Coltrane, whose own was so unobtrusive that only a close examination would reveal its existence.

Trane was now smiling more often, for the band was sounding better every night. Kuhn was a subtle but delicate pianist, while Tyner, no less subtle but much stronger, was performing his chordal accompaniment much closer to what Coltrane wanted to hear. Davis was a powerful, swinging bassist with an excellent knowledge of harmony; he filled in the rhythm section with great finesse and dexterity, closely following the leader's solos and giving him firm, supple support.

But John Coltrane wasn't smiling nearly enough.

Not that he ever did, in public. But in private, as he listened to the band behind him, he could feel, even with the improvements, that something wasn't quite right. Tyner and Davis were fine so far; LaRoca, crisp and swinging but not *strong* enough, not possessing enough *power*. Not like Philly Joe Jones, when Trane had worked with Miles, loving his sound but loathing his undependability. Nor like Jimmy Cobb, or Elvin Jones, about whom John Coltrane was thinking constantly.

But Jimmy Cobb was still with Miles. And Elvin Jones was still in jail.

Gerald McKeever was out of jail.

He was called Spliby, which means a "fly," as in *Superfly*, kind of guy; or his nickname could also stand for the sounds he made while playing makeshift drums. He learned those while in jail for five years on a burglary charge. Confined in upstate New York, he'd picked up his rhythmic feel from listening to a late night jazz show, by playing with his bare fingers on the cold metal of his cot.

McKeever was a lean, expressionless, tough-looking man with the cold eyes of an ex-con. He was bitter, hostile, and unemployed, living with his mother in a Brooklyn housing project. He cared for and about nothing and no one; with two, and only two, exceptions.

His mother; he loved her; she was good to him.

John Coltrane; he worshiped him; Trane was God to him.

Spliby had heard *Kind of Blue* while in prison. Trane's solo on "So What" had grabbed him; its driving, energetic outpouring of notes, all with such tight, incredible control, the intelligence behind the passion, the discipline that controlled the creativity.

McKeever was hanging out one night in a Greenwich Village bar, listening to some Coltrane music on the jukebox. The bartender, noticing, said, "If you dig him that much, man, you should catch him in person."

"Huh?" Pause. "*Where?*"

The bartender told him.

Minutes later, Spliby was standing in line outside the Jazz Gallery. Twenty minutes later, he was paying his dollar-fifty admission and crowding into the "bleachers," a section where one could simply listen without purchasing a drink. On the bandstand, at the very back of the tunnel-shaped room, was the John Coltrane Quartet. The musicians were dressed in dark suits, as their leader preferred, looking neat and nice. The ex-con, sitting in faded jeans and a shirt with two buttons missing, scuffed shoes with worn-down heels, felt the difference, became uncomfortable, wondered what he was doing there; in his own mind, he looked more bedraggled than a Bowery bum.

Until Trane started playing.

The song was "Summertime."

"I was sitting there, *digging . . . screaming . . . crying . . .*" Spliby says. "I *felt* so much of what he was saying, I had so much *I* wanted to *say* to the whole world . . . *and I didn't know how to get it out!* He was *my God!*"

The club closed at four; Spliby was still there. When Trane had played the last tune, Spliby walked up to the bandstand and said, "Mr. Coltrane, you are *my God.*"

Coltrane looked at him, his eyes compassionate, his voice soft, as he said, "Please don't call me that."

"I can't *help* it, that's the way you make me *feel,*" McKeever said and walked away.

The next night, he came back with his kazoo.

Just a little green kazoo, a child's toy, \$.49 at Woolworth's. He sat on the bleachers as before; during intermission, he stayed there, playing Coltrane tunes on his kazoo. He'd been woodshedding with it; he was good, his ear was sharp and his mouth was supple. He worked on the changes to a ballad the saxophonist liked to play, "I Want to Talk About You."

Again, he stayed there until closing, then went over to talk with Trane, this time refraining from the God-talk. The saxophonist was touched by him, empathized with his situation, intuitively feeling that Gerald McKeever was, in effect, laying his secret soul on the line by calling him "God" as he did, as if he were a Catholic confessing his sins to John Coltrane.

(Gerald McKeever would go through many changes in the process of getting close to John Coltrane. Through Trane's influence, Spliby learned to lessen his hostility against society and to love more people than he had thought possible, but without sharing the saxophonist's ingrained naïveté about the way the world is. Musically, he became so involved with Trane's tunes that he learned, and strictly by ear, the proper chord changes to such lyrical compositions as "Naima," "Dear Lord," and "Wise One," playing the songs on kazoo in perfect unison with the saxophonist's recorded solos. He also stopped drinking and taking drugs—until John Coltrane's death, after which Gerald McKeever, seeking something to fill the immense void in his life caused by Coltrane's passing, went back to the bottle and the needle. Today, he no longer drinks or takes drugs; not when his kidneys are in such shape as to require two or three days of dialysis in the hospital each week. And when not hospitalized, Spliby sits quietly at home, still living with his mother, still playing his kazoo to Coltrane solos, and still sustaining himself on the music and memories of John Coltrane.)

John Coltrane was sufficiently touched by Spliby to take him to a restaurant and buy him a meal. Then, Trane gave him a ride home to Brooklyn, while Spliby played a full chorus of "Cousin Mary" on kazoo for John Coltrane, as they drove along.

As he dropped Spliby off, Trane said, "You know my music better than I do."

The John Coltrane Quartet was on tour.

Riding in the leader's Mercury station wagon, the musicians

headed west. They were earning a minimum of $200 per week, more when the club would pay is excess of $1,250 for the entire band. They stayed in hotels that catered to musicians, sometimes spending as little as $6.00 a day. They often ate in ethnic restaurants for $1.25 a meal. Except for Trane; he'd head for a health food store and a drug store, the former for his raw carrots and prune juice, the latter to stash away a supply of Butter Rum Life Savers.

When Coltrane wasn't playing or writing out a new tune, he was off in a corner of the club, or alone in his hotel room, practicing, often on tenor, but now more frequently with his soprano. He'd been studying and working with the small, straight horn for more than a year; it was a difficult instrument to keep in tune, due to its extremely high register. In addition, a smaller, tighter embouchure was needed to play it properly.

The band played the Minor Key in Detroit; and there, in the Motor City, Pete LaRoca got the wheels put under him.

Trane just wasn't hearing LaRoca any more; he discharged his drummer and gave him severance pay and plane fare back to New York. The saxophonist got in touch with Billy Higgins, a drummer who'd been working in Los Angeles with Ornette Coleman, and made arrangements to use him when the band arrived in L.A., their next stop. Higgins made the first rehearsal, but the same problem emerged yet again; the drummer didn't sound as right as Trane had thought he would. Where LaRoca played behind the beat, Higgins was right on top of it.

That wasn't what John Coltrane wanted, either. It was one of those times in his life when he didn't know for sure what he really wanted until he got it.

Coltrane happened to meet Thad Jones, Elvin's brother, who was playing trumpet with Count Basie in Los Angeles while Trane was there. Thad told him that Elvin was just getting out of jail and gave him a number where the drummer could be reached. Higgins accompanied the band to San Francisco, their next engagement, where Trane called once—and sometimes two or three times—each day to New York, trying to catch Elvin Jones.

Finally, at the end of the first week of a two-week engagement, Trane got Elvin on the phone.

"Elvin?"

"Yeah . . . *hey,* is this . . ."

"John Coltrane" Pause. "Elvin, are you clean?"

Long pause. "I'm . . . *clean.* . . ."

Long sigh. "Can you join the band in Denver next week?"

"Hey, *Trane,* I'll play with you *anywhere* . . . even the men's room!"

Now Coltrane got busy; he shipped Billy Higgins back to Los Angeles and had Elvin Jones flown to Denver. Upon arrival, Jones found a new set of drums waiting for him on the bandstand, courtesy of Coltrane

Davis recalls, "That first night Elvin was in the band, he was playing so strong and so loud you could hear him outside the club and down the block. But Trane wanted it that way. He wanted a drummer who could really kick, and Elvin was one of the strongest, wildest drummers in the world. After the gig, Trane put his arm around Elvin, took him to a barbecue place around the corner, and bought him some ribs. Trane and Elvin were tight from then on."

The band's next date was Chicago's Sutherland Lounge.

There, in addition to playing three sets each evening, incessant practice on both tenor and soprano, and filling up on health foods at Miss Fortune's restaurant at Cottage Grove and Sixty-third Street, Coltrane found time to talk with Don DeMicheal, managing editor of *Down Beat,* who had just joined the magazine. In 1961, DeMicheal would be named editor and *Down Beat* would become the only regular outlet for jazz journalism, with *Metronome* going out of business that same year. Therefore, *Down Beat* was of more than minor importance to musicians and fans, though hardly beloved among the former due to its penchant at the time for uninformed criticism of the new music. That is, many white critics had barely digested Bird's music, and here came Trane hitting them right between the typewriter keys while they were wondering whether they should listen to him seriously or simply dismiss him as a man who just played weird sounds.

This dilemma would never be resolved satisfactorily for either party, white critics or black musicians. However, DeMicheal, a tall, lean man with thick black hair flying continually in his face, a Southerner sympathetic to jazz in general and black musicians in particular, was sincerely interested in understanding Coltrane's music.

But his first reaction to hearing the saxophonist live was, "What is he playing all those notes for?"

The music disturbed him and made him uncomfortable on several levels. He listened hard, fighting the urge to walk out. But, as the same song had touched black Gerald McKeever, so also did "Summertime" reach white Don DeMicheal (who'd later hire Bill Quinn as assistant editor, making Quinn the first black writer so honored by a white magazine).

Then, just as DeMicheal was becoming acclimatized to Coltrane's interpretation of Gershwin, the saxophonist startled him all over again by playing some high notes followed by a coarse honking sound that the journalist thought was in terribly bad taste. However, during intermission, Coltrane explained by saying, with a tight smile, "Oh, that was just to pull the rhythm section together."

To DeMicheal, such an open display of honesty, with none of the subterfuge common in countless other musicians he'd come in contact with, made him want to write an article and show the magazine's audience what Coltrane and his music were really like. John was hesitant about this prospect, but Don visited the Sutherland night after night, explaining the format he had conceived for the piece. John would talk about himself and his music in the first person; he'd get the by-line, with Don's name as collaborator. Finally Coltrane, who had on occasion considered the idea of doing some prose writing himself, agreed.

The article appeared in the September 29, 1960, issue of *Down Beat.* As DeMicheal had hoped, it was as revealing of the man as the musician. Speaking of Johnny Hodges, for example, Coltrane said, "And the confidence with which Rabbit plays! I wish I could play with the confidence that he does." Of his respect for musical tradition and his continual studying, he said that "I've found you've got to look back at the old things and see them in a new light. I'm not finished with these studies because I haven't assimilated everything into my playing."

But probably the most important statement he made—and the one that would haunt him for the rest of his life from the combined forces of critics, musicians, and the audience—was this:

"I want to progress, but I don't want to go so far out that I can't see what others are doing."

> We were driving out of Denver in the station wagon, one day just before dawn. John wanted to get some sleep, so he let Elvin take over. I was sleeping in the front seat, with John and McCoy in the back, but I woke up shortly after Elvin started driving. I looked at the speedometer and Elvin was doing 90, he was working out on the steering wheel and accelerator like a set of drums. I woke up McCoy and he woke up John, and the two of us talked John into taking over the wheel again.
>
> STEVE DAVIS

> Once I borrowed Trane's car to go on a date, and after I took her home I was in a hurry to get home myself. I was driving too fast, and I skidded off the road and hit a tree. The car was a total wreck, but I walked away with just bruises and scratches. When I told Trane about it, he said, "I can always get another car, but there's only one Elvin."
>
> ELVIN JONES

Like Steve Davis and McCoy Tyner, Elvin Jones studied privately while in high school. He once had designs upon becoming a doctor rather than drummer. But a shortage of family finances and a wealth of percussion talents moved him into music; those same factors may have also caused him to quit high school after the tenth grade. He then worked at a variety of manual labor jobs while studying drums with private teachers, and like John Coltrane he read all the music books he could find.

At six feet and 150, he's extremely slim, and his unusually long arms can cover a lot of percussion territory. His style is almost atavistic, with a raw, primitive power; he plays cross rhythms, constantly stimulating himself with a succession of sixteenth notes, accents, and fast breaks that cause him to sweat away two or three pounds each evening. Some perceptive critics have also said that whatever Trane was doing on saxophone, Elvin was duplicating on drums.

Of the four musicians in Coltrane's band, Jones is the only one with any exterior animation. That is, John and Steve and McCoy look like very straight guys while on stand, as if they were three-fourths of the Modern Jazz Quartet, while Elvin's white-toothed grin and exclamatory grunts set him apart as much as his ferocious playing.

With Jones on drums, Coltrane's quartet was now sounding the same way the saxophonist was hearing his music in his head. That fall, when they played New York's Half Note, everything was very much together, especially Trane's soprano, now sounding like a spirit's cry at the top of the register and a child's sob at the bottom. Like Sidney Bechet, his original inspiration, John Coltrane was using frequent trills and arabesques, but his style was closer to the sound of an oboe, to an Indian drone effect than Bechet's studied breathiness. With Trane, the soprano wailed and screamed as he split high notes and overblew the lows, using the horn primarily on songs that offered simple, lyrical lines for his multinoted excursions.

Tyner recalls, "It was a song plugger, I think, who brought us the sheet music at the Jazz Gallery. I didn't like the tune at first but John did, so we started playing it and it began to grow on me. The audience really liked it, the way we played it in three-quarter time. It was probably the only jazz waltz they'd ever heard since Sonny Rollins' 'Valse Hot.' So John decided to record it on his next album."

That song was "My Favorite Things."

During three hectic days in October 1960, the quartet recorded enough material to fill three albums. *Coltrane Plays the Blues* and *Coltrane's Sound* were not released until a year later, but *My Favorite Things* was in the record stores and on the radio stations within months; it sold more than 50,000 copies during its first year of release. For a jazz album to do better than 5,000, or twice that much at most, is roughly equivalent to a million-seller by the Rolling Stones.

C. H. Garrigues said, in the San Francisco *Examiner:* "It is, without question, the best Coltrane album to date and—almost equally without question—one of the most important of the 1960s."

He continued, "If one listens to Trane's long, complex solo, then follows through and hears how skillfully pianist McCoy Tyner lays an implacable foundation for Coltrane's second—long, complex, masterful, and exceedingly logical—solo, it becomes apparent that marvelous things have happened to the Coltrane horn."

In the Minneapolis *Sunday Tribune,* Charles Hanna commented, "Coltrane is not an artist you can listen to casually. You must give him your undivided attention to even begin to appreciate his talent. He emits a stream of musical consciousness that could, I suppose, be likened to some of the writings of James Joyce. He produces music that might be incomprehensible to some listeners, but its value and meaning lie in his compulsion to weave an entire piece of musical cloth almost instantaneously."

He concluded, "*My Favorite Things* is one of his best recordings."

> I first heard John Coltrane when his record of *My Favorite Things* was released in France in 1962. I was impressed; no, I was amazed how he could obtain such beautiful intonation on his horn. I knew Sidney Bechet's music well, because he had lived in Paris for so many years. But until Coltrane I had never heard the soprano saxophone played like this, with no vibrato yet such a clear, singing sound.
>
> JEAN-PIERRE RAMPAL

Bill Harris plays acoustic guitar, but to call him a classic guitarist is like referring to J. S. Bach as a church organist or describing John Coltrane as a bebop saxophonist. The guitarist usually includes the music of both Bach and Coltrane in his recitals; as he explains, "They were both great artist of their time, and the music of a great artist is always timeless."

Harris, who lives and teaches in Washington, D.C., first met Coltrane when the latter was playing with Johnny Hodges. As Bill recalls, "I used to sit in the hallway outside John's hotel room and listen to him practicing. He'd leave the transom open, and I just sat there with my back against the door and listened for hours."

In 1962, he recorded several of the saxophonist's songs, including "Naima" and "Syeeda's Song Flute," on a "demo" disc which was never released publicly. All the tunes were transcribed for solo guitar. He played the record for Coltrane, who, after listening closely, commented, "You know my music, Bill."

Harris also knew that the saxophonist had more than a passing interest in guitar players. Grant Green and Wes Montgomery both had sat in with Coltrane, who once asked Montgomery to work with him. The guitarist declined; as Wes told Bill, "Too much music there. I just couldn't handle John's music and my own all at the same time."

John Coltrane always had more than a passing interest in listening to other musicians, for reasons both personal and professional. Toward the end of 1960, he was listening intently to bassist Reggie Workman and drummer Roy Haynes at a now-defunct Village club. He knew of Haynes's work with Bird, among others, and he'd known Workman from Philadelphia. As Steve Davis recalls, "Reggie had really developed. I think he was coming on stronger, playing more upfront than I was. I know some people were telling John they couldn't hear the bass. Maybe this influenced him in his decision, but I'm not sure."

What Davis is sure of, though, is that when the quartet played a gig in the Quaker City shortly after the first of the next year, John put his arm around Steve, and took him aside after the last night of the job, and said, "Steve, I'm going to make a change." He also said, "There are some things you have to do, even though you don't want to."

So Steve Davis was out.

And Reggie Workman was in.

> I remember Coltrane and I were once on a tour that included several saxophone players, and Lester Young was one of them. We were on the bus, heading for the final gig, when one of the guys got so restless that he started walking up and down the aisle, playing every bop cliché he could think of. We were all watching, not saying anything. He wasn't getting a rise out of anybody, so he stuck his horn right against Lester Young's ear and played the most weird Bird runs he could

remember, for about five minutes. Then, he stopped and said, "Hey, how about that? Doesn't that grab you, baby?" Well, Pres just looked up with that all-knowing smile of his and said, "Yeah, man . . . but can you sing me a song?"

STAN GETZ

Stan Getz is a singer of songs, and that is why John Coltrane listed him among his four favorite saxophonists, for Coltrane would have been a singer if he had not become a saxophone player. As McCoy Tyner once said, "John would be driving along while we were traveling, and suddenly he'd break into 'O Solo Mio.' He was kidding us a little because he didn't have that great a voice, but he was serious, too, because he'd try to sing right on key."

Getz can come in on any key, and his lyrical, melodic improvisations, strongly influenced by Lester Young, are still sufficiently individualistic and certainly compelling enough to attract and hold almost any audience's attention. There is also a lingering melancholy, a visceral sadness in Getz's sound—"Of course you hear sadness there; I've had a lot of sadness in my life"—that was similar to the increasingly profound melancholy in Coltrane's music.

Stan's sadness was, as he said, his own, accruing to no one else except himself. However, John's melancholy was of a more universal nature, not so much from his own experiences as from the suffering and sadness of others, the wasted lives and worried people he'd observed during his years of traveling. He was, in the continuing quest for perfection in his music and compassion for others, acquiring a preacher's consciousness; not pejoratively, not in telling others not to do this or that, but in trying to make other people's lives more meaningful through music. And those who listened closely to Coltrane could tell, could certainly *feel* the persuasive intensity and personal message of his music; he was "talking" with his saxophone voice, and his sound so perfectly expressed what musicians called "the cry" of a preacher, a mystic, or a prophet.

"I want to be a force for good," John Coltrane often said.

He was doing good for Stan Getz, among others; the two saxophonists often shared the billing at such clubs as the Jazz Gallery. Getz, the reigning white saxophonist—as, say, Sonny Rollins was *the* black tenor player before Trane came so strongly on the scene—was winning most of the polls. And with good reason; pianist Oscar Peterson had not given him his nickname, Stanley the Steamer, simply for alliterative purposes. Stan could wail just as powerfully on up-tempo tunes as he could rhapsodize a ballad without dragging the rhythm to death.

As Getz says, "I used to close the bill because I was the established star, but the mood of the crowd was strongly for Coltrane as the underdog. I'd come in early and listen to John during his set, and he'd be playing so beautifully in his style that he inspired me to push myself all that much harder when it was my turn to play. There was no cutting contest involved, though some critics and fans might have thought so. I was really pleased that the audience could dig both of us, two different tenor styles, because that's what music is all about—a lot of guys saying different things their own way, and saying something worth listening to."

As for the polls of that period, some of them make most interesting reading. Especially the *Playboy* listing, which shows Stan Getz holding down one of the two tenor chairs in the All-Star Jazz Band from 1957 on.

John Coltrane took the other tenor chair from 1962 forward, ironically replacing that first titan of the tenor saxophone, Coleman Hawkins.

John Coltrane won the *Down Beat* poll on tenor for 1960, both the general poll and the special listing for the opinions of the International Critics. The latter also voted him tops in the combo category and best on miscellaneous instrument (soprano).

In addition, he also won the love of a lady, who shall remain nameless at her request. There were no explanations, only circumstances, and Naima had nothing to do with these circumstances. It was John, not she, who was the changeable, the restless, the searching one. As if, despite the apparent stability and solidity of his southern upbringing, there was a driving force that he could not control; as if his life was one long quest for what he once asked from Steve Kuhn, among others (and the way he asked it), "Tell me something new."

In this case, the "something new" in Coltrane's life was a white woman we shall call Trane's Lady, who moved to New York during the late 1950s to work as a secretary and be near the music and musicians she had learned to love. She met John Coltrane through Sonny Rollins, but it was at Benny Golson's urging that she began to listen to and learn to like his music—and her own urging that caused her to love the man.

She was tall and slim, the way Coltrane liked his ladies, with a sweet face and a gentle disposition. In fact, as well as in persona and personality, she was much like the man himself.

She kept a diary for every year she spent with John; that was what she always called him, John.

5/21/60: I got up early and went to Brooklyn to learn how to make sweet potato pie from Mama Gracie. Went to Jazz Gallery, spoke to John after first set. "I've brought you a present." "You?" "Me." He tasted the pie I'd baked for him, licked his fingers, and said, "Let's talk sometime."

5/31/60: At Jazz Gallery with my girl friend, Dee. We didn't have a chance to talk there, so John drove me home. He kissed me tenderly, and said he'd call me. I got to bed at 5:15 A.M.

6/2/60: John called about 8:15 P.M. He asked me, "Could I put you on short notice?" I said, "Yes."

6/8/60: John called at 2:15 A.M., wanted to see me. He picked me up at 4:30 A.M., took me to a Harlem hotel. He was more than considerate with me, knowing of my inexperience, and initiated me into his ways of extreme tenderness. It took me less than a week to fall in love with him. And it all started right after I had taken him the sweet potato pie.

7/4/60: John called at 2:20 A.M., wanted to see me this afternoon. I suggested Mama Gracie's place for us. He called me Honeybun. Called back 5:30 P.M., said he'd slept all day. His mother had called from Philadelphia and asked him to visit. He was going, said she might have a plain white cake for him, no frosting. Said frosting spoils a cake. He'll try and smuggle me a piece, will call me tomorrow.

7/5/60: Opening night at Small's Paradise. John didn't call.

7/16/60: John called 1:20 A.M., will see me at Doris' apartment at

3 P.M. I brought him oatmeal banana bread. He's going on the road next week. Said this might be last time he'll see me.

9/16/60: John called 9 A.M., stopped over an hour later. Gave him ledger for bookkeeping, to use for paying musicians in his band. Gave him whole wheat fig bars, he's on a diet. Said he weighed 190.

9/22/60: I met John, gave him birthday present of Irish linen handkerchiefs. Said they were too nice to use, he'd put some cologne on them and keep them. Used English Leather until I switched him to Bergdorf's Men's Cologne.

Trane's Lady also persuaded him to become a customer at Breidbart, a posh men's store on Avenue of the Americas and Forty-sixth Street, where silk-and-mohair suits were then being sold for no less than $200. It was necessary for the saxophonist to purchase dozens of suits from the store, for in common with Alfred Hitchcock, John Coltrane owned two separate wardrobes, his thin and his fat. His weight problem, so it seemed, was always with him.

And his feet often gave him trouble, too; a familiar situation for anyone who works at what was essentially a stand-up job. His means of alleviating the strains of standing on his feet all night long were not to the liking of Trane's Lady. The footwear he chose did not blend, was not co-ordinated with the classiness of his suits. No matter; comfort was what he sought and comfort was what he got. In spite of her disapproval, Coltrane continued to wear on his weary feet, night after night: Hush Puppies, priced at $4.95 a pair.

> The most impressive thing about working with Trane was a feeling of steady, collective learning.
>
> ELVIN JONES

> When I saw Elvin the first time, I flipped out. He sounded like thunder. Every time he'd crash the bass drum, I'd holler, *"Thunder!"*
>
> GERALD MCKEEVER

You must carefully listen to John Coltrane's sound.

You can't be put off by the hard, abrasive exterior of his music; his melodic lines are like a wave effect, each new musical explosion cresting, then collapsing, then cresting again, this time more powerful than the preceding wave. And that is only the surface of his sound, as the waves are only external manifestations of the ocean; it is like the earth's outer shell, where the impact of those thickly textured notes and the density of his music can collide head on with the unprepared listener. For he is a time traveler; his music is of the past and future tenses as well as present. He takes the listener back to a time when the earth's crust was barely cooled and the sea creatures had not yet begun their long walk on the land; and forward to an era yet uncharted and unpredicted where music may be transmitted from mind to mind in such an instantaneous accomplishment that there will no longer be any need for musical instruments as such.

Now, cut through to another level, corresponding to the earth's second layer, that of dense rock. Here are the chords, the triads, climbing their vertical hills, creating vast open spaces between those multitudinous notes and allowing the listener to get inside the musician a little more.

Then, slip into another layer; like the earth's oxide-sulfide zone, here are the rhythms of nature, the life-and-death cycle preordained from the very beginning. Still more space. Closer . . . closer . . . to the core of John Coltrane.

Like the nickel-iron core of the earth, boiling liquid radiating outward. As does the musician's spiritual, selfless essence, his overpowering desire to bring peace and good will to all.

The soft, sensitive core of John Coltrane.

Zita took me to see John many times. I'm not a connoisseur, but the emotional impact of his music overwhelmed me and almost made me too nervous to sit still. We talked a few times, and he treated me with so much courtesy he made me feel more like his mother than Zita's.

LUCIA CARNO

When my mother was seventy-five, she stood in line for forty-five minutes to hear John Coltrane. She's eighty-seven now, and she's still nuts about all the people I'm nuts about.

JIMMY ROWLES

A musician, another saxophonist, entered Coltrane's life—first as compatriot, then as collaborator. And the quartet became a quintet with the addition of Eric Dolphy.

For a long time Eric Dolphy and I had been talking about all kinds of improvising techniques. Finally, I decided that as long as my band was working steadily, it made sense for Eric to join us.

JOHN COLTRANE

I wrote a book about Eric Dolphy, but I'd also been listening to Coltrane ever since "Good Bait" on the *Soultrane* album wiped me out. I loved them both, but for different reasons. Trane was really into existential anguish, screaming from the depths of his soul, whiel Eric's music came through with such tremendous joy.

VLADIMIR SIMOSKO

Eric Dolphy, two years younger than John Coltrane, was born in Los Angeles. He lived there until he came to New York with the Chico Hamilton Quintet, settling there in 1959.

Like Coltrane, Dolphy started on clarinet, later switching to alto saxophone; he also learned flute. He studied with Buddy Collette, a well-respected reedman working the studio scene, at Los Angeles City College, and with conservatory teacher Lloyd Reese. Clarinetist Merle Johnston, at Collette's recommendation, taught Dolphy the techniques of handling the tricky, quirky bass clarinet, the instrument Adolphe Sax had spent so much time trying to perfect.

His parents, who lived in Watts, built their son a studio behind their house, and there he practiced, studied, and rehearsed. Altoist/vocalist Vi Redd recalls, "If someone played four choruses, Eric would play eight. That's the way he was. He'd work harder than anyone else." Tenor saxist Clifford Solomon, who worked with Dolphy in the Roy Porter band, adds, "Eric was the best reader in the band, with the best technique. But he always helped other people when they needed it. Everybody respected him."

Dolphy had known Coltrane since the latter's days with Hodges in 1954. When Eric arrived in New York, Trane helped him find work by introducing him to people who could do him some good. But the person who did him the most good was John Coltrane himself.

He hired Dolphy to write the arrangements for the *Olé* and *Africa/Brass* albums, both featuring large ensembles backing the basic quartet. He loved Eric's speechlike, rapid-fire figures on alto; his liquid, trilling flute work; and the reedy, throat-clearing sounds he coaxed from the recalcitrant and rarely used bass clarinet. When the club owners screamed at Dolphy and the critics praised him—the opposite usually happened to Coltrane—John backed Eric all the way by hiring him and keeping him as a steadily working sideman during 1961–62.

In 1961, John Coltrane signed his first contract with Impulse Records. The company had been created by the American Broadcasting Company as a spin-off from their ABC-Paramount label, which was primarily for popular music, and was structured to concentrate on the burgeoning jazz market. The company was located at 1501 Broadway, the Paramount Pictures building, where they remained until moving to the ABC Building at 1330 Avenue of the Americas upon its completion in 1965. When Impulse came into existence in 1961, the first artist they signed, that April, was John Coltrane.

The contract was the result of a many-sided negotiating session involving Harold Lovette, the Shaw Agency, Impulse president Larry Newton, and of course Coltrane himself, whose Atlantic contract was expiring and who was ready to make a change. After the final terms were agreed upon, John Coltrane had a contract that would make him, with the exception of Miles Davis, the highest-paid recording artist in jazz.

It was a one-year contract with two one-year renewal options, but considering Trane's increasing popularity this was, in effect, actually a three-year contract, calling for a minimum of two albums each year. The advance was $50,000, structured at the rate of $10,000 for the first year and $20,000 each year for the next two years. However, in order to avoid the tax bite that so much advance income would subject him to, Coltrane was paid $10,000 each year at $2,500 per quarter; whatever monies were still due him would be paid in full at the expiration of the final contract three years hence.

He recorded his first album for Impulse during May and June. Called *Africa/Brass,* it was Trane backed by a large ensemble, hinting at both African rhythms and Indian ragas in the title tune. The setting was more conventional for "Greensleeves" and "Blues Minor," the latter an incredibly visceral, "shouting" line that was probably the most basic, if not the most interesting, cut on the album. Creed Taylor was the producer, but he left the company shortly thereafter. His replacement was Bob Thiele; this was the start of the Thiele/Coltrane association that would last for the rest of the saxophonist's life.

Thiele produced all of Coltrane's Impulse record dates from the first "live" session at the Village Vanguard on. He had previously done the same for such artists as Joe Sullivan, James P. Johnson, Louis Armstrong, and Lester Young, and for such firms as Decca, Dot, and Roulette. This stocky, pipe-smoking man was intensely aware of what he called the New Black Music and was especially interested in signing as many of its practitioners as possible for Impulse. Examples were Pharoah Sanders, Archie Shepp, Albert Ayler . . . and of course John Coltrane.

In his contract, Coltrane had complete approval of all aspects of the record album itself, such as graphics, layout, and packaging. The latter especially intrigued him; Impulse was the first to use double-sleeve packaging for just a single album, using the extra space for photos, liner notes, and personnel credits. The company also charged an extra dollar, retailing their albums at $5.98, the highest price then posted for jazz records; but, according to the accountants, Impulse didn't lose any money on the deal.

The Shaw Agency didn't lose any money on Coltrane's bookings, either.

John Coltrane *wanted* to work; he was extremely puritanical about the work ethic and always had been. Day after day in the recording studio, night after night on the bandstand, he was *there,* his audience could count on him to show for the gig, and that's one reason his fans were so loyal. He delivered for his audience, always. The agency was extremely pleased with such a situation; they were getting their 10 per cent commission for each date booked, plus the same amount for setting up his Impulse recording contract.

Larry Myers and Jack Whittemore booked the saxophonist into such clubs as Olivia's Patio in Washington, D.C., the Crawford Grill in Pittsburgh, Cleveland's Cotton Club, Chicago's Plugged Nickel, Shelly's Manne-Hole in Los Angeles, and others already mentioned. They got him $2,500 to $3,000 a week and usually kept him working, week after week. Once, they packaged a Miles-Mulligan-Monk show at the Apollo Theater. When Trane heard about that, he asked them to arrange some theater or concert dates for him, too.

They did; he played several concerts at Philharmonic Hall in New York. His audience was large and loyal enough to fill, or nearly fill, the 2,700 seats there.

From the diary of Trane's Lady, for the year 1961:

2/11: John called, said our relationship couldn't continue due to other pressures in his life. Told me, "I wish it could have happened some years ago." Started to say, "I don't know what to say, I'm losing a friend. . . ." Corrected himself to say, "No, I know that's not true."

3/20: Elvin said he'd get me in at Apollo. Asked for him, out came John. Said it was too much of a hassle and gave me $5.00 to buy a ticket.

7/8: John came by, apologized for not calling and said, "Don't cut me." Recorded big band session, didn't come off as he'd hoped. Said he was feeling confused.

8/7: Nat Adderley called from Detroit, said Cannonball gave John some diet pills and John got dizzy. Nat thinks he took two instead of one. Remembered John once said he doesn't believe in taking one of anything. Nat said audiences screaming for "My Favorite Things" the way they did for Bobby Timmons' "This Here."

8/25: Randall's Island Jazz Festival. John got polite reception, Cannonball got good reception, Horace Silver broke it up with "Filthy McNasty."

10/16: John in San Francisco. Met Ralph Gleason, who was impressed when he interviewed John there. Ralph said John told him about books he wanted to read and asked good questions about them. Also said John never says anything unless he's sure of what he says, is careful and thinks for a long time before making a decision.

10/30: John visited me for two hours. Worried about his music, wants something different but likes money, too. Dieting, but I fed him pie anyway. I got lipstick on his shirt when he grabbed me, because we hadn't seen each other for a long time. Noticed Bible in my library, said, "Are you a Christian? Because if you're not, we're through." I said I was. End of discussion.

11/10: John on *PM West* TV show with Carmen McRae. Did "My Favorite Things" and looked nervous. Opened and closed show, suffering from such insults as "far out" and "will put us into space."

I was practicing drums, using other people's on jam sessions, playing drumsticks against the sofa at home along with Trane's records. One night at the Half Note, Elvin said to me, "I want you to play the next set for me; I've got some business to take care of." He left, and I told John what he'd said. John said, "Do you want to play?" I said, "I'd like to, if it's all right with you." I got behind Elvin's drums, and Trane played "Softly, As in a Morning Sunrise," "I Want to Talk About You," and "Naima." All quiet things, but I was listening to the other guys, and we made it through all right. John thanked me, and asked me if I read music. I said, "No." He said, "Well, Spliby, you've got a lot of good feeling there." Then, as I was coming off the bandstand, I saw Naima and Cousin Mary, who both looked so surprised to see me and not Elvin on drums.

GERALD MCKEEVER

On the nights of November 2 and 3, 1961, two people were listening closely to John Coltrane at the Village Vanguard for reasons other than pleasure. Bob Thiele was there to supervise the recording of Trane's first live album, with Rudy van Gelder to make the actual recording.

It was a reunion for Coltrane and Van Gelder, since the majority of John's Prestige albums had been recorded at Rudy's studio in New Jersey, at that time the living room of his parents' home in Hackensack. Originally an optometrist, Van Gelder became, after several years of recording his friends as a hobby, a self-taught sound engineer, and his consuming passion for music culminated in the opening of his own recording studio in Englewood Cliffs.

Thiele, sitting at a front table and sipping a drink, was enjoying the music but not understanding much of it, not yet. He was feeling vaguely apprehensive about recording Coltrane, yet was still sufficiently perceptive to read the saxophonist's attitude as "You're supervising the recording, so you must know what you're doing." Van Gelder, with one two-track machine and several microphones, was working off spurts of nervous energy; he moved quickly, his hair falling frequently into his eyes, chasing after Trane as he moved around on stage, changing the microphone positions every few minutes to make sure the band was being picked up properly.

Club owner Max Gordon, a diminutive, white-haired man with the expression of a cautious gnome, was wandering around as usual. He occupied himself with counting the house, watching the musicians, checking the bar, and finally sitting down at a rear table to listen to the music, his head nodding and a child's pleased smile sneaking across his face.

Both John Coltrane and Eric Dolphy (only heard on "Spiritual" in this recording) were standing in front of the rhythm section, opening with tight ensemble figures and segueing into long solo statements, one after the other, for chorus after chorus. McCoy Tyner and Reggie Workman were feeding the saxophonists the most sympathetic chordal, harmonic accompaniment, while the primitive power of Elvin Jones was hard-driving the entire band. Elvin was beginning to showcase himself more and more, his increasing loudness and nonstop drumming nearly overwhelming the two horns most of the time.

"Softly, As in a Morning Sunrise" was smoother, though. Elvin's brushwork started out crisp and flowing, moving the melody along behind McCoy and Reggie and switching to sticks when John came in on soprano for one of his incantatory chants.

And then, it was time to record what was to become "Chasin' the Trane."

It was a blues, and as Coltrane said, "You never have to worry about the blues. In this case, however, the melody not only wasn't written but it wasn't even conceived before we played it. We set the tempo, and in we went."

Out Tyner went; Coltrane wanted him to "stroll," that is, to lay out completely, and he did as he was told. So the as yet unnamed "Chasin' the Trane," using a Debussy figure as its theme, was just Coltrane, Workman, and Jones for fifteen minutes and fifty-five seconds of energetic, expressive changes and counterchanges, interpolations and improvisations in a continuous stream-of-consciousness creation that would leave listeners shaking their heads not in negation but disbelief that such a difficult project had not only been attempted but had also emerged with such musically successful results.

Max Gordon was nodding his head so forcefully that it seemed ready to snap off.

Bob Thiele was tapping his feet hard enough to wear down his heels, puffing so fiercely on his pipe that he nearly insulated himself in a smoke screen of his own making.

Rudy van Gelder was a study in near-perpetual motion, following Coltrane around as closely as a bill collector and keeping one of his microphones just inches from the leader's tenor saxophone at all times, even though he had to climb over half the customers to do it.

And when the tune was finished and no one could think of a name to call it, Van Gelder, thinking not only of the music played but also about the efforts he had expended in order to get it on record, suggested the title as strictly what he felt he was doing all night long. So the song became "Chasin' the Trane."

We were all young Jewish guys, growing up in New York and listening to Coltrane. His music helped open us up to our own feelings, get rid of our collective guilt, and make us think about creative ways to express ourselves. I was playing drums with Damita Jo when I first heard "Chasin' the Trane," but my ears weren't ready and it was too much for me. It took me a few more years to really get into it, and when I did I'd use it for a spiritual uplift. Because I got to thinking, no matter the odds, Trane was doing his thing, so why shouldn't I?

LES PERLMAN

At Hollywood's Renaissance Club, I heard musical nonsense currently being peddled in the name of jazz. There should be a collective blend among the individual players, transforming the music into that elusive element, swing. Coltrane and Dolphy seem intent on deliberately destroying this essence, this vital ingredient. They seem bent on pursuing an anarchistic course in their music that can but be termed anti-jazz.

JOHN TYNAN

The John Coltrane Quintet toured Europe that same November of 1961. It was their first overseas engagement, and Coltrane was so pleased with the band that he increased the musicians' salaries to $300 a week. Norman Granz promoted the tour, taking the group into England, France, Germany, and Scandinavia. The European critics were more responsive than the U.S. critics to the music for what it was, an art form and not simply sounds to drink beer by, and they wrote some excellent reviews. More important, though, the audience appreciated the band sufficiently to set up a continuous hand-clapping, foot-stomping demonstration that made the musicians feel very much wanted.

France was the exception. Paris, a city normally cultivated and discriminating enough to appreciate such varied artists as Bechet, Picasso, and Voltaire, could not apparently accept Coltrane. During an extended version of "Impressions"—ironically enough, based, like "Chasin' the Trane," on a Debussy whole-tone scale—some clods threw pennies on the stage at the Olympia Theater, thus financially putting down the musicians. As Elvin said afterward, "We can always use the money, and it could have been worse—they could have thrown wine bottles."

England proved more hospitable. Bob Dawborn of *Melody Maker* interviewed Coltrane; the saxophonist, as if offering a possible explanation for the Parisians' rudeness, simply said, "We're very inexperienced at playing concerts. We're used to playing at great length in clubs, and it's hard to cut down to concert time limitations, especially with Eric."

> When I came to New York from Pittsburgh in 1961, the only two people I wanted to play with were John Coltrane and Ornette Coleman. I'd heard that John was looking for a bass player, so I called him and he invited me over to his house to audition. He played both saxophone and piano while I improvised on the changes he set up. He was very nice to me, but I got the feeling that I hadn't really gotten my message across and that I wasn't really as good as I'd thought I was. I went home to practice and study more, and later I joined Ornette.
>
> DAVID IZENZON

> I believe Reggie Workman went with Art Blakey after he left, and Jimmy Garrison came to us from Ornette Coleman. This was around December 1961. I don't remember exactly why Reggie left, but I'll say this about Jimmy, his time and choice of notes was the best of all the bass players John had used. He stayed more in the background, and that was what John really wanted.
>
> McCOY TYNER

Since "Chasin' the Trane," where he was conspicuous by his absence, McCoy Tyner was moving more into the background himself, as Coltrane's solos got longer and Jones's drumming got louder. The quartet might have become a duet if Dolphy hadn't been working with them, and when he left in mid-1962 that's just the way the band was sounding, with John and Elvin almost overwhelming McCoy and Jimmy to the point of obscurity.

While Eric was still with the band, the five presented an incredible *visual* contrast on stand.

John was crouching more in his playing, dropping some of his formerly perfect posture to move both his horn and body more, as if dancing to his own music. Elvin was sitting tall behind his drums, sweating and screaming, his face contorted into indescribable expressions that some called nothing less than demonic. McCoy was leaning over the piano at a right angle, his head held closely to the keys. Jimmy, called "Half Pint" by Spliby, and a good eight inches shorter than his bass, was mostly hidden by his instrument but let an occasional grin flash across his face. (Off the stand, Garrison was hanging out with Jones and snorting heroin, unfortunately influenced by the drummer's habits, for Elvin, despite his promise to Trane, was still staying high on more than music.)

And Eric, taller than an upright bass, long and limber as a stretched-out sausage, barely moved as he played, his huge luminous eyes absorbing everything around him (almost as much as his leader, and in a similar manner) and his bristly beard sticking out like a paintbrush from his jutting jaw. As gentle as he was joyous, Dolphy loved to play with Coltrane as much as he loved the man himself.

As Trane's Lady once said, "John always told me that outside of Sonny Rollins, Eric Dolphy was his only true friend."

> When I knew them, Trane and Eric were listening to tribal recordings of South African pygmies. Trane was really into African rhythms. He told me that each drummer has a certain rhythm to play and doesn't try to play all the rhythms at once. What he heard was several drummers playing polyrhythms. But what he wanted in his band was Elvin playing polyrhythms all by himself.
>
> LEON THOMAS

> I own a clothing store in Johannesburg, South Africa, and I play my own records while I'm working during the day. I do business mostly with blacks, and these guys really listen to their music. I play a lot of Coltrane, especially *My Favorite Things,* but the strangest thing is that these guys don't dig Coltrane half as much as Jimmy Smith or James Brown. I can't understand that at all.
>
> GERRY ROSENBERG

Don DeMicheal was concerned about some of the adverse criticism that Coltrane and Dolphy were receiving, separately and together. To counter this, he scheduled a special article in which the two of them could express themselves on the subject of their music. The article was published in the April 12, 1962, issue of *Down Beat*. What is notable is that while Dolphy concerned himself more with the technical and interpretive aspects of the music, Coltrane was the more philosophical of the two, expounding primarily on the music's abstract and mystical qualities.

Eric talked about imitating birds, especially on flute; he said that "birds have notes between our notes, like between F and F♯, and so does Indian music, with different scales and quarter tones." To John, music was "another way of saying this is a big beautiful universe we live in. Music is just a reflection of the universe, like life in miniature. You take a life situation or an emotion and put it into music."

And Eric closed with his own complaint about the critics, suggesting that "the critics should ask the musician about his music if he doesn't like or understand it. Sometimes it really hurts, because a musician not only loves his work but depends on it for a living."

> Coltrane and I used to get together and talk about mouthpieces and reeds and music. One night we were down in the Village listening to Max Roach, and John talked about how he felt "up against the wall" in his music because a lot of musicians had told him that what he was doing "wasn't hip enough." Talk like that used to give John a bad case of the blues.
>
> RAHSAAN ROLAND KIRK

Three reviews for *Coltrane Plays the Blues:*

James Scott of the Kansas City *Star* said, "Coltrane's tenor saxophone sounds like an ill-tuned cello ineptly scraped. His soprano sax is surer, but the message is the same sing-song, oriental chanting that is supposed to be the wave of the future." Comparing Bird with Trane, he concluded, "Parker's goal was beauty and what is different is not necessarily beauty. Coltrane is different but so is a sonic boom."

In the Providence *Sunday Journal,* Philip C. Gunion called the album "something which you could play over and over and all that would be worn out would be your stylus. A fine collection of stuff, all by Coltrane, except for the first named, written by Elvin Jones."

Don DeMicheal reviewed *Blues* for *Down Beat,* pointing out "though not a blues player as Milt Jackson is, Coltrane evokes a blues feeling within a more abstract, musically sophisticated framework. His upper register rasp is the same effect a blues singer gets with his voice. This is Coltrane at his best, creating great excitement." But, he concluded, on a dissonant note, "How much longer can Coltrane continue to find new and exciting things in what has become a limited approach, as stimulating as it may be?"

> I was a waiter at the Village Vanguard in the early 1960s, and to me Coltrane was like Bach; for me, there's no one after either of them. The thing I liked best about Trane was that he came on like a real person. Even if we weren't talking, I could still feel that he was communicating with me. And when we'd talk, on occasion, I always felt he meant what he said. What I could never understand, though, was how such an essentially decent man could function in the high-pressure world musicians live in. It's simply a miracle that Coltrane managed to survive in that world as long as he did, and still remained completely himself.
>
> BURT BRITTON

Some excerpts from the diary of Trane's Lady for 1962:

5/4: I visited San Francisco, John staying at Civic Manor Motel. Gave him Bergdorf Goodman Cologne which he liked a lot. Ralph Gleason took me to Jazz Workshop to see John.

6/1: Back in New York, John called 11:15 P.M. Still having mouthpiece trouble. Described himself as a nervous little man running around with a saxophone, but not showing it on outside. Will talk with Jack Whittemore about getting more money so he can hire

Wes Montgomery. Said he's lost weight, hopes to be down to 170 soon.

7/31: Shaw claims no bookings for John next week.

12/7: Learned Elvin got busted for possession and smuggling of dope, coming back from Europe. Believe it happened in Boston.

> I was in Indianapolis once when John was playing at a club there, and I listened to him getting into these different harmonic explorations of his. The next night, at my own engagement, I noticed that some of his ideas had affected my own playing; my harmonies were more complex and I was stretching out more on my solos than before. Then, I started listening to "Giant Steps" more and more; I transcribed it from the record and started experimenting with its chord structure. The next thing I knew, I was playing it as a ballad. The chords were so beautiful I hated to hear them go by so fast, but at the slower tempo I could really enjoy playing them.
>
> MARIAN MCPARTLAND

In the early 1960s, John Coltrane was becoming so fanatical about recording continuously, as well as becoming involved in stretched-out solos, that Bob Thiele often brought him into the studio late at night to record. Since the saxophonist's contract only required two albums per year, it was not surprising that some Impulse executives complained about the amount of recorded material that Trane and Thiele were amassing. Nonetheless Coltrane recorded three albums during 1962 and all three affected his career in varying degrees.

The first, simply titled *Coltrane,* featured a churning, convoluted solo on "Out of This World" that really was out, so far out that it seemed as if there were two separate bands, Coltrane by himself and the rhythm section, for the saxophonist was deliberately playing rubato (out of tempo), with stunning effects. Also included were two dedicatory songs, "Miles' Mode" for his former employer, and "Tunji," named after the Nigerian drummer and musicologist Olatunji, whose native African rhythms were influencing Coltrane's conceptions like a drum choir inside his head.

The *Ballads* album was Thiele's suggestion; he wanted Trane to try for a broader (read more affluent) audience. Unfortunately, Coltrane must have had little to say about the selection of the songs. "Too Young to Go Steady" is a dog tune, "Say It Over and Over Again" is as monotonous as its title implies, and "Nancy" seems like a too-obvious attempt to appeal to Sinatra fans, due to Frank's close identification with the tune.

Then, *Duke Ellington and John Coltrane* was recorded.

This was *the* album of the year, a choice combination that worked out well for all concerned. It was Thiele's idea, again; he was particularly concerned that Coltrane should modulate his hypercritical attitude toward his own playing. It was probably the saxophonist's paradoxical balance of insecurity and perfectionism that was increasingly causing him to do retake after retake, making record dates not only time-consuming but also unnecessarily expensive. Ellington, as the combined genius and pragmatist that he was, would show Coltrane the better way, Thiele thought. And the music each could stimulate the other to create; the results had to be nothing less than beautiful.

Rudy van Gelder recalls, "John was really awed in Duke's presence, especially since Duke was wearing his best clothes and John was just dressed in shirt and slacks. Ellington entered the control booth to talk to me, and I thought he was going to compliment me on my recording techniques, as most musicians do. But all he wanted to know was where the bathroom was."

Coltrane's playing on the date was strangely "conservative," using the positive definition of that term, for he was conserving the best musical ideas of the past and incorporating them into his sound and conception. He stayed close to the melody, no doubt due to his respect for Ellington. Of the seven songs recorded, all except one were either Duke Ellington or Billy Strayhorn tunes, the exception being Coltrane's composition "Big Nick," dedicated to the lush-toned tenorman Big Nick Nicholas, a long-time favorite of Coltrane's.

After the first take of "In a Sentimental Mood" was recorded, this is what those concerned had to say:

Bob: "Duke, what do you think?"

Duke: "That's fine."

Bob: "John, do you think we should do it again, or not?"

John: "Well . . ."

Duke: "Why play it again? You can't duplicate that feeling. This is it."

And it was.

After he heard the record, Johnny Hodges said, "As long as I've know this song, I think Coltrane gave the most beautiful interpretation I've ever heard."

Hodges should know; "Mood" was his featured solo in the Ellington band for decades.

> When I got out of the service in the early 1960s, I brought home a Coltrane record. When I played it, my mother asked, "What's that?" I said, "A new Coltrane record." She said, "Don't you already have that one?" She thought all his music sounded the same.
>
> BILL COSBY

Bill Cosby used to hang out at Birdland in the days when he was known as the young black comic who didn't tell racial jokes and specialized in comedy sermons such as his hilarious, poignant version of *Noah*.

When Cosby walked into the club, he'd often joke with manager Johnnie Gary; sometimes the two of them would still be talking when Coltrane arrived. The saxophonist then pulled out peanuts from his pocket, still in their shells, and offered them to both. Then Coltrane would continue on to the dressing room, where he'd check on the latest baseball scores with the attendant, who usually had a transistor radio tuned in to a game.

Birdland, so called in honor of Charlie Parker's nickname, was located on Broadway at Fifty-third Street. It was a basement club holding four hundred, charged $2.00 admission, and, like the Jazz Gallery, offered a bleachers where one could simply sit and listen and not be obliged to buy even a soft drink.

Coltrane knew Cosby; once, he'd invited him to the bandstand during a set and said, "Bill, entertain the people while I take a walk."

Cosby had been secretly practicing a Coltrane imitation, a complex mimicry involving himself assuming the position of Trane playing tenor and making strange, scat-singing sounds in his throat that were a chillingly close approximation of the way Coltrane played tenor. The moment seemed appropriate, so the comedian went into his Coltrane bit, and the audience (including Coltrane) enjoyed it.

Cosby stopped by Birdland whenever he was in town; if Coltrane was playing there, the comedian would usually be invited to portray the saxophonist. Cosby used the rhythm section in his act, and they'd propel him into some startling pyrotechnics that sometimes sounded like yodeling.

One evening, Cosby came in earlier than expected and found Coltrane's rhythm section on the bandstand but no saxophonist in sight. He was feeling in the mood to do his Coltrane imitation, so he asked Elvin, who just grinned as he glanced at the other musicians and said, "Think we should audition this cat as Trane's replacement?" The others agreed, so the comedian climbed on the bandstand. Pee Wee Marquette, the diminutive emcee whose raucous falsetto was powerful and penetrating enough to crack the walls of the Brill Building, crooned into the microphone, "And now . . . ladies and gentlemen . . . Birdland, the Jazz Corner of the World . . . proudly presents"—pause—*"The Bill Cosby Quartet!"*

Cosby went into "Out of This World." He had the Coltrane stance, the Coltrane sound down; he was standing straight up with arms out front as if fondling a tenor sax, fingers flicking over imaginary keys, eyes closed and teeth biting over nonexistent mouthpiece, as his voice was wailing, note for note, the exact Coltrane recording with even the most minor nuances duplicated.

Two minutes passed.

Cosby was bending down in a crouch, his expression dissolving into an ecstatic, sweating semblance of Trane's transcendent mannerisms. The audience was with him, all the way.

Four minutes passed. Then, with Cosby reaching a grand, exuberant climax, from backstage came . . .

The sound of a tenor saxophone, playing in perfect unison with whatever sounds Cosby was creating.

Cosby stopped, standing stiffly as if captured on fast film; the saxophone in his ears stopped simultaneously. He started again, picking up the solo where he'd broken it off; the saxophone came on again, matching him note for note.

And Coltrane, as if himself mimicking the well-known Sonny Rollins grand entrance, walked on the bandstand while still playing, his real sound blending perfectly with Cosby's imitation of that sound. He got close to the comedian, his tenor only inches away. They continued their duet while the audience, mesmerized as if Trane were twins, burst into loud, spontaneous applause.

Naima accompanied John on the band's November 1962 European tour. It was her first trip overseas, but her husband didn't have time to show her the sights; he was busy writing, rehearsing, playing, and being interviewed. But she was beside or near him most of the time, and she was content with that.

What she was not content with was the growing feeling she was getting that they were drifting apart.

Not that John said or did anything different from what he had said or done before. It was just that, for some inexplicable reason, she couldn't feel him communicating with her in his usual way. She asked him about that. Her two miscarriages, in 1957 and 1961, had made her wonder whether he was becoming distant due to those misfortunes; and was there something she'd said or done, or hadn't said or done, that he didn't like? "No," he said, dismissing the matter, but still, as if Monk had taught him more than music, "disconnecting" from her in such a detached way that made her nervous enough to start biting her nails.

Yet after they returned to New York, he disappeared for nearly an entire day and only returned around suppertime—with a new Chrysler station wagon. He then took Naima and Toni out to dinner at an Indian restaurant. His involvement in the cuisine was increasing proportionally to his absorption in the music, thanks to a continuing and growing correspondence with Ravi Shankar.

But he still remained incommunicado with her. So while John played the blues, Naima experienced them.

In 1959, a linenkeeper walked off a freighter at the docks in Buenos Aires, Argentina, and handed his friend Leandro Barbieri a package containing, among other records, Miles Davis' *'Round about Midnight* and John Coltrane's *Soultrane*. Barbieri was studying saxophone privately and playing lead alto with Lalo Schifrin's band.

When the linenkeeper next met his friend Leandro in 1961, his friend was calling himself Gato and had switched to tenor saxophone. The record Gato got this time was *Giant Steps* and when Barbieri heard this one, he almost switched right back to alto again, so much tenor did he realize that he still had to learn.

He soon left Argentina for Europe. But before he did, he sent Coltrane, through his friend the linenkeeper, a present, to express his love for and learning from Trane's music.

It was a tenor saxophone case; hand-made from green leather, a silk lining inside, the word TRANE gold-lettered outside, bought and paid for by Gato and his wife, Michelle.

The saxophone case was delivered, but Coltrane didn't know who had sent it, for the Barbieri note read, "From a friend in Buenos Aires."

The following year, the Barbieris moved to Rome. When they discovered that John Coltrane was playing a date in Milan, they came to hear him. They went backstage to meet him, and there, in a corner of the dressing room, they saw the saxophone case they had sent him.

"Oh, you're from Argentina?" Coltrane said, after they were introduced. He pointed at the saxophone case and commented, "Someone from Argentina sent that to me. I use it all the time."

When Barbieri confessed that someone was he, Coltrane thanked him and said, "It's beautiful." Then, his voice humorous but his eyes serious, he asked, "Do you think you could send me one for my soprano, too?"

> The little drum was beating out a gay rhythm, and presently it was joined by a reed instrument; together they filled the air. The drum dominated, but it followed the reed. The latter would stop, but the little drum would go on, sharp and clear, until it was again joined by the song of the reed.
>
> JIDDU KRISHNAMURTI

John once told me, "The ending of every song is Elvin."

TRANE'S LADY

Elvin Jones is Mercury. Like the planet nearest the sun whose geophysical quirk makes it rotate in such a manner that one side is always facing the blistering sunlight while the other is perpetually bathed in the freezing cold of night.

Thus Elvin has his bright and his dark side; and seldom, if ever, does it appear that a border compromise is possible. He is either/or; his duality is almost schizophrenic in its sharp dividing lines, his Yang and Yin permanently disconnected. When he is feeling fine, he is one of the most beautiful people in the world. But if his mood is darker than mellow, then there is no meaner man around.

Away from music, his interests at that time were liquor, drugs, and women. He could drink a quart a day, shoot up six bags and scream for more, and walk out on his wife as quickly as a band groupie might spend a set or two hanging around his drums and then ask, "Elvin, can you fuck a woman like you've been fucking those drums all night?"

Some unspoken, perhaps unknown, inner source of frustration fueled him. When he'd get angry about something, he'd walk off the bandstand, stripping off his shirt on the way. He'd grab a triple gin from the bar and stride outside into the chilling temperatures of a winter night, waves of steam rising from his bare chest.

He'd show up late or not at all. If he did show, then he'd leave early, winking at the girl sitting at a nearby table who'd quickly follow him out the door.

Once, a too-noisy customer almost got decapitated, as Elvin unlatched a cymbal and pitched it in his direction. The cymbal missed the loudmouthed patron by inches.

Elvin split with his first wife Shirley, a white woman nearly as tall as himself. After Trane's death, he married a Japanese girl named Keiko. In between those two occurrences, there were women from all places and all races, digging this drummer, the power center of the band.

For Elvin Jones was John Coltrane's chief accompanist, not McCoy Tyner or Jimmy Garrison. This was most unusual; even such drummer-leaders as Max Roach and Art Blakey had *never* brought the drums into such prominence as Coltrane did with Jones. John wanted a strong, screaming drummer behind him, and he got one; Elvin often played at such incredible levels of volume that the leader could barely be heard on tenor and was often drowned out on soprano.

Yet Elvin truly loved John. His ambivalent attitude toward his employer/friend often had him asking, "Hey, Trane, can I get an advance on my salary this week?"

Last week, next week; the same.

That didn't seem to matter to Coltrane. Having Jones on drums, no matter how overwhelming he got, was what the saxophonist apparently wanted. For Jones had balls, musically speaking; he could ride out those forty-five minute solos and keep perfect time and adventurous accents behind his boss, later commenting that "it just seemed like a flicker of time to me."

John would often use those long solos to "sober Elvin up," and one of his favorite techniques for doing this was to "blow in Elvin's ear." As Spliby recalls, "One night Elvin took off on break and came back high. Trane started playing 'Mr. P.C.' and after about ten minutes, he motioned to McCoy and Jimmy to stroll. It was just Trane and Elvin after that, and Trane was watching Elvin really close. Every time Elvin would start to nod out, Trane would blow his horn in Elvin's ear and wake him up."

> When you work you are a flute through whose heart the whispering of the hours turns to music. Which of you would be a reed, dumb and silent, when all else sings together in unison?
>
> KAHLIL GIBRAN

If you are a saxophone player, you will have mouthpiece trouble sooner or later. There is no avoiding it; that's the way the saxophone is structured. And whether your mouthpiece problems become serious or remain trivial is simply up to you.

> Coltrane visited the Otto Link factory in Florida in 1963. We make him some special mouthpieces that gave him a broader

These men should be smiling. The other three, besides Coltrane, were instrumental in securing a renewal of the saxophonist's recording contract with Impulse Records. And Coltrane had every reason to look happy; under the terms of his new three-year contract, he would receive an advance of $25,000 each year. Left to right: Harold Lovette, Trane's manager; producer Bob Thiele; Coltrane (standing). Sitting: Larry Newton, Impulse president. COURTESY OF BOB THIELE.

John Coltrane played his first—and only—engagement at the Antibes Jazz Festival, Juan-Les-Pins, France, in July 1965. Randi Hultin journeyed from Oslo to cover the event as a journalist. Hultin and Coltrane celebrated their reacquaintance in style; she cooked Norwegian soul food for him at her hotel, Les Pergolas. PHOTOGRAPHER: RANDI HULTIN.

Even at home, Coltrane was always experimenting, always searching for a new sound. Eddie Harris and Sonny Stitt were playing the electronic Varitone saxophone attachment in public, but Trane preferred to work with it in private. PHOTOGRAPHER: TONY RULLI. COURTESY OF THE SELMER DIVISION OF THE MAGNAVOX COMPANY.

John and Alice Coltrane making love with music at a concert in Madison, Wisconsin, during 1966. Replacing McCoy Tyner on piano, Alice played with John's band for a year and a half, until his death. REPRINTED COURTESY OF "DOWN BEAT."

According to several polls, John Coltrane was the most popular jazz musician in Japan. Therefore, the band's welcome upon arriving in Tokyo on July 8, 1966, for a three-week concert tour was both gracefully Japanese and tumultuously American. PHOTOGRAPHER: TAKASHI ARIHARA. COURTESY OF "SWING JOURNAL."

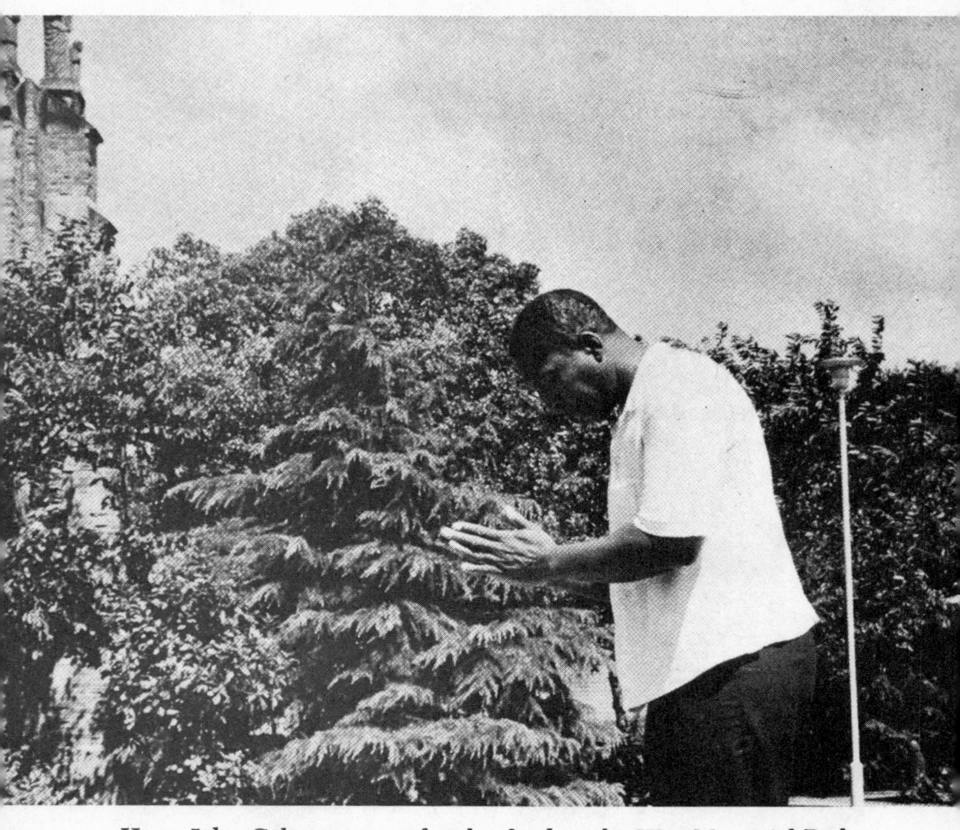

Here, John Coltrane prays for the dead at the War Memorial Park in Nagasaki, where the second atomic bomb of World War II was dropped on August 9, 1945, killing more than 150,000 people. COURTESY OF BOB THIELE.

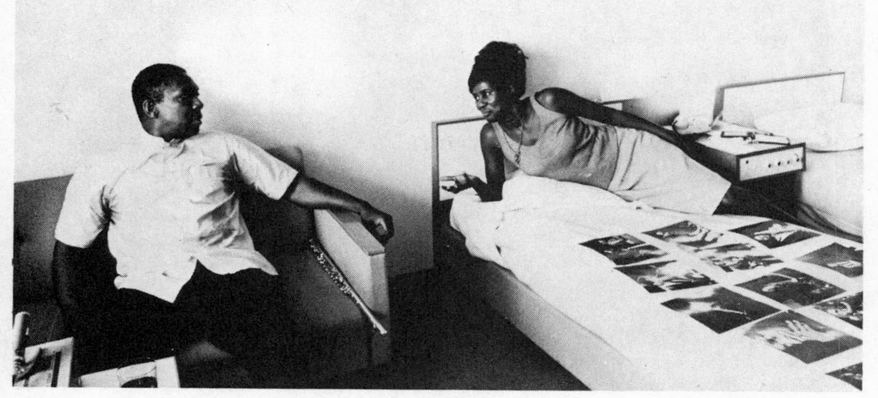

No rest for the Coltranes, not even in their hotel room. Their concert schedule in Japan called for one performance each day and two on Sunday, with no days off. They're both taking care of business; Alice is conferring with her husband about photo selection, and John has Eric Dolphy's flute handy in case he feels like practicing. PHOTOGRAPHER: TAKASHI ARIHARA. COURTESY OF "SWING JOURNAL."

Always willing to help his friends, Coltrane climbed out of a sick bed to inaugurate a Sunday concert series at the Olatunji Center of African Culture in Harlem, founded by Nigerian percussionist and teacher Michael Babatunde Olatunji (and partially funded by the saxophonist's regular contributions). Ironically, it was Trane's last date—May 23, 1967—his final public performance before he died on July 17. Left to right: Pharoah Sanders (tenor sax), Jimmy Garrison (bass), Algie DeWitt (bata drum), Alice Coltrane (piano), Rashied Ali (drums), Coltrane (tenor sax). COURTESY OF THE OLATUNJI CENTER OF AFRICAN CULTURE.

St. Peter's Lutheran Church
The Rev. Ralph E. Peterson, Pastor

Lexington Avenue at 54th Street
New York City

11:00 A.M.

July 21, 1967

Service for John Coltrane

A LOVE SUPREME

The Albert Ayler Quartet

Invocation

Words from the Bible — Rev. Dale R. Lind

A Love Supreme — Mr. Calvin Massey

Meditation — Rev. John G. Gensel

Prayer

The Ornette Coleman Quartet

Benediction

JOHN W. COLTRANE

1926 - 1967

Funeral services for John Coltrane
COURTESY OF REVEREND JOHN GENSEL.

John W. Coltrane the only son of John Robert Coltrane and Blair Coltrane was born in Hamlet, N. C., Sept. 23, 1926. His early childhood was spent in High Point, N. C. where he graduated from the William Penn High School. In 1943 he moved to Philadelphia, Pa. where he attended the Ornstein School of Music. He served in the U. S. Navy during World War II.

He is survived by his wife Alice and three sons John Jr., Ravi, and Oran and two step daughters, Antonia and Michelle; his mother Mrs. Alice Blair Coltrane, and his Aunt Mrs. Minnie Fowler, Norfolk, Va.; Mr. William Blair, Orange, N. J.; Mr. John Blair, Hamlet, N. C.; and his favorite cousin Mrs. Mary Greenlee, and a host of relatives and friends.

Not asleep, no.
Awake and more alive than ever before.
In the consciousness and
at - one - ment with
the One & only all - pervading,
all - embracing Ultimate Truth
and only Reality, God;
our own true self.

The family and relatives of John express gratitude to the multitudes who have indicated their deep sympathy to them in so many ways. The Lord Bless You!

We appreciate the musical praise to God and the honor rendered John by his colleagues: Albert Ayler, Milford Graves, Donald Ayler, Richard Davis, Ornette Coleman, Charles Haden, David Izenzon, Charles Moffett.

The photograph on the front cover was taken by John's close friend, Bob Thiele.

Funeral arrangements in charge of the Richard W. Hasgill Funeral Home, 155 Sunrise Highway, Amityville, L. I., N.Y.

Interment: Pinelawn Memorial Park, Farmingdale, N. Y., July 21st, 1967.

New York sculptor Bradford Graves paid his respects to John Coltrane by dedicating a sculpture to the late saxophonist. Called "Trane," this monument measures nine by six feet and weighs eight tons; the sculpture currently resides where it was created during 1968, in the Carpathian Mountains of Czechoslovakia. PHOTOGRAPHER: BRADFORD GRAVES.

sound, and he used them during his last years of playing. Later that same year, Coleman Hawkins was here, and he asked me, "What is John doing, and what is he doing it with?" I told him. Hawk, knowing how much more energy a large bore mouthpiece requires, said, "If he keeps that up, he'll soon have as big a sound as mine."

BEN HARROD

I was living in San Francisco in 1963, and I saw Coltrane at the Jazz Workshop. Afterward, I talked with him and he invited me to his hotel room to talk about mouthpieces, because I was having trouble with mine and I wanted his advice. When I got there, he dumped out two airline bags of mouthpieces on the floor and said, "Take your pick." I tried them out until I found one I liked. While I was doing this he was practicing on his tenor, and I suddenly noticed, being so close to him, how long and tapered his fingers were as they curved around the keys, almost like they were sculptured. For a saxophone player long fingers can be a problem, because the key positions are structured for medium-sized hands. Actually, his fingers looked like they belonged to a piano player. I asked him, "Could I look at your hands?" He looked me over with those huge eyes of his, and then he held out his hands. I told him what I'd been thinking, and he said, "Did you ever see Bird's fingers?" I said, "No." He said, "Bird had short, stubby fingers."

DEWEY REDMAN

March 6 and 7, 1963, were two days that John Coltrane pretended that he was a singer. He was; his tenor was singing the lines like a second voice when he recorded an album with vocalist Johnny Hartman.

Though he once sang with Dizzy Gillespie, Hartman considers himself a ballad singer, and his enunciation, crisp delivery and resonant baritone tell the story. Coltrane, too, had always wanted to record with a vocalist. He also wanted to help Hartman out during some tough times in the singer's life.

John suggested Johnny to Bob Thiele; the producer agreed on a recording, and the date was set. Their collaboration would be like the *Ballads* album with vocals added, impressionistic and lyrical songs selected by the three of them. It would be structured this way: Hartman would sing a full chorus on every song—except for "Dedicated to You," where he only got through the first verse before turning the tune over to Trane—followed by Coltrane's tenor solo and concluding with another Hartman vocal. One song, "Lush Life," that Trane had previously recorded on Prestige would get an updated treatment; otherwise, there would be new versions of such tunes as "They Say It's Wonderful" and "Autumn Serenade."

Hartman listened intently to Coltrane's solos in the studio. But too much so on "My One and Only Love," which opens with a brief saxophone solo, for he recalls, "I was enjoying his playing so much I forgot to come in for my closing vocal, and we had to do it all over again."

Then, he smiles as he says, "Everything was a first take, except for 'You Are Too Beautiful.' We were doing the second version and had almost finished with a perfect rendition when Elvin, who'd been clowning around, dropped a stick on his cymbal right at the conclusion of my final syllable."

From the diary of Trane's Lady for 1963:

2/15: John called to wish me Happy Valentine's Day.

2/28: John stopped by after second set at Birdland. I gave him tea with honey. Disturbed about his weight and his inability to stop eating.

5/23: Saw John at Birdland, with Philly Joe Jones on drums. Heard Elvin was in Lexington. Later, John stopped by, said he was sorry he missed my birthday again. Talked about confidence, said sometimes he feels he's already done his best work.

6/9: John called me at 5:30 A.M., came over and stayed three hours. Talked about adversity, said he wouldn't have discovered some good things if certain situations in his life had worked out better. I fed him sweet potato pie, then he asked for raisin nut bread and tea.

7/18: John working at Birdland opposite Terry Gibbs. Stopped by later, told me he'd talked with Alice McLeod, who's playing piano with Gibbs. Said he had a headache, then we had a spat about him standing in front of my air conditioner which wasn't good for him.

8/8: Saw Philly Joe Jones in subway, he said Elvin's back.

8/11: John came by and ate more than half a pie. We sat around nude and read magazines. He'd often sleep nude if he was going out. He didn't like clothes, too binding.

11/26: John playing at Jazz Workshop in San Francisco. I was there to give him delayed birthday present of cologne. Said he'd left home two months ago and was living with Alice McLeod. Getting ready to tape TV show for Ralph Gleason.

> John Coltrane taped a thirty-minute TV show for me. It was part of my *Jazz Casual* series, and was shown over National Educational Television. I usually do a five-minute interview, then the rest is all music. But just before taping, John told me he didn't want to be interviewed. So I had to give a thirty-second comment on his importance as a musician, and then his quartet just played. Like all other shows I've done, that appearance was televised on more than two hundred educational stations around the country.
>
> RALPH GLEASON

That was a rarity for John Coltrane: a television appearance on which he felt comfortable enough to play without pressure, and one that promised him an attentive audience. In America, educational TV was the best visual medium for such an uncharismatic man and his music. His only network appearances occurred when he was working with Miles Davis, and that was primarily due to Miles's mystique, not Trane's.

> Playing with John Coltrane was like a beautiful nightmare.
>
> ROY HAYNES

Roy Haynes, whose drum style is as crisp as that of Philly Joe Jones, as flexible as that of Max Roach and as strong as that of

Elvin Jones, once played with Charlie Parker. Ironically, he was born in Boston, the city where Elvin Jones's drug bust resulted in his facing a court-ordered alternative—jail or rehabilitation.

On the one hand, Rikers Island; on the other, an institution called the National Institute of Mental and Clinical Research Center, located in Lexington, Kentucky, and generally known among those knowledgeable about drugs as simply Lexington. Among its facilities are those for curing drug addicts on a "voluntary" basis. However, like Jones, most of those so confined are usually volunteers more in the military manner.

Jones spent three months there, from May through August 1963. In the meantime, Coltrane had to use those few drummers whose sound and strength he could depend upon to keep driving him along, such as Louis Hayes and Philly Joe Jones; though more the former than the latter, for Philly Joe was still just as likely as not to miss a gig. So it was Haynes upon whom Coltrane primarily depended; ironically again, he was playing with Stan Getz and could work with Coltrane only when he had some free time coming from Getz's commitments.

Haynes did record with Coltrane, his most memorable date being a "live" version of "My Favorite Things" during the Newport Jazz Festival on July 7, 1963. Though still utilizing the three-four meter, Haynes plays in a more free and flowing exposition that makes the song sound as if it were actually written in four-four time.

That August, Elvin Jones returned.

John and Elvin embraced like long-separated brothers—they were no more than three years apart in age—and from note one when Elvin got back behind his drums again, it was as if he'd never been away at all.

> The first time I really became aware of Coltrane's genius was when I heard a live recording from Birdland, a ballad called "I Want to Talk About You." At the end, he played a cadenza that was much longer than the song itself. It impressed me so much that I transcribed it for my students at the Royal Academy of Music in London. I use it as an instruction

piece, so that I can always call Coltrane to the attention of my students.

JOHN DANKWORTH

I like to fantasize when I listen to music. When I saw Coltrane at Birdland, I saw him as an angel and Elvin Jones as a devil. Coltrane seemed so sweet and gentle, while Jones had a macabre, almost evil appearance about him. I got the feeling, throughout the music, that the drummer was trying to dominate the group. In some strange way, I felt that I was watching a musical contest between good and evil, between Coltrane and Jones.

DICK RICH

During the fall of 1963, while Coltrane was recording the "*Live*" *At Birdland* album, Dick Rich—later to become better known as one-third of Wells Rich Greene ad agency—happened to wander into the club one evening with a blind date. He didn't even know that Coltrane was on the bill.

Rich was, that evening, enveloped in a miasma of deep frustration, due to a bad marriage heading for divorce and a dull job heading for termination. So, as he recalls, "my date was smart enough to shut up and leave me alone while I got lost in Coltrane's music for three sets."

The tune that turned him around was "My Favorite Things."

Rich continues, "The way he played that song was a prime example of musical excellence. I've always prided myself on achieving excellence, and here was this master musician demonstrating for me just how great someone could be if he only tried. I'd been feeling sorry for myself for months, and that night Coltrane inspired me to seek out excellence for myself. It was a real turning point in my life."

A few months later, Rich was sufficiently stimulated to create an award-winning commercial for Alka-Seltzer, a commercial involving half a hundred different stomachs, each and every one calling for salvation (with the implied aid of the sponsor).

Still later, Dick met an Italian lady named Sylvia, whom he also introduced to the music of John Coltrane.

I was in Dick's apartment when I saw the album of *My Favorite Things*. He had mentioned his identification with the song before, so I put it on the phonograph. I had never heard Coltrane's music before, but when I listened I got a mental image of him as a tortured, shy, lonely man. I learned to love his music as much as Dick. After Coltrane died, I spoke with several people about him and they said, "Who is John Coltrane?" To me, that was like saying "Who?" when you mention Michelangelo.

SYLVIA RICH

It was, then, sometime during 1963 that John Coltrane entered one lady's life as he was leaving another's. It was an odd juxtaposition; neither woman knew of the other's existence. Yet one discovered him through music as the other lost him from marriage.

Sylvia Rich learned of John Coltrane the musician; Naima Coltrane lost John Coltrane the man.

I could feel it was going to happen sooner or later, so I wasn't really surprised when John moved out of our house in the summer of 1963. He didn't offer any explanation. He just told me there were some things he had to do, and he left with only his clothes and his horns. He stayed in a hotel sometimes, other times with his mother in Philadelphia. All he said was, "Naima, I'm going to make a change." Even though I could feel it coming, it hurt, and I didn't get over it for at least another year.

NAIMA COLTRANE

John Coltrane toured Europe without Naima in October 1963, and was introduced to Randi Hultin in Oslo, Norway. A petite, effervescent brunette who writes, photographs, and talks about music, especially American jazz, whenever and wherever she can, Hultin made a point of inviting Coltrane to visit her at home. There, when he signed her guest book, he filled in the first few bars of what had become his favorite song.

"Naima."

Her home, a two-story house located on top of a hill outside of Oslo, was a living museum of painting and sculpture, music and photography. John sat in her living room, listening to Norwegian folk music while munching on herring and goat cheese.

Tyner stayed at the hotel, his choice; Garrison and Jones went partying, their choice. But John Coltrane, though he did not tell Hultin about his marital situation, was simply happy to relax and be himself inside someone's home, since he no longer had a house of his own in which to do this.

Randi had American music, too, tapes she'd made herself when visiting musicians had passed through town. When she played some of them, John seemed most interested in the offbeat effects of several musicians he knew who had been recorded vocalizing, even if only kidding around. Art Taylor, Kenny Dorham, Milt Jackson; all singing, or attempting to.

"Do you sing?" she asked him.

He smiled, almost in embarrassment, as he said, "Well . . . my voice isn't much good for that sort of thing." Then, he added, shyly, "I guess you'll have to say the only singing I do is on my horn . . . hopefully."

On the Sunday morning of September 15, 1963, a dozen sticks of dynamite were planted in the basement of the 16th Street Baptist Church in Birmingham, Alabama. At 10:25 A.M. an explosion took place, blowing several man-sized holes in the church walls, injuring fourteen parishioners, and killing four black girls, aged eleven through fourteen, who had just finished their Sunday school lesson, *The Love That Forgives.*

John Coltrane heard the news that afternoon on a radio broadcast. Not anger but melancholy, not an urge toward violence but a feeling of sadness descended upon him. To kill anyone for a cause, no matter what, revolted and jolted him as much as if he were a devout Buddhist and someone had stepped on an ant in his sight. He was a complete pacifist, but he was not a political man; he was aware of the stupidities committed against others in the name of race, creed, or color. But he was, and would always remain, naïve in the sense that he believed people could and should love one another and that peace would then come about throughout the world.

A personal statement was called for; he would make one, in his own way, the best way he knew how, through music.

During the next few months, he took time to sketch out a song. On November 18, he recorded two tunes to fill out the *Birdland* album. One of them was his eulogy, a lament and an elegy, for the four murdered children in that Birmingham church: "Alabama."

More than any other Coltrane composition during that period, it expressed the deep, profound melancholy that was revealing itself more and more frequently. People listened, and asked, "Why the sadness?"

In the 1940s, it was just a family restaurant and bar located in the warehouse district near the Manhattan waterfront, on the southwest corner of Spring and Hudson streets. In the 1950s, it was called the Half Note and was making its name as one of the most offbeat and relaxed jazz clubs in New York. And in the very late 1960s, it moved midtown to West Fifty-fourth Street as if singlehandedly attempting to revive the fabled Swing Street formerly located two blocks farther south.

However, when Coltrane played the Half Note in the early 1960s, the club was still located on Spring and Hudson. It was managed, and still is, by the Canterino family: dark-haired Mike, whom you could tell apart from brother, Sonny, by the former's mustache, and blond sister, Rosemarie.

For a street corner location, the club was quite dark inside; the windows and walls were painted black, and the lights were kept low. The Canterinos built the bandstand from Coke boxes, knocking a hole in the wall that divided the club's two rooms so that those in each section could view, in effect, only half of the band at a given time. The decor was album covers and murals donated for payment in drinks.

Mike Canterino had been exposed to jazz while serving in the Navy during the early 1950s. He was stationed in Florida, where he met, among others, the piano-bass team of Dwike Mitchell and Willie Ruff. Upon his return to New York, he persuaded his family to convert their restaurant into a jazz club, and in 1957 the Half Note was born.

The audiences at the Half Note were mixed. As Mike recalls, "We seemed to attract the most politically advanced blacks whenever Trane was appearing. He'd take a long solo, probably close to an hour, and these guys would be shouting 'Freedom now!' all over the place. It was like they were using his music as a rallying cry for whatever political movements they were into."

Since the club was so casual, it was only natural that many hungry young musicians dropped by to sit in. A few customers might complain that they had come to hear Coltrane, not so-and-so or such-and-such taking up most of their time. But the saxophonist was generous in allowing the younger musicians a chance to blow, though sometimes too much so. Nevertheless, if some querulous customer were to continually question the wisdom of such a situation, Coltrane might break his customary silence and say, right from the bandstand, "Well, these young musicians have to start someplace, like I did. You don't think I just walked up to Miles or Monk and got the job like that, do you?"

When not on the bandstand, Trane might be in the kitchen, talking with the Canterinos' parents, who did the cooking. They'd fix him pizza with green peppers; he'd thank them and sit quietly in a corner and thumb through his Bible while eating the pizza.

But when the saxophonist returned to the bandstand, as Mike Canterino remembers, "Trane played for a long time. The veins were popping in his forehead and he was sweating up a storm. He'd play every tune as if it was the last number of the last set, with so much intensity and feeling he must have thought he was going to die before he'd completed his solo."

When I first heard Coltrane with Miles, he sounded ugly to me. I'm from the Lester Young school of subtle, mellow intonation, and I prefer brevity in my solos. John's reedy, raspy sound and extended solos turned me off at first. But I kept listening to him, because his ideas were so advanced. Eventually I got used to his sound, and I began to understand that his bold, flat statements were as if he was standing naked on stage, the music coming directly from the man, not the horn. Later, I heard hundreds of other tenor players emulating him, copying him note for note. Sometimes I feel like saying, "There is only *one* John Coltrane; you should listen and learn from him and otherwise let him be."

JIMMY GUIFFRE

More and more working musicians such as Jimmy Guiffre were now comprehending John Coltrane's music. So were more academic musicians, those who taught rather than played for a living. Among the latter, David Baker is one of the most outstanding; a former trombonist with George Russell who gave up the horn due to medical problems, he switched to the study of classical cello and the teaching of music at a Midwestern university. Thus Baker is in an excellent position to comment on Coltrane's contributions, especially his advanced musical techniques.

For the first time, *Grove's Dictionary of Music and Musicians* is going to list jazz musicians in the next edition. I'm writing about six, and one of them is John Coltrane. His major contributions, I think, are these: using multiphonics, playing several notes or tones simultaneously; creating asymmetrical groupings not dependent on the basic pulse; developing an incredibly sophisticated system of chord substitutions; and initiating a pan-modal style of playing, using several modes simultaneously. I've transcribed some of his solos for teaching my students at the University of Indiana. I think all musicians should study Coltrane solos the way we now study the etudes of Bach and Brahms.

DAVID BAKER

Among those in agreement with Professor David Baker was Doctor Lyn Christie of Sydney, Australia. There, at a place called Club El Rocco, a quartet led by bassist Christie was playing such Trane tunes as "Giant Steps" and "Naima," for an audience that was appreciative but more than a little puzzled at hearing, for them, such strange sounds.

Christie was a graduate of the University of New Zealand Medical School, a physician by day and a musician at night. He is now in New York, practicing not medicine but music, full time.

While still in Sydney, though, Christie was playing jazz. "We get our records a year or two after they're released in the States," he explains. "We weren't able to hear 'Giant Steps' until late in 1961, but as soon as we got the record our tenor saxophonist, Graham Lyall, was studying it day and night until he had it down. I certainly listened to the album for many hours before I could write an arrangement that all of us could play."

They played it, too, nearly every night, passing on Trane's torch each time they did. As Christie says, "None of Coltrane's music ever drove any of our audience out the door."

> When you hear music, after it's over, it's gone in the air. You can never capture it again.
>
> ERIC DOLPHY

> When I thought thoroughly about it, I realized that there is usually an essential difference between composing a piece and listening to it. The composer knows his piece as a forest wanderer knows his path, but the listener is confronted with the same creation the same way as a stranger in a forest.
>
> JOHN CAGE

> Some people like their musical communications in a disciplined manner: systematic, consequences, intellectual control, law and order. This in a Bach fugue is highly pleasing. Others are looking for the undefined: openness, broadened sensibility, intuition, and freedom. For example, the uncertainty of John Cage. Coltrane's music contains both a complicated but consequent form and a dimension of hypnotic and almost metaphysical mystery.
>
> GUNNAR LINDGREN

John Coltrane was more mystic than musician.

This is the only logical explanation for the effects his music had on many members of his audience; in fact, many of them knew nothing whatsoever about any kind of music, including jazz, yet they were mesmerized, entranced, and quite often, like Dick Rich, had their lives changed from continuous exposure to Coltrane's music. There had to be something else *besides* music there; in reality, there was a force *beyond* music that was communicating with Trane's audience on quite a different, higher level of meaning.

Call it Universal Consciousness, Supreme Being, Nature, God. Call this force by any name you like, but it was *there*, and its presence was so powerfully felt by most people that it was almost palpable.

John Coltrane was a mystic, somehow attuned, as are all mystics, to the Ultimate Reality.

And the Ultimate Reality is Death.

> We were both traveling in a particular spiritual direction, John and myself, so it seemed only natural for us to join forces. It was like God uniting two souls together. I think John could have just as easily married another woman, though. Not myself and not because I was a musician, but any woman who had the particular attributes or qualities to help him fulfill his life mission as God wanted him to.
>
> ALICE MCLEOD

Like Trane's other ladies, Alice McLeod is tall (five-nine), shy, and musically inclined. She was born in Detroit, Michigan, on August 27, 1937. There, she attended Cass Technical High School with such other musicians as Bob Friday, a bass player, and drummer Earl Williams, all three of them playing at school dances while still in their teens.

Pianist Hugh Lawson also attended Cass. He was in the same class as Alice, both of them graduating in 1955. He recalls Alice as "a very introspective girl who kept mostly to herself or a very few friends. She was so shy we'd have to coax her to play in public."

She played various engagements around the Motor City until 1959, when she went to Paris to study with Bud Powell, returning the following fall. Before becoming Mrs. Coltrane, she was briefly married to another musician; she has a daughter, Michelle, from that union.

Alice McLeod originally met John Coltrane in 1960, when he played a date in Detroit. She was at a party and someone said to her, "I thought you were working tonight, Alice. I wanted to hear you play." John, standing nearby, looked at Alice with those luminous eyes of his and said, with interest, "I didn't know you were a musician; tell me more." As Alice recalls, "From the way he looked at me, I knew we would be meeting again."

They did; their next encounter took place at a considerable distance, for she was attending a concert by Miles Davis at the Olympia Theater in Paris. Coltrane was then with Davis; of that experience, she says, "I felt I was receiving a message from John through his music, as if he was talking to me personally."

Their next face-to-face meeting did not take place until July 18, 1963, at Birdland. There, Alice was playing piano with vibraphonist Terry Gibbs's quartet, and the Coltrane band was on the same bill. One of Gibbs's crowd-pleasers was called the "two vibes" routine; that is, he and his pianist would play four- and eight-bar exchanges on the vibraphone, using a special arrangement and performing in such a manner at least once during the evening. Of course, Gibbs's pianist would require at least a rudimentary knowledge of the vibraphone in order to bring this arrangement off successfully, and since Alice had once studied vibes she was well equipped to trade musical breaks with her boss. (Some say too well equipped; when Gibbs was outclassed too often, he usually fired the pianist responsible, and this happened to Alice later that year.)

The audience was impressed by the two-vibes routine, and so was John Coltrane. During intermission he sought Alice out and said, with admiration, "I never knew you could play vibes." She replied, "You never knew a lot of things about me." To that, as if accepting what sounded like an implied challenge, he said, "Well, I'm going to make it my business to find out all I can about you."

Later, Alice McLeod confided, "John didn't talk much, but when he did he always had something to say. One thing I learned from him was how to communicate fully without words. You might also say that I learned to appreciate quiet men because of John Coltrane."

They were married in Juarez, Mexico, sometime during 1966. Harold Lovette arranged both the union and the disunion, for John's divorce from Naima occurred simultaneously with his marriage to Alice. Prior to 1966, the New York State law specified adultery as the only legal grounds for divorce; however, the statutes were changed that year to allow such other qualifications as separation.

John and Alice Coltrane moved into a palatial suburban residence in Dix Hills, Huntington, Long Island, New York, which Lovette had arranged for them to purchase from, ironically, a dentist, who wanted a quick sale. The original price of the house was $75,000; the sale price, $40,000.

The first two items of furnishing John bought for Alice were a grand piano and a harp; she had also learned to play the latter. Then, he purchased enough contemporary furniture to outfit the ten-room, split-level, brick ranch house in style. A two-car garage was located on the first floor. Inside, the living room featured knotty pine paneling and brick walls; in fact, there was paneling in every room, including the dining room and kitchen. The master bedroom was downstairs, with four smaller bedrooms upstairs. The house also included a basement, attic, and study; it spread over four acres of land and was quite isolated from the nearest neighbor.

When the Coltranes moved in, the area was almost rural in its ambience, with open spaces and rolling hills. A black developer had purchased several tracts in the area, selling them to brothers and sisters first. Thus, there were several black families living in Dix Hills prior to the Coltranes' arrival.

As Alice recalls, "The new development that opened up across the street brought in mostly white families. So, in a sense, it was the whites this time who were integrating the neighborhood."

> I can only recall one negative aspect of my relationship with Coltrane, and it happened in the summer of 1964. I had booked him for an outdoor concert in Cincinnati and Montreal, on two successive evenings, at $7,500 for both nights. He didn't show at Cincinnati, and he gave me no indication that anything was wrong. I had to make a 1 A.M. announcement in

Cincinnati, and we had to give some refunds. I showed the local press the signed contracts, and I alerted Montreal not to expect him; he didn't arrive there, either. When I was finally able to get John on the phone, he just said he wasn't feeling well, and that was all. I'm still surprised; the money was excellent and he had always showed up before.

GEORGE WEIN

My wife Carmela and I badly wanted to see Coltrane, so we drove to Chicago from Wisconsin, where I teach, on the only night I had free. Naturally, our car broke down on the way, but we managed to hitch a ride and arrived at the Plugged Nickel during the last number. We got in without paying admission but we only heard about five minutes of music. He'd finished on tenor, and we really wanted to hear him on soprano. The other guys were walking off the bandstand when I went up and talked with Coltrane. I just said hello and mentioned what had happened to us on the way down. When I was finished, he said, "If you can stay for a few more minutes, so can I." He went back on the bandstand, picked up his soprano, and played an unaccompanied version of "My Favorite Things" for the next ten or fifteen minutes. It was so beautiful, so incredibly exciting that the rest of the audience, ourselves included, gave him a standing ovation when he was finished.

TOM THOMAS

During the 1960s, John Coltrane's trajectory intersected with the lives of two other men who were also crossing each other's paths, bassist Art Davis and violinist Sanford Allen.

The Indian musical influence had given Coltrane the idea of using two bass players, one in the usual harmonic/rhythmic function and the other as a drone, sometimes playing countrapuntally with the first. Art Davis, the first black bassist on the NBC staff, worked with Coltrane from 1961 to 1965. As he recalls, "John really liked Ravi Shankar's tabla player, Alla Rakha, and was always talking to Elvin about him. But he didn't always want me to play like the drone effect of an Indian tamboura. I started playing tonalities with both Reggie Workman and Jimmy Garrison, and sometimes we'd sound more like two members of a string quartet than bassists."

Davis was militant as well as musical, a well-educated and experienced musician who could work a Max Roach gig one night and make a symphony rehearsal the following morning. One racial situation in particular aroused his indignation. As he puts it: "Lincoln Center was being built with Federal money and there were Federal laws against racial discrimination. Yet I saw no black musicians in the New York Philharmonic at that time, and doubted if I'd ever see one soon."

So Davis and cellist Earl Madison later sued the orchestra itself because they had auditioned, made the finals—and then learned that someone else was hired without their even being advised. Ironically, violinist Sanford Allen had previously been hired as the first black member of the orchestra. He was engaged as a substitute in 1962, becoming a regular the following year. But it was Davis' contention that this was mere tokenism, and after his traumatic auditioning experience, he sued.

But he got more reaction than he had bargained for. Counterpressure was put on him, causing him to lose his studio job and many of his playing gigs. Today, he is primarily engaged in teaching.

Sanford Allen, however, was recently promoted from second to first violin section; though he's still the only black musician in the orchestra, as one glance during a concert reveals.

"I don't play jazz; I don't improvise well," he says. "But I listen to a lot of jazz, and when I first heard 'My Favorite Things' I really listened closely to Coltrane. His music stopped me from whatever I was doing at that time. It excited me; more than anything else, the emotional content reached me, and Coltrane is still the only jazz musician who does that to me all the time."

Allen is also intrigued by Coltrane's "scientific" approach to music, "as if he's investigating a particular problem that has to be solved. His constant experimentation is an excellent illustration of this approach."

Coincidentally, he is married to an Indian, and he knew of Trane's interest in the music of that country. He comments, "I've listened to Indian music for years, but I can't really make a strong connection between Coltrane and Indian music. However, I do think the sound he gets on soprano often reminds me of an Indian oboe called the shenai."

I live in Santa Monica, but I often go into Los Angeles to hear jazz at Shelly's Manne-Hole. I'd been listening to Coltrane since I caught him with Miles in Ohio. For five hours, I sat on a stool at the Manne-Hole listening to three sets of Coltrane. Not only was my ass numb but also my mind, from all the stunning music I'd heard. At one point I suddenly realized that I'd been staring at his horn while he was soloing, and I hadn't moved for at least ten minutes, as if his music was hypnotizing me. The same principle as the snake charmer and the snake. On a subsequent visit, I became convinced that this is what actually happens between Trane and his hard-core followers—such as myself.

Joe Corso

From the diary of Trane's Lady for 1964:

2/19: I watched Jazz Casual show featuring John on Channel 13.

3/13: John called on this Friday the 13th. Said he owed me an explanation. Has been very confused, doesn't understand me and doesn't want to, just "enjoys" me. I told him I was leaving the country in a few weeks and would be living overseas for a year or longer. He laughed; more shocked than humored.

I was going through a change of life when I started listening to Coltrane's music. His music reflected this change and furnished me with a new aesthetic outlook. It's music without *pre*conception and *pre*meditation. The structure of his horn lines reaches so deeply that it symbolizes nothing, just wonderful ornaments melting into even more wonderful ornaments. Coltrane creates the way the world creates—naturally. The way a tree grows branches or a cloud shapes itself, unconsciously but perfectly *right;* the same way Coltrane plays music.

John Okas

I booked John Coltrane into the Village Gate from 1961 through 1965, and I remember him as a quiet, courteous artist who was always on time and always interested in working. Once, I booked him as part of a triple bill with Carmen McRae and Dick Gregory. However, the event that I recall most vividly was the time he played here on the same bill with Odetta. She was recording for Vanguard, and their party included some visitors from France who sat through Odetta's performance and then started to leave when Coltrane came on. I walked over to their table and asked them to wait a few minutes and give John a chance. It was, in retrospect, a strange double booking, involving two totally different audiences. But I guess they were both available at the same time and that's probably how it happened. Anyway, the Vanguard people stayed for a full set of Coltrane, and at the end they thanked me for introducing them to his music.

ART D'LUGOFF

John Coltrane was pleased, in general, with the way his Impulse recording contract was working out. He liked the people, the production . . . and the pay.

From time to time, John Coltrane would borrow money from Impulse, and we made those loans because of his substantial record royalties. We did this to help him with his taxes. If we paid him royalties, that's income; but the interest on a loan can be deducted for tax purposes.

ALAN BERGMAN

Coltrane's album sales were around 25,000 to 50,000 over a year's time, which was tremendous for a jazz album. *A Love Supreme* was his best seller, going into six figures. I was amazed, because I'd never heard much of his music on radio and I wondered, "Who's buying all these records?" Then, I visited several colleges as part of an educational package, and I saw that almost all the student musicians had Coltrane records. I think young musicians were probably the first to buy his records.

BOB THIELE

In April 1964 John Coltrane's Impulse recording contract was renewed. And, although the structure of the contract remained the same, one-year plus two one-year renewal options, the advance was substantially increased: to $25,000 a year for each of those three years.

With Coltrane's new contract came a concomitant increase in recording activity. So many records were eventually released that even dedicated Coltrane connoisseurs were struggling to keep up-to-date on the saxophonist's latest stylistic changes and musical growth. Not so Spliby; he was close enough to the man and his music to notice every nuance. He heard the increasingly melancholy tones in Trane's music; they mystified him, made him think and feel that something strange was happening or about to occur.

Especially when he listened to the album called *Crescent*.

Not too many people picked up on the *Crescent* album, but I sure did because that's the most lyrical and the most melancholy I'd heard so far. There's one tune, "Wise One," that starts off slow and moody, then goes into a Latin rhythm on the bridge. But when Trane comes back to the melody I hear a message, a question, "Why?" Later, I got the feeling he might have written that tune for Eric Dolphy.

GERALD MCKEEVER

Crescent was recorded on April 27 and June 1, 1964.

Eric Dolphy died on June 29, in Berlin, Germany, of complications resulting from diabetic and coronary problems.

John Coltrane wept for his deceased friend, his treasured friend whom he would never see or hear again. Eric's parents presented John with their son's flute and bass clarinet. Coltrane then started playing both of these instruments, recording "To Be" on the *Expression* album as a flute fantasy, and using bass clarinet on a selection from the *Cosmic Music* album dedicated to, and titled for, "Reverend King." Reverend Martin Luther King, Jr., who would, of course, himself die on April 4, 1968.

> I hesitate to use the word "genius," but I would certainly call John Coltrane a great craftsman and a highly specialized person. I listen to the new music, including his, but the public, whose ears are not so specialized, takes a long time to make the historical discovery of the obvious. Also, as an artist, Coltrane was creating in public and was not expecting to create a classic each time he picked up his horn. But he was going to try each time for a classic performance and hope before he was through that he'd say a few things worth while. I think John Coltrane said more than a few things worth while.
>
> ARTIE SHAW

> John Coltrane was a musical force, a pure, powerful force that influenced everyone around him and must have, in some way, influenced everyone who ever heard him. Even the people who write the music for TV commercials or put together the Muzak you hear in an elevator are bound to have been influenced by his musical force. If you know and love music and are aware of contemporary developments, there's no way you cannot be influenced by the music of John Coltrane.
>
> ARNIE LAWRENCE

John Coltrane was at times influenced by the music of Sun Ra, for he once said, "Sun Ra told me that anything I could play he had something to do with, something that will fit with whatever I'm doing."

And Sun Ra said, "Coltrane's music, like mine, is cosmic and spiritual. But there is a strong romantic strain in his music that I hear and love. All his music is interesting to me, but I liked 'My Favorite Things' better than anything else because this song brought out the romantic in him."

Sun Ra is not romantic himself; he is beatific, a gentle, Buddha-like man in physiognomy and philosophy. He leads a band that ranges from eight to twenty-two and is called by many names but, most frequently, usually preceded by a battalion of adjectives, the Arkestra. In this band he has gathered around him some of the most advanced musicians this side of Juilliard or the Paris Conservatory. They assist their leader by researching the music and instruments of various countries so that Sun Ra, like Nero Wolfe solving a particularly puzzling problem, can eclectically create into a vast musical collage all these sounds and scales, notes and rhythms, and call it what music is supposed to be—a universal language.

His name, Sun Ra—Ra is one of the Egyptian sun gods—reflects his universal belief that the source of life is the same as the source of music. Like a wandering band of minstrels, the Arkestra is a commune of men and women musicians, dancers and singers who sometimes prick our consciousness by chanting, "If you are not in reality, whose myth are you? If you are not a myth, whose reality are you?" As the band's theme states: *We Travel The Spaceways.*

On stage, they are dressed in the wildest dreams of any chic boutique—fur hats, flowing robes, print shirts, beads and bells—and perform on Chinese flute, Indian oboe, European bassoon, Japanese koto, and African kora. Sun Ra himself, wearing in addition to his flowing robes a glittering metal skullcap he calls his Sun Helmet, plays piano, clavinet, and several electronic synthesizers.

Pharoah Sanders and Rashied Ali played with the band before joining John Coltrane, as did many other outstanding musicians, especially saxophonists. Sun Ra's reed section (with the exception of Ellington's) is the best in the business; collectively and individually, the musicians can play sounds that purists will claim exist nowhere on the saxophone register. And almost every member doubles on exotic percussion of all kinds, much like the African drums that Trane was always hearing in his head.

John Gilmore, Sun Ra's tenor saxophonist, recalls, "I used to rehearse with Miles Davis before he hired Trane. When the band moved from Chicago to New York in 1960, I'd play the Monday night sessions at Birdland. Sometimes I'd see Trane there and ask him to stop by and listen to a band rehearsal. Trane knew Sun Ra from Chicago, and he finally started visiting our studio on West Eighty-second Street. Sun Ra gave him literature on outer space and we talked tenor while I showed him some of the things the band and myself were doing at that time."

Gilmore showed Coltrane how to reach certain notes in the overtone series that some critics claimed weren't even on the horn. But they were; Gilmore was certainly playing them and Coltrane was definitely hearing them. In return, Coltrane taught Gilmore some of his harmonic discoveries, which the latter often used with startling effects.

"Trane really wanted to play more avant-garde music, but he didn't get the foundation until he listened to Sun Ra a lot," Gilmore concludes. "I think we helped him get his Oriental and African music together, too. I'll tell you this, whenever I saw him after he'd studied with Sun Ra—he was *smoking*."

I recall that for almost a year, from summer 1963 through the following spring, I'd see John and say hello and he'd just nod and walk off. I asked Elvin what was the matter, and he said, "John wants you to know he still likes you." I thought that was a strange way to show it, but Elvin explained, "He feels he can't talk with you because you're with *Down Beat*. Even though he likes you personally, he's decided that jazz criticism is all wrong and since you're a critic he just can't talk with you any more." Later in 1964, John sent me a letter asking me to forgive him. He said he'd lost God before and had just now found God again.

DON DEMICHEAL

John Coltrane listened to everyone, including God. And though everyone did not necessarily return the favor, many people throughout the country *were* listening to John Coltrane; some in the most unlikely locations.

Portland, Oregon is not the greatest place for jazz, but I got a show going on KBOO, a Pacifica-type station there, and once did a four-hour program on Coltrane. I was really surprised to find such incredible devotion and interest; I got hundreds of calls and letters about the show. Then I tried to put together a forty-eight-hour program on the fourth anniversary of his death, and the station manager vetoed it. But the music director, who's strictly classical, and the program director, a blues man, were both strongly in favor. To me, that was a fantastic illustration of Trane's unusual, universal appeal.

DON KROM

You don't hear much jazz in Las Vegas, but my father, a radio announcer, brought some Coltrane albums home when I was eleven. The importance of what I heard, the seriousness and dedication of his approach; these things helped get me through puberty. That was a big enough drag by itself, but a hundred times worse if you're a white eighth-grader who didn't like the Beatles and all of whose idols in 1964 were black.

TOD CARVER

Young people, even children, were now listening to John Coltrane's music. But Coltrane had no children of his own, and in common with most men he wanted to pass on his heritage to a son.

At last, a child was born to John and Alice Coltrane on August 26, 1964. They named the boy John, Jr.

My feeling is that Coltrane was trying to get at nothing less than the absolute truth, that his horn was the vehicle he was using to go beyond just music. I'd compare what he was doing with the meditation processes Martz talks about in his book, *The Poetry of Meditation,* and some of the procedures Castaneda talks about in the Don Juan books.

JOHN TAGGART

It is the darkest hour before the dawn, 4 A.M., the Hour of God. John Coltrane has risen on this fall day of 1964 and is sitting on the carpeted floor of his paneled study, a silk bathrobe wrapped around his body as, his head bowed, his arms and legs crossed, he begins his period of meditation.

Quiet envelops the room. All he can hear is the sound of his breathing; all he can feel is the stiffness of his muscles as he sits and concentrates on stopping his mind and receiving communications from the cosmos.

He wishes to talk with God if he can; at the very least, he wants a message from God, informing him whether he is going in the proper direction or not. He is so confused, he tells himself; he desires clarity and the knowledge that he is traveling on the right path. Give me guidance, God, he prays.

Minutes pass, changing into hours as he sits there, mute and unmoving, as if he has been turned into stone. His mind and body have temporarily ceased to exist for him; if he feels anything, it must be only what a pure spirit would perceive—a floating freedom.

His meditation is deep now, the longest, most sustained period he has ever spent. He hopes for a directive from God; nothing less will satisfy him now.

Absolute quiet prevails.

Suddenly, music fills the space around him and the spaces inside him; melodies and harmonies and rhythms integrate themselves into his consciousness. This must be the Word of God, commanding him to create a composition as homage to the Supreme Being. The feeling he is receiving is beyond feeling itself; the communication being delivered to him is indescribable.

And, awakening from this profound meditation with its paradoxical emphases on exultation *and* melancholy, he knows that from this moment forward the music he writes will reflect this duality, these contradictions, as his life reflects them every day that he awakens from his short night's sleep.

As he later confided, "For the first time in my life, I have the whole album from beginning to end."

A Love Supreme was recorded the following December as John Coltrane's gift to God. As he believes, "This album is a humble offering to Him."

He received great assistance for this composition from his reading of the Kabbala.

"Where philosophy ends, there the wisdom of the Kabbala begins," a sage once said. He was referring to a series of books—primarily the *Sefer Yezirah,* the Book of Creation, and the *Zohar,* Hebrew for splendor—that were written from the seventh to the eighteenth century and are used as the basis for a particular brand of Jewish mysticism that assigns each word, letter and number in its language an occult meaning. That language is Aramaic, the tongue of Christ.

By the numbers, then; if you listen carefully to the continuous chanting of "a love supreme" that separates the first and second sections of the composition, you can count the repetition of this phrase nineteen times.

Separate that number; one means alone, nine stands for universal. One creative man alone, either with or against the universe, but definitely of the universal consciousness.

One plus nine equals ten. And, in addition, according to the Kabbala, there are ten manifestations of God.

I joined a record club that had so many choices I got confused. So I sent for a Coltrane album because I'd heard his name mentioned somewhere. The album was *A Love Supreme,* and when I played it the first time, I kept asking myself, "What is *this?*" Then I listened three or four times in a row, and it got to me so much I wanted to "be" the music. I realized you've got to be all musician or none at all. I started transcribing a few of his solos for trumpet, which I play, because trumpet and tenor are both B♭ instruments. Now I'm trying to get inside his music as it sure got inside me.

STAN CHOVNICK

"A Love Supreme," to me, is repetitious but not monotonous. I can sing it; it's like a chant or a spiritual, and very African in feeling. Now, the way I would sing it is like this: I'd use my voice like a horn to cover the full range of the music, which is considerable. I can picture myself dressed in African robes with a battery of percussionists around me and myself right in the center of the audience. I'm letting my version of, "A Love Supreme" radiate through the audience like ripples in a a lake, and I'm giving them my love through this music as John Coltrane gave his love to me and to everyone else who ever heard his music.

STELLA MARRS

Love, Devotion, Surrender; this is the philosophy of guru Sri Chinmoy, whose disciples include, among others, John McLaughlin and Carlos Santana. And like "A Love Supreme," these three words are also the title of a record, this time featuring McLaughlin and Santana together. If you pay particular attention to the first selection on this album, you will hear the *Acknowledgment* section (the first part) of "A Love Supreme."

The philosophy, the music, the words utilized in both of these albums represent an unquestioning acceptance of God's will. In short, when God calls, you come. And, again, this message can have only one ultimate meaning—Death.

I remember talking with Coltrane outside of Birdland one night, not long after he'd recorded *A Love Supreme.* He was talking about death in a philosophical way, just like it was a subject of ordinary conversation. I was young, in my twenties, and he scared me. I said, "Why talk about death, when there's so many beautiful things in life?" I tried to move the conversation back to music, but he would keep bringing up the subject of death every few minutes. I think he must have known then that something was wrong and that he wouldn't have long to live.

ROBIN KENYATTA

Once in a while I'd go back to Philadelphia to visit, and sometimes I'd talk with John's mother. I remember her telling me about *A Love Supreme* and how she was wishing he'd never written it. I was surprised to hear her talking like that, but she told me John had a vision of God before he composed it. She also said John told her that he was seeing these visions of God a lot of times when he was playing. She was worried to death, because she said, "When someone is seeing God, that means he's going to die."

BOBBY TIMMONS

There is death and life, dark and light throughout our expanding universe. John Coltrane was attuned to these universal truths, as was the man he most admired, Albert Einstein. And, as Coltrane paid attention to, and learned from, his musical predecessors, so also did Einstein, who studied the accomplishments of Max Planck in particular. As Planck stated in his Quantum Theory of 1900, light is not transmitted in a solid mass but in waves or particles.

Five years later, Einstein proposed his Special Theory of Relativity, based on further experimentation with photons (energy particles). This theory states that all phenomena, all systems of nature, move with uniform relativity to one another, and that time is not absolute but a form of perception or an order of events.

This was, in short, his famous formula; $E=MC^2$.

Following this, in 1915 came the General Theory of Relativity, stating that the laws of nature are the same for all systems regardless of their state of motion. Einstein also formulated the Principle of Equivalence of Gravitation and Inertia, which states that there is no way to distinguish motion produced by inertial forces from that caused by gravitational forces, for the effects of both are exactly the same. Proceeding further, he declared that the movements of the stars and planets are determined by the metric properties of the space-time continuum, and that a gravitational field has as much reality as an electromagnetic field.

Now, an interesting parallel exists between Einstein's mathematics and Coltrane's music. For music is mathematical and so is physics. The laws of the one interrelate with the axioms of the other. And Coltrane was into metaphysics as much as music.

Think of Trane this way:

An electromagnetic field pulls in particles that are attracted to its positive charges, as Coltrane drew people who were attracted to his music. A gravitational field brings a body or bodies into its orbit that fall into its sphere of influence, as Trane did to people who were similarly inclined. And there are the constantly changing structural values of his music as the notes are emitted from his horn; the effect is like that of light waves pouring out in searing, convoluted streams of pure energy, the matter of the man radiating them like a nuclear reactor. Time, too, was broken up by Trane, stretched and contracted; especially when he was taking a super-long solo. How many people were cognizant of the length of time it took the saxophonist to thoroughly explore each composition, each improvisation? The fact is that the passage of time during the period that people listened to his music was fluid, plastic, and often caught them unaware; some might glance at their watches and say, "Is it *really* that late?"

John Coltrane was, in his own way, a walking, playing, living example of Einstein's theories in action, a spiritual and spatial force, closely following the principle of the First Law of Thermodynamics: heat can be turned into mechanical energy, and the converse, with a perfectly constant rate of exchange.

In short, energy can never be destroyed, only changed.

And John Coltrane went through his own kind of changes, day after day.

> I remember talking about Einstein with Coltrane while we were having an egg cream at the drugstore on St. Marks Place and Second Avenue. Actually, he was talking about numbers and their relationship to music, how intervals affected certain kinds of chords and how they could be used to create a different order in music. He brought up the theory of relativity. To him, it meant that many things already existing had a relationship in music, and it was up to the musician to discover these relationships and express them musically. I saw Coltrane for the last time in March 1967 at the health food store on Broadway and Fifty-seventh Street. We picked up the same subject of relativity almost exactly where we broke off our previous conversation. More than anything else, I recall him saying, "The universe is always expanding."
>
> David Amram

I was brought up on classical music, and I was interested in "legitimate" tonal qualities. Then I heard Coltrane with Miles on the *'Round about Midnight* album, and what caught my ear more than anything else was the break going into his solo on "Dear Old Stockholm." It was so *coarse* I didn't think anybody would have the *nerve* to play like that. I started transcribing his solos, just to see what they looked like on paper. After listening to and writing down his solos for years, I found it was Coltrane's texture that interested me the most, the actual technical construction of building a melodic line from the chord structure and the succession of notes as he played them. I discovered, contrary to my first impression, that the quality of his ideas and phrases was of the highest. He was consistently playing against himself, not wanting to be stuck into just one groove, as if he was playing the total antithesis of himself at all times.

ANDREW WHITE

Andrew's Musical Enterprises, Inc., of Washington, D.C. is exactly what it appears to be, a one-man corporation. Its business is the production and distribution of the transcribed saxophone solos of John Coltrane; its chairman, president, and chief executive officer is a thirty-two-year-old saxophonist, bassist, and composer named Andrew Nathaniel White III.

White has been around; he's played with the J.F.K. Quintet, American Ballet Theater Orchestra, Stevie Wonder, Birmingham City Symphony Orchestra, and the Fifth Dimension, to name a few. However, the preoccupying passion of his musical life has been the providing of transcribed Coltrane saxophone solos for study and practice.

"I've transcribed 209 solos from fifty albums," he says. "Not the compositions, just the improvised solos on each one. About three-quarters of them were done prior to 1960, because I started college that year and got pretty busy with the books. But in 1971 I had enough money to take off for a couple of years, so I refined what I'd already done and added some new solos. After September 1973 I had it all together, and I let people know that these Coltrane solos were now available."

His purpose was educational more than financial; to upgrade the literature of the working jazz musician, whom he thinks "needs more discipline and more knowledge of the total jazz repertoire." White considers Coltrane as an excellent academic source for learning how to play properly, and he rates him accordingly. "On a scale of one to ten, in twentieth-century music, I'd say he was third. But," he adds, "if you're talking strictly about jazz and improvising music, I'd put him *above* Number One."

The two saxophonists met only twice, both times in D.C. where White was playing and Coltrane was visiting. The first time, Andrew was listening to John at a club where the latter was working, but he was so overawed that he couldn't think of anything musical to ask him, and all Trane said was, "Just keep on playing." On their second encounter, Coltrane caught White playing a transcription of his "Giant Steps" solo, followed by Andrew's improvisation on John's improvisation. This time Trane said, "I see you're playing all those hard tunes."

White does not agree with those who become obsessed with the emotionalism in Coltrane's music. He believes that a musician must remain emotionally apart from the execution of his music; to him, the actual act of creating is based on objective, not subjective, experience. One must feel the emotion first and *then* attempt to recreate that feeling. He does not see how Coltrane, for example, could be feeling and playing at the same time, considering the incredible effort involved in creating the feeling and the playing and then projecting both simultaneously. He simply says, "It can't be done."

He concludes, on a strangely prophetic note, "John Coltrane was either a demon as a saxophone player or just a good saxophone player. According to the way I see it, if what we're hearing is the opposite of what he was, he was a musical demon. Otherwise, he would have just laid back and played, which I don't think he ever did, because he was always, to me, playing at the top of his form with no release. I think I'll have to say that we were confronted with a musician of demonical powers, and who is to say who needed the exorcism, Coltrane or us?"

During the turbulent 1960s, the Vietnam war was of course going on. And when someone once asked John Coltrane about that subject, he said, simply, "I am opposed to war; therefore I am opposed to the Vietnam war. I think all wars should be stopped."

> I remember talking with Trane about the Vietnam war in 1965. He was really unhappy about the war and the state of the world in general. He was almost crying when he said to me, "Why can't people learn to love each other?"
>
> GERALD MCKEEVER

> John Coltrane helped keep me alive when I was in Vietnam. I heard him everywhere I traveled before I was shipped out, and I brought some Coltrane records with me to Vietnam and listened to them constantly. His music was like life to me, and death was just down the road a few hundred yards away.
>
> FRANK LOWE

Eric Drosin is practicing.

He is sixteen, a Manhattan resident and high school student. He is practicing in the school's music room, struggling with the size of the upright bass that is six inches taller than himself.

Because of John Coltrane.

The previous year, when Drosin was attending boarding school in Florida, a teacher introduced him to Coltrane's music. A great leap forward from the Jefferson Airplane to John Coltrane.

"'Softly, As in a Morning Sunrise' was the first record I heard," he says. "Then I started listening to 'My Favorite Things,' the Newport version, and 'Bessie's Blues,' which was such a blunt statement it smacked me right in the face."

Eric Drosin does not neglect the ballads. "Lush Life," the Prestige version, kept him up until six one morning, not so much listening as attempting to transcribe the solo for practice purposes.

He continues now, practicing from the "Blue Train" solo, for he insists that "Trane's solos have such beautiful bass lines I can learn more from them than from a classical bass practice book."

Jazz has nothing to do with composed music and when it seeks to be influenced by contemporary music it isn't jazz and it isn't good.

IGOR STRAVINSKY

John never spoke more highly of any classical composer than Stravinsky. Once, when we were visiting his mother, he brought out a record and said, "I think I've found my universal musician." Then he played Stravinsky's *Firebird Suite*.

ALICE COLTRANE

A different, but genuine, kind of firebird, a fellow some called Little Rock, was playing tenor saxophone in New York City during 1965 when he started working with John Coltrane. Later—and better—known as Pharoah Sanders, he was born in that Arkansas town with the name of Ferrell. Some people simply nicknamed him after his home town; eventually, however, Ferrell was metamorphosized into Pharoah, and the latter stuck.

Spliby met Sanders when the Arkansas musician was "working at the Playhouse Cafe on MacDougal Street, sleeping under the stage because he didn't have a place to stay." Pharoah was short, compact and distrustful of any other sounds but music. He spoke only with his eyes and with his tenor. His sound was a squawking, screeching, top-of-the-register explosion that involved an extensive use of the overtone series and considerable overblowing of the horn. Spliby could dig that, and he introduced Pharoah to Trane, who was always interested in listening to the younger players. Coltrane let Sanders sit in with him, and complimented the younger saxophonist on "his spirit and eagerness to learn."

And because John Coltrane had been missing the much-needed thrust of an additional horn since Eric Dolphy's death, he invited Pharoah Sanders to join his band.

I am seventeen, white and live in Birmingham, Alabama, hardly a center of jazz development. But a friend turned me on to *A Love Supreme,* and when I listened it really spoke to me. Other people *knew* what this man's spirit was crying out. Now I know, too, and I love the man for that.

BART GROOMS

Two young Parisian gentlemen were listening to John Coltrane during the 1960s. While they did not consult Marcel Mule for his approval, they have this to say about Trane:

I first heard *A Love Supreme,* and I liked the last part best, "Psalm." I tried to play this part on trumpet, at which I am an amateur, but I found it too difficult. I listened to other records, especially *Impressions,* and I can hear the Debussy influence there. Now when I listen to Coltrane, I feel a quiet happiness, like repose, from his ballads. But when he plays fast and starts from low pitch running into high pitch, he makes me straighten my back and sit on the edge of my chair.

BERNARD PILLE

Bernard introduced me to Coltrane's music, starting with *A Love Supreme,* but I like *Om* the best because of its mystical qualities. I am an amateur painter, and when I paint I put on his music to stimulate my creativity. My style is abstract, and Coltrane makes me think of blue and orange colors. If I ever feel confident enough to dedicate a painting to him, I would call it *My Favorite Things.*

GILBERT KUBIS

Cecil Payne's immediate family is Barbados-born. He played and recorded with Coltrane on the album *Dakar*. That music was not quite so African as the title implies though Payne's baritone sax solos have the flowing, dancing feeling of his heritage, and he remembers Coltrane well.

"The last time I saw John Coltrane was in church," he recalls.

"St. Gregory's Catholic Church in Brooklyn. John, Roland Kirk, and myself were playing a benefit. The church needed money to build a schoolyard for the children to play in, and Cal Massey, who was a member of the church, promoted the concert. John recited the poem from *A Love Supreme,* then he played the entire piece from beginning to end. I believe this was in the summer of 1965. I remember John seemed so happy to be in church that his face was shining like an angel."

Alto saxophonist Gary Bartz also remembers John Coltrane, particularly in connection with two different "walkouts" that occurred when he was listening to Trane's music.

"One summer I was with Art Blakey and we were on the same bill as Coltrane at a jazz festival in Cincinnati," he recalled. "I saw people walking out because he was playing long solos. I thought that was rude, not giving him a chance to develop what he was trying to say."

Later, back in New York, Bartz and a friend were listening to Coltrane at the Village Gate, when Gary's buddy suddenly said, "Let's take a stroll."

"*What?*" Bartz replied, angrily. "When Trane's right in the *middle* of his solo?"

"I got my reasons. Come on outside and we'll talk about it."

Gary Bartz demurred; he stayed right there while his friend split. During intermission, he wandered outside. He spotted his buddy standing on the corner and was ready to read him off when the other said, almost apologetically, "Hey, man, you know how much I dig Trane. But sometimes he's *too much.* Like he's coming on so long and strong and I get so high on his music I just got to take a walk and cool myself down." He paused, adding, "Sometimes I just can't handle all that music at one time. You know, like my circuits get overloaded."

The jazz band is a real creation in novel tonal effects, whether you like them or not.

AARON COPLAND

Whenever I make a change, I'm a little worried that it may puzzle people. And sometimes I deliberately delay things for this reason. But after a while I find there is nothing else I can do but go ahead.

JOHN COLTRANE

John Coltrane went ahead and recorded *Ascension* in the summer of 1965, adding seven musicians to his basic quartet. Not quite a big band, not quite a small ensemble; just John Coltrane and friends.

Like most of his music, *Ascension* was a simple lead sheet but with additional voicings blocked out for the extra instruments. The saxophonist also set up tonal and atonal passages in such close juxtaposition that they created a quality similar to the parallel octave runs of African vocal music, with intense, explosive dialogues between the soloists and the rhythm section. The probable precursor of this composition, so totally different from any previous Coltrane creation, was Sun Ra, with his concepts of collective improvisation. Two complete takes were recorded, and the leader authorized the release of Take 1.

After the album was released, Coltrane called Thiele and said, "That's not the master." When Thiele protested that Coltrane himself had chosen this take for release, the latter said, "Well, I'm sorry, but I've been listening to the other take and I think it's better. Let's release that one instead." Impulse did, and on each record is inscribed "Edition II."

I was on LSD the first time I heard Coltrane, and the record was *Ascension*. I was nineteen, had a full tab of acid under my belt, and heard this overpowering musical force filling my head to overflowing. When I got straight again, I listened to the same music stone sober, a year later. It affected me so much I stopped getting high on anything except music, especially Coltrane's. And when I heard "Spiritual," I knew then what Coltrane really was—a spirit.

LARRY HICOCK

Once, as I was listening to *Ascension,* I went into a kind of trance and saw myself flying over Africa. I could feel the spirit of the entire continent and its pulsating, teeming life; I could hear African music and Coltrane's music simultaneously. But I couldn't see the people; only the jungle and savannas, even though I was no more than fifty feet above the ground. It was John Coltrane's music that carried me there, as if he was leading me by the hand.

JOHN MCLAUGHLIN

The John Coltrane Quartet played the Antibes Jazz Festival in Juan-Les-Pins, France, on the sun-swept Côte d'Azur for two evenings, July 26 and 27, 1965.

Randi Hultin was there; she and John talked on several occasions. He allowed her to complete a sketch of him for an oil painting, a portrait of Coltrane that she later mailed to him which, for some reason, he did not receive. He asked her why she wasn't painting more, and she said, "I'd rather do natural painting, and that takes so much more time than abstract, which others want me to do. But I just don't feel I have the right imagination to do something exceptional in abstract art."

He replied, "Strange, that's how I often feel about my playing." He expressed a desire to stop playing for a period, time enough to return to school and "learn about everything I could use in future musical expressions."

The musicians roomed at the Grand Hotel. Since Coltrane was practicing when he wasn't playing, few members of the press were allowed to disturb him. But Randi Hultin got invited, as did Mike Hennessey from England's *Melody Maker,* who asked the saxophonist, "What new combinations do you think you'll use in your next album?" The question was appropriate enough, but Hultin, perhaps in an impish mood, blurted out, "He's going to add an accordion to the band."

Despite the weather's warmth, John insisted on wearing tuxedo and black tie and made his musicians do the same, as if he thought the audience would expect the band to appear dressed for a dinner party. Hardly; most people were wearing little more than shirts and blouses, Bermudas and short shorts, plus the expected scattering of swim trunks and bikinis. As if physically unsettled by this strange fashion show, the saxophonist played unevenly throughout the entire score of "A Love Supreme" at the first concert. Hultin commented, "He charged like an angry bull with his tenor." Coltrane admitted, "I played too long, and I think I played very badly," adding, "I have to give a better concert tomorrow."

Randi, knowing that "Naima" was still his favorite composition, asked him to play the song during the next day's concert. Or, if not "Naima," then "My Favorite Things."

"We'll see," he said.

On the following evening the audience, Randi included, heard him open with "Naima"—and close with "My Favorite Things."

> What I'm most afraid of, at this moment, is losing the musicians I have with me. Especially Elvin, in spite of his unpredictability.
>
> JOHN COLTRANE

> I attended John's Paris concert after Antibes. There, I saw Elvin become irritated about something, kick his drums and walk angrily offstage. McCoy Tyner and John had been laying out, so Jimmy Garrison was left alone with the audience. While he was trying to play a bass solo, Elvin emptied a big trunk of drum equipment backstage, making a thunderous noise.
>
> RANDI HULTIN

Prior to August 11, 1965, few people, including most Americans, had ever heard of Watts, a sprawling black ghetto near Los Angeles. But that was the first of six straight days of rioting, because of a man named Marquette Frye being arrested on the trivial charge of loitering. Frye was one harassed black person too many for the overpoliced residents of the neighborhood, especially since he was grabbed by a white cop. The ensuing Watts Riot resulted in 33 dead, 812 injured, more than 3,000 arrested, and $175 million worth of damages.

When John Coltrane heard about Watts, he expressed himself not politically but personally. He immediately phoned Eric Dolphy's parents to make sure that they were all right.

Then there was the near-riot in Chicago at the *Down Beat* Jazz Festival on Sunday, August 15, reported by Buck Walmsley in the September 23 issue of that magazine:

"After intermission the John Coltrane Quartet, with Archie Shepp as an added starter on tenor, gave as tasteless a display of musicianship as I've ever heard. Not that all the members of the group played junk, for pianist McCoy Tyner and bassist Jimmy Garrison both took solo turns of beauty and imagination. But Shepp and Coltrane seemed to be more interested in trying to out-honk, out-squeal, and out-blast each other than in playing music. The one-tune, 45-minute set was a bomb as far as most of the concert's 7,500 attendees were concerned."

A second son was born to the Coltranes on August 6, 1965. They named him Ravi; after Ravi Shankar, a man that John still had not met.

> I love flying, and Trane's music gives me the feeling of flying. It scares me and thrills me, just as flying does.
>
> RODGER MCGUINN

Roger McGuinn, then one of the Byrds, was touring the country with the band that same summer. The musicians were traveling in a mobile home, with only two cassettes to serenade them during that month-long road trip. One cassette included the Coltrane songs "Africa" and "India," the other featured Ravi Shankar ragas.

The band members listened to both, but McGuinn was extremely entranced by Trane and "the way he'd go off on a completely different track from anyone else, almost screaming on his horn." They were all collaborating on some songs, and McGuinn suggested working in a few Shankar and Coltrane phrases, especially the latter. If you listen carefully, you can hear those influences in the Byrds's mesmerizing, memorable recording of "Eight Miles High."

"The first break is a direct quote from a Coltrane phrase," McGuinn explains, "and throughout the rest of the song, we try to emulate the scales and modes that Trane was using. Especially his spiritual feeling, which got me into transcendental meditation not long afterwards."

> When I heard John Coltrane on record, there was tranquility and serenity in his music. I do not recall the kind of restlessness in John Coltrane's music as I have heard in other types of music and from other musicians.
>
> SWAMI SATCHIDANANDA

> I was much disturbed by his music. Here was a creative person who had become a vegetarian, who was studying yoga and reading the Bhagavad-Gita, yet in whose music I still heard much turmoil. I could not understand it.
>
> RAVI SHANKAR

In November 1965, after the mutual exchange of many letters and experiences, Ravi Shankar and John Coltrane, master musicians from two totally different and contrary cultures, met for the first time in New York, where Shankar was appearing in concert.

As Ravi recalls, "Meeting John was a great surprise. Most jazz musicians I have met were not interested in anything outside of their own musical world, but here was a humble and self-effacing man with an interest in other people and their cultures like few I have ever met."

They dined together. Coltrane ordered vegetable cutlet, but Shankar asked for chicken, apologizing, "I like chicken when I am on a rigorous touring schedule. It helps me keep up my strength."

The saxophonist sighed, thinking of his weight. He was at nearly two hundred pounds and was desperately trying not to gain any more.

The next day they had a long talk together, the first of many. Coltrane explained some of his music to Shankar, but the great majority of their time together, at John's request, was taken up with Ravi's discussion of his country's musical heritage.

As, for example, these specifics:

Indian music contains 72 parent scales, 120 talas (time measures), 22 semitones, 66 microtones, and seven whole tones. These are all used for the six basic ragas (melodies with a minimum of five notes each), and can be expanded to cover the more than seven hundred ragas still being played. However, this includes only the Karnatic music of South India; the Hindustani ragas from the North are another musical experience. In addition, Indian music is not structured on Western chordal harmony; that is, it does not modulate. Yet the use of spontaneous improvisation often occupies from 80 to 90 per cent of a raga's playing time, and in common with its African cousin, Indian classical music is based on vocal music and structured on one continuous melodic line.

Or, as Shankar quoted from an ancient Sanskrit saying, "That which colors the mind is a raga."

To John, Ravi's sitar playing was comparable to the rich, resonant sounds plucked by Carlos Salzedo, his favorite harpist. Coltrane asked him how he could bend notes on the sitar, the traditional Indian string instrument equipped with seven playing strings, up to thirteen sympathetic, and from nineteen to twenty-three frets. So Shankar sat down with his sitar and showed him, adding such exquisite embellishments to his basic improvisations that the saxophonist was moved to tears. In gratitude, he invited Shankar to hear his new band—augmented by Archie Shepp and Pharoah Sanders on tenor, altoist Carlos Ward and drummer Rashied Ali—at the Village Gate.

Shankar accepted; he heard, and liked what he heard. And yet, on another level of awareness, he didn't.

Ravi recalls, "The music was fantastic. I was much impressed, but one thing distressed me. There was a turbulence in the music that gave me a negative feeling at times, but I could not quite put my finger on the trouble."

John Coltrane was a preacher on his horn and always sounded that way to me, from the first time I played with him in the fall of 1965 to our last date together in early 1966. Even now,

I am still inspired by every note on the records he left behind. I remember that we often talked about cause and effect, being able to sow the seed in order to reap the harvest. I learned so much from him that I hope I can someday pass on to others what Coltrane passed on to me.

CARLOS WARD

The band at the Village Gate also included, as mentioned, drummer Rashied Ali, a Philadelphian whom Coltrane had known for several years. This was Trane's first experience with a two-drum format; he wanted to recreate the rhythmic sounds he was still hearing inside his head, that quintessential choir of African drummers. Since Ali had started on congas before switching to traps, he seemed like a logical choice to bring into the band.

Or so John Coltrane thought; but Elvin Jones believed differently.

Ain't playin' *shit!* Trane's got this jerk on drums with me and he's got me goin' for hours on one tune, wearin' me out. *Still* ain't playin' shit!

ELVIN JONES

I didn't want to play with any other drummer, but I sure wanted to play with Trane, so I took the gig when he offered it. The cats in the band, especially, Elvin, thought I was pretty arrogant, and I probably was, because I had my attitude and they had theirs. But we got along musically, if not personally. Sometimes Elvin and I would switch parts just for the change, because I usually played the ensemble passages with him but only Elvin would back the horns and piano in their solos. I can play with just about anybody who wants to play with me, but I don't have to talk with him afterwards, either.

RASHIED ALI

Rashied Ali is taller and lankier than Elvin Jones, but Ali has huge eyes that are reminiscent of the luminous eyes of his leader.

He moved to New York in 1963, after studying harmony and counterpoint at Granoff School in Philadelphia. Despite formal training, he considers himself primarily self-taught on percussion. Ali played with Coltrane for the first time on a fall evening the following year, when Jones was late for a Birdland date. That is, Ali asked Coltrane if he could sit in—his third request in as many months—and this time the saxophonist said, "All right." The band played "Greensleeves" and part of another tune until Elvin arrived and claimed his chair. But, as Rashied recalls, "I felt pretty good playing with Trane. I'd finally broken the ice and he could hear how I sounded with him. I remember his soprano was so strong it was dominating the whole band."

Sheed, as he is often called, was truly a different drummer; as different from Elvin as Jimmy Garrison was from Steve Davis on bass. Ali was avant-garde, less concerned with basic pulsation than Jones and more involved with melodic improvisation. He liked to stretch and contract the time, constantly shifting his rhythmic accents and sometimes playing more like a bassist than a drummer. He was neither as loud nor as strong as Elvin—few drummers, if any, are—but, as John later described him, "Rashied is a multi-directional drummer. Any direction I go in, he follows right along with me."

Recalling Coltrane's drum fixation, Ali says, "He always played off the drums. He told me the drums freed him, he didn't have to worry about chord changes. He got the freedom to play what he wanted from working directly off the drums."

> Afro people in America are learning about their roots. Musicians like John Coltrane did so much to make this connection between African people and black people here in the States. Even if he didn't say it in words, he said it with his instrument. You know, in North Cameroon we have hautboy (African oboe) players who sound exactly like Coltrane, without ever having heard him.
>
> MANU DIBANGO

John Coltrane is always trying to learn from others. He is so humble in his way of asking that others usually tell him everything he wants to know. For instance, he asked me about Africa. I gave him books on African cultures and languages and records of African music, and then introduced him to my African friends. He told me, "I must go back to the roots; I'm sure I'll find what I have been looking for there."

BABATUNDE OLATUNJI

Michael Babatunde Olatunji has a master's degree in Public Administration, but he is more likely to be seen in his role as public performer. A rotund man with a round face, he radiates an infectious joy, and his mellow, mellifluous voice sings as he speaks of his West African heritage. He lectures on African culture and leads a drum ensemble that includes dancers (as in his native Nigeria), usually playing the talking drum and allowing the music to speak for itself.

Olatunji—some, like Trane, call him Tunji—and Coltrane became friends in 1959, when the Nigerian's *Drums of Passion* album was released on Columbia. During the ensuing years Trane tapped Tunji's knowledge of African percussion, following his drum fetish through history (he did not travel to Africa) to its logical conclusion, the continent and culture where it all began. Oddly enough, the two men never played together, perhaps because Coltrane was pursuing his drum fantasies in private until he could feel confident enough to display some concrete results of them in public.

In 1965, Coltrane and Olatunji shared some serious conversations about the increasing necessity of "making a change."

As Trane said, "I'm used to the critics complaining about me, and sooner or later they should understand my music. If they don't, there's nothing I can do about it. But what's really bothering me is the way I have to move around, New York today, Detroit tomorrow, San Francisco the day after that. It seems to me I've been using up so much energy traveling from place to place that I hardly can find time for writing any new music or even thinking about what I'm going to do next."

Tunji agreed. "I know what you mean, and I would like you to think about an idea that I have had for years. Perhaps we could work together and make an African cultural center a reality."

Then Olatunji told Coltrane about the money he had saved from his performances at the African Pavillion of the New York World's Fair, and from his record royalties. He wanted to establish a center for the study of African culture that would include a rehearsal/performance room where not only Coltrane but any other musicians, well-known or not, who wished to use the facilities would be welcome, free of charge.

They went ahead. Olatunji invested a five-figure sum and Coltrane contributed on a weekly basis, usually about $250. Yusef Lateef also became interested in participating, so an informal agreement was reached among the three musicians. They would combine their financial resources, book their own groups, rehearse their music at the center, and eventually form their own recording company.

As Olatunji emphasized, "We must put on our own concerts. It is time for us to take these risks ourselves. If we lose money, then that will be our bad luck. But if we are successful, then the profits will be ours, and we will not be making booking agents and concert promoters rich in the process."

With Coltrane and Lateef in agreement, Olatunji booked all three groups into Philharmonic Hall for a two-show concert on January 14, 1968, paying a $1,000 deposit to hold the hall.

But the concert would never take place. John Coltrane would pass on six months too soon.

John Coltrane: Five Years After.

The title of a two-hour show produced for the Canadian Broadcasting Corporation in Winnipeg, Manitoba, and broadcast over Canadian radio stations during July 1972.

Because someone, at least a few in this case, cared. Three Canadians, one Dutchman. Gren Marsh and Lee Major took care of the commentary, while Larry Hicock supplied the script, research, and production. Michiel de Ruyter of Radio Nederland provided several important interviews with Coltrane, Tyner, and Jones, none of them previously available to Western audiences and all taped in Holland from 1961 to 1965.

> Sometimes I wish I could walk up to my music as if for the first time, as if I had never heard it before. Being so inescapably a part of it, I'll never know what the listener gets, what the listener feels, and that's too bad.
>
> JOHN COLTRANE

In 1965, *Down Beat* proclaimed John Coltrane as "Jazzman of the Year," elected him to the Hall of Fame, awarded him first place on tenor saxophone, and named *A Love Supreme* as Record of the Year. The latter award also occurred in the International Critics Poll. In addition, the critics voted Trane second place on soprano.

It is interesting to note, however, that in the breakdown of the International Critics Poll that shows the voting members' country or continent of origin, these figures stand out: only nine of twenty-nine Americans and Canadians (32 per cent) voted for Trane on tenor, while seven of eleven Europeans (64 per cent) named him number one on that horn.

McCoy Tyner left John Coltrane in December 1965, to form his own group. He had been thinking of leaving for some time; not because Coltrane's solo space was stretching out in inverse proportion to his, but because he wanted to follow his own musical directions. However, the fact that Alice Coltrane was also a pianist may have contributed to his decision.

Tyner once said, "A musician such as John shouldn't have to depend on the piano all the time. Sometimes it's better to work without it, because the piano, as an orchestral instrument, can get in the way of the soloist, especially a horn player. John and I would decide on which tunes I'd play and the ones on which I'd lay out."

But now McCoy was taking a permanent stroll.

And Alice Coltrane walked in as McCoy Tyner walked out.

> Trane was very strict about his music. If we were doing it wrong, he'd point it out to us and ask us to play it right or

not at all. He never raised his voice, but he got the message across. He once told Alice, "You're playing the wrong chords; please get them straight."

RASHIED ALI

George Wein, the producer of the Newport Jazz Festival, also puts on other concerts of a similar nature. He remembers one affair in particular where Coltrane and Monk shared the bill, their first appearance together in almost ten years.

"This was in February 1966, at Cobo Hall in Detroit," Wein recalls. "We got hit with an all-day snowstorm, but surprisingly enough we had a crowd of 11,000 out of 15,000 capacity. Monk and his band made it, but John's rhythm section was snowed in and only John and Alice were there. Monk went on first, but by the second half John's men still hadn't showed up and I was getting worried."

In order to alleviate such worries, Wein asked Coltrane if he would mind playing with Monk to close out the concert. Monk, hearing this, immediately danced his approval and gave his former sideman an affectionate hug, while the saxophonist nodded his assent. They played mostly Monk's music, in particular those tunes from their 1957 collaboration. For the last few numbers, Alice sat in on piano, joining her husband for some of his own songs.

Afterward, in the dressing room, Wein, who'd really enjoyed Monk and Trane together, thanked the saxophonist and said, "I'm rather glad your rhythm section didn't make it tonight."

"I thought you'd feel that way," Coltrane replied. Then, he said, reflectively, "You know, I often wonder whether what I'm doing now is the right way to play. Sometimes I feel this is the way I want to go, but other times I'd rather return to the way I used to play." He paused, adding, "But for now, I think I'll continue in the direction I'm going and see what happens."

From the diary of Trane's Lady, the closing entry:

5/3/66: John called me at work and asked if he could see me. I said, yes, then thought better of it. He called me at home that evening. I said I didn't want to become emotionally involved again, but he insisted on stopping by. He stayed an hour and a half, listening while I did most of the talking. I mentioned Beatles and Rolling Stones; he was surprised I was interested in rock. We decided to end the affair then and there. As he was leaving, he asked me, "Do you have any sweet potato pie around?"

In March 1966, John Coltrane played a two-week engagement at San Francisco's Jazz Workshop. Elvin Jones and Rashied Ali were both on drums, earning, as did the other musicians, $500 a week.

An excellent salary, but apparently not excellent enough, financially or psychologically, for Elvin, who abruptly gave notice after the first week and took off for Europe to join Duke Ellington. And as Jones departed, he passed on his professional opinion of Coltrane's current musical direction:

"Only poets can understand it."

I sat in on drums with Trane in San Francisco after Elvin left. I was working with Archie Shepp at the Both/And, and I knew Trane was used to having two drummers behind him. While we were playing, I got so involved with the energy level of his music that in my excitement I knocked the beater from my bass drum and a cymbal off its stand. Suddenly Trane stopped playing, as if he heard instantly that something was wrong. He looked at my drums, then he got down on his hands and knees, trying to fix the drums while I was still playing like mad.

BEAVER HARRIS

In May of that year, John Coltrane recorded his second "live" album at the Village Vanguard. It contained only two tunes, "My Favorite Things" on one side, "Naima" on the other. And Alice was on piano, playing John's favorite song; the song dedicated to his first wife.

I'll never forget July 1966 at Newport, when I approached Coltrane with a photograph I'd taken months ago in Chicago.

He was backstage with his tenor around his neck, blowing scales and listening to a record man talk business. He looked at my picture, said "Plugged Nickel," signed it with a "Thank you," and walked off to play a solo.

JIM KAY

It was Sunday afternoon, the last day of Newport, and I told him, "John, play as long as you like, there's no time limit." The band played about forty-five minutes on one tune. Suddenly, the music stopped, then John took an unaccompanied solo that was the most lyrical thing I'd ever heard in my life. He played alone for about five minutes, then he and the band took the tune out.

GEORGE WEIN

Hai is Japanese for "Yes," and that was what John Coltrane said when the Shaw Agency asked him if he'd like to tour Japan during July 1966. Not only would he have the chance to play for his Japanese admirers in person—according to *Swing Journal*, a Japanese jazz magazine, Coltrane was "the most popular musician in Japan"—but he would also have the opportunity to pursue his Eastern studies close up, something that he could never even approach by reading books back in America.

However, had he been given advance notice of his daily schedule as arranged by the Japan Booking Corporation, he might possibly have changed his mind.

This was the itinerary for his Japanese tour:

7/8: Check into Tokyo Prince Hotel upon arrival.

7/9: Press Conference, 1 P.M.

7/10: Concert at Sankei Hall, 6:30 P.M.

7/11: Same as 7/10.

7/12: Bullet train to Osaka, check into Osaka Grand Hotel; Press Conference, 5 P.M.; concert at Festival Hall, 6:30 P.M.

7/13: Check into Hiroshima Grand Hotel; concert at Municipal Concert Hall, 6:30 P.M.

7/14: Check into Nagasaki Grand Hotel; concert at Municipal Concert Hall, 6:30 P.M.

7/15: Check into Hakata Imperial Hotel; concert at Citizen's Concert Hall, Hakata (Fukuoka), 6:30 P.M.

7/16: Check into Osaka Grand Hotel; concert at Daini Hall, Kyoto, 6:30 P.M.; midnight concert at Osaka Schochiku Theater.

7/17: Check into Kobe International Hotel; concert at Kobe International Hall, 6:30 P.M.

7/18: Check into Tokyo Prince Hotel; concert at Kosei Nankin Hall, 6:30 P.M.

7/19: Concert at Kosei Nankin Hall, 6:30 P.M.

7/20: Check into Osaka Grand Hotel; concert at Festival Hall, 6:30 P.M.

7/21: Concert at Municipal Concert Hall, Shizuoka, 6:30 P.M.

7/22: Check into Tokyo Prince Hotel; concert at Kosei Nankin Hall, 6:30 P.M.

7/23: Check into Nagoya International Hotel; concert at Aichi Bunka Kodo Hall, 6:30 P.M.

7/24: Midnight concert in Tokyo.

When the Japan Air Lines aircraft carrying the John Coltrane Quintet touched down at Tokyo International Airport around two in the afternoon of July 8, several thousand Japanese, as if expecting a world statesman, surrounded the plane, and then started singing like an official welcoming committee for their honored guests. As they were walking down the ramp, Jimmy Garrison nudged John and said, "You know of any big shot on this plane they might be looking for?"

Coltrane was about to shrug "I don't know" when the musicians spotted the banners that read:

WELCOME JOHN COLTRANE QUINTET
Impulse/King Records

In Japan, his albums sold as many as 30,000 copies each; almost the equivalent of his American distribution, but in a country with only half the population.

Life-sized posters of the musicians were in abundance. As their host rolled out a red carpet from the ramp through the airport terminal doors and out to their waiting limousine, several schoolgirls presented them with bouquets of flowers.

The girls bowed; the musicians did their best to bow back.

The following day, a press conference was held in the Magnolia Room of the Tokyo Prince Hotel. Correspondents from the major Japanese media, as well as a variety of foreign reporters, were in attendance. It was as if the musicians were visiting potentates preparing to sign a peace treaty. Harold Lovette, who was accompanying the band, said, "In Europe, we were treated like artists, and that's the way it should be. But here, you'd think we were their *brothers*, the way they gave us such personal attention."

Only in Japan; never in America.

Though Coltrane still disliked speaking in public, he consented to the press conference as a matter of courtesy and perhaps with a touch of curiosity about what his hosts might ask him.

Kiyoshi Koyama, editor of *Swing Journal*, asked him, "What would you like to be ten years from now?"

Without hesitation, John replied, "I would like to be a saint."

> Trane was no saint; he was just a man. Some people might call him a saint, but to me he's still a man—the best, most beautiful man I ever worked with.
>
> RASHIED ALI

The Japanese, too, thought of John Coltrane as a beautiful man. And they have their own ways of saying, and showing, so.

> These things most impressed me about Coltrane. When I met him at his hotel room, he was wearing just a shirt and pants, with leather sandals on his bare feet. This was so unlike Miles, who was always dressed in expensive suits. After hearing Coltrane play, I liked his technique and ideas, and also his willingness to play harder and longer. He seemed to give more of himself than any other musician I ever saw.
>
> KIYOSHI KOYAMA

> John gave out a lot of autographs after our first Tokyo concert. Just as we were getting into our cab to leave, a young boy came running up but the driver pulled away too fast for him. He was still running when we were blocks away. Then, after we were back in our hotel room for about twenty minutes, we heard a knock at the door. It was this Japanese boy, who had apparently run all the way. He had followed us for miles just to get John's autograph.
>
> ALICE COLTRANE

Wherever the Americans went, the Japanese welcomed them. Fans stopped them in the streets, taking off their own shirts and asking John and the others to autograph them. If they entered a restaurant and the people recognized them, the musicians were asked to sign their names on the wall, if not the menu.

And, during those few free hours they could find for themselves:

Harold and Jimmy got juiced, checking out all available liquids from sake through Suntory scotch.

Rashied complained that his Japanese guide stuck so close he had no chance to "walk around town and rap with the people." He assumed, of course, that some of those people spoke English, which the great majority did not. Nevertheless, he'd sneak out on occasion and stop at the coffeehouses, conversing mostly with students who were learning English.

Pharoah said nothing and did less.

Alice asked John if they could see the Kamakura Buddha; he said, "If we have time."

They didn't; but in Nagasaki John took time to visit the War Memorial Park, where the second atomic bomb of World War II was dropped on August 9, 1945, killing more than 150,000. There, he prayed for the dead and, with his deep humility and great respect for all human life, John asked God to grant the world what he had named a recent composition: "Peace on Earth."

After the first Tokyo concert, several Japanese musicians asked to sit in. Coltrane was doubly honored, for the Yamaha Instrument Company had given both Sanders and himself alto saxophones, a new model they wished John to try and advise them about. So Coltrane and Sanders played their Yamaha saxophones during that Japanese jam session.

Sleepy Matsumoto, one of Japan's best-known tenor saxophonists, was there. He requested "Lullaby of Birdland," George Shearing's dedication to Bird's namesake, and Coltrane, perhaps remembering many pleasurable hours of music-making there, obliged. After the tune, on which Matsumoto got off some stomping choruses of his own, he said, "John Coltrane is *shibui*," a word difficult to translate but essentially signifying taste and class. He also said, of Trane's sound on the Yamaha horn, that it was like "liquid fire."

Before the band returned to America, Coltrane bought a koto, a Japanese string instrument with a harplike sound. He also purchased a sitar, recalling an earlier suggestion by Ravi Shankar, for he so loved the shimmering sounds of strings—*all* of them.

At almost every concert, while satisfying the constant requests for "My Favorite Things," he also featured two recent compositions, "Leo" and "Peace on Earth." The Tokyo concert of July 22 was taped, and these two selections were released posthumously on the album *Concert in Japan.* "Leo" included a Yamaha saxophone duet of Coltrane and Sanders, with "Peace" portrayed by John on tenor.

The sound and feeling John Coltrane creates on "Peace" is an extraordinary testament to the Japanese, whose attention, love, and respect he must have both welcomed and absorbed, for it is his most inspired "live" performance on record. He is "talking to you," speaking so directly and passionately that the music sounds like a gentle whispering in your ear; he is asking you to love all people and is hoping they will love you in return.

That, sad to say, was the tragedy of John Coltrane's life; he wanted to solve the world's problems through music and art, peace and love. Like a preacher, or a teacher. And this simple, exquisite cadenza with its countless, spiraling variations that he called "Peace on Earth" was his way of saying, "I want to love all people, and I want them to love each other."

A beautiful fantasy, however naïve the reality.

In a subsequent issue, *Swing Journal* published a cross section of opinions about Coltrane's music. Of the four summarized here, the first person is a pianist, the second a tenor player, and the latter two are members of the audience:

> I was surprised, because Coltrane's music seemed very naïve to me. It is mostly technique applied to simple music, but there is no relationship among the musicians on any one song. Both Coltrane and Sanders keep repeating the same phrases all the time. I think they are playing more for themselves than for the audience.
>
> YAGI

> His music is very avant-garde but I like it. It is one step forward from Charlie Parker's bop. I am never concerned about beat or rhythm or phrase with Coltrane, but I do prefer his "old style" music better, such as "Giant Steps" and "Good Bait."
>
> GIRO INAGAKI

> Coltrane has the power to impress the audience with simple melodic lines. But his sound is so insistent that I feel confusion and depression in his music. There is too much reality in his music for me to bear when I hear it, and I do not usually listen to music to hear these things in it.
>
> YUKITAKA TSUTSUI

> Contemporary jazz is not beautiful or happy. I hear emotional excitement and passion in Coltrane's music, but I do not feel it as intensely as I expected to. His music is like a religious ceremony, not yet established but still changing and growing. It is not completely fulfilled yet, and therefore it does not completely fulfill my aesthetics.
>
> SHINICHRO NAKAMAYA

The John Coltrane Quintet returned to New York. There, Rashied Ali, who had been snapping photos of his boss with a camera he'd bought in Japan for a friend, developed his film and kept some of the pictures as souvenirs.

After Coltrane's death, Ali was looking over the photos one day when he was jolted by something that had escaped his scrutiny on previous occasions. As he points out, "About half of those pictures showed Trane holding his hand over his liver, like he was trying to stop the pain he must have been feeling all by himself."

I haven't had much leisure time for the past fifteen years.

JOHN COLTRANE

When Coltrane returned from Japan, I called him and asked him to tour Europe that fall. He said he wasn't feeling well, and he really sounded tired, so I offered to pace the tour any way he wanted. He said he wasn't sure he wanted to go, that he was feeling weak. When I asked him why, he said, "I'm not eating." I was shocked; I asked him what kind of diet he was on. He said, "I'm not on any diet; I'm just not eating." "*Anything?*" "No, I'm trying to clean out my system."

GEORGE WEIN

Weak or not, eating or not, John Coltrane took his musicians into the recording studio during late 1966 and early 1967 because he recognized his obligations and responsibilities as a leader—to keep his men working so they could be paid. He had turned down all bookings for an indefinite period. He wanted time to create some new music, time to read and meditate, and simply time to walk around inside his own head and see what was happening there.

He was forty years old, and he sensed that some important changes were coming into his life. Whatever they were, he wanted to be ready.

He was not ready, however, for the increasing frequency of the headaches he was having. They had started in Japan, slowly, like a gentle knocking on the door; now they were arriving like a narcotics squad, beating on his head until he was gulping aspirin by the bottle and causing Alice such alarm that she finally suggested that he see a doctor.

"No," he said, firmly. "I'll be all right."

When he wasn't recording, he was reading, studying Sufism in particular, at the suggestion of bassist Donald Garrett, who had played and recorded with Coltrane just the year before. Garrett had recorded three albums with the saxophonist during 1965, playing not only bass but bass clarinet, Eric Dolphy's bass clarinet that Coltrane had asked him to try out (Garrett had also started his musical studies on clarinet). One of the records was called *Kulu Se Mama,* conceived by percussionist and poet Juno Lewis as a dedication to both his natural and his earth mother. Garrett had become for that short interlude, as Art Davis had been before him, the second bassist in the band. Of that period, he says, "I always thought using two basses sounded like an African water drum."

Like the Kabbala, Sufi is a form of mysticism, in this case inspired by Islam. It stresses knowledge and enlightenment, requesting its adherents to secure for themselves Oneness of Being and thus experience Absolute Reality. As the *Treatise on Oneness* says, "When the secret of an atom of the atoms is clear, the secret of all created things both external and internal is clear, and you do not see in this world or the next anything besides God."

As the eighth-century Sufi Hasan Al-Basri said, "He that knows God loves Him, and he that knows the world abstains from it."

Or as Garrett said to Coltrane, "You've got to go to the source to learn anything, and Sufi is one of the best sources there is."

Garrett and the saxophonist had once gone directly to another source while working in Seattle, during the fall of 1965. There, they had taken LSD before recording an album. Contrary to current opinion, this occurred *after,* not before, *Ascension* was recorded. Of that record, many had thought, and some, such as Grace Slick of the Jefferson Airplane, had said that *Ascension* was "Coltrane's acid trip." However, the pervasive influence of ingesting acid may have produced the eerie, mystical vibrations that emanated from their recording of *Om,* which included, in addition to some of the freest and strangest music Coltrane ever recorded, the chanting of selected verses from the Bhagavad-Gita. And when Trane returned from his LSD trip, he said, as if quoting a Sufi sage, "I perceived the interrelationship of all life forms."

One day toward the end of 1966, the telephone rang in the Coltrane home.

"John, this is Tony Rulli. I've got something here I think you might be interested in."

Rulli was talking about the Varitone electronic saxophone attachment, similar to the equipment that Sonny Stitt and Eddie Harris were using. But this was a more advanced model, extremely experimental and capable of creating a galaxy of unusual, unearthly sounds.

Coltrane immediately drove into midtown Manhattan, where Tony had a room at the Victoria Hotel. When John arrived, he didn't even bother to remove his coat. He immediately stuffed the saxophone into his mouth, started adjusting the controls, and went right into a workout that lasted for three continuous hours. This was necessary; the Varitone was equipped with its own separate saxophone, and those who wished to utilize this model had to adjust their embouchures to the new horn in order to enjoy its electronic benefits.

Trane was so entranced that he took the Varitone home, new saxophone included. He practiced incessantly for the next six weeks, concentrating on mastering the use of the octave control. This control could create a unison sound an octave lower than anything he was then playing on the saxophone itself; it sounded as if he was playing two saxophones simultaneously. In short, he was playing parallel octave runs, a traditional African technique, with American electronic equipment.

When Rulli stopped over to take the Varitone back to the factory for additional refinement—later, a model was developed that could be connected to a musician's own horn—Trane was truly sorry to give it up. The electronic invention had stimulated his creativity enormously, and he wanted to suggest it to Sanders. But the Varitone had to be returned, and the next working model was not made available for another year, too late for Trane.

I returned to New York at the end of 1966, and I called John at once. I invited him to visit me in India, and he said he would seriously consider my offer. He sounded very sad, and I told him I was disturbed after hearing the latest record he had sent me. He told me that he was feeling extremely frustrated, that he was still trying for something different but he did not know what he was looking for. I was preparing to open a school of Indian culture in California, so I asked him to visit me there if he could not come to India. He said he would, and he sounded as if he really meant it. Then I went out on another concert tour, and when I returned to New York again, John was gone.

RAVI SHANKAR

I haven't heard anything higher than "The Father and the Son and the Holy Ghost" from the *Meditations* album. I would often play it at four in the morning, the traditional time for meditation. I could hear God's mind in that music, influencing John Coltrane. I heard the Supreme One playing music through John Coltrane's mind.

CARLOS SANTANA

Meditations was reviewed by *Down Beat* in the December 1, 1966, issue, in a double discussion, side by side. It was like a courtroom contest between defendant and prosecutor; the former, Don DeMicheal, gave the album five stars (tops), while the latter, Bill Russo, awarded only one (bottom).

DeMicheal claimed, "I do not pretend to understand this music. I doubt if anyone, including those playing it, really *understands* it, in the sense that one understands, say, the music of Bach or Billie Holiday. I *feel* this music, or, rather, as I said, it opens up a part of my self that normally is tightly closed, and seldom-recognized feelings, emotions, thoughts well up from the opened door and sear my consciousness."

Russo countered, "Coltrane lacks the spirit of the idiom he attempts. He gets stuck, repeating figurations time and time again, as if such repetition could somehow improve what little they had to offer the first two or three times they occur. It doesn't, obviously."

The bata drum is a holy drum from Africa by way of Haiti. Bata means "baby" and has vibrative rights on the human heart. I play it because I'm a priest in a voodoo cult, the same as they have in Haiti. To me, voodoo means "Who are you?" or

"Who you?" as in hoodoo. It's the only cult in the world that makes you identify yourself and say who you are.

ALGIE DEWITT

Algie DeWitt and John Coltrane met in Philadelphia during November 1966, when the latter appeared as a guest soloist at a concert sponsored by the Church of the Advocate, and the former was among several participating Philadelphia musicians.

DeWitt is tall and slender, his body supple from years of dancing and his movements as graceful as a swaying snake. His face, complete with bristly beard, is wreathed in what seems a permanent expression of wonderment, as if he is perpetually engaged in the cultivation of the marvelous. He plays bata, an hourglass-shaped drum about three feet long, his lean fingers tapping out primitive tempos from ancient times, now on the treble head, then on the bass, and sometimes on both simultaneously.

After listening to Algie's drumming, John said, "I liked your sounds. You blended well with what we were doing." The drummer replied, "Trane, you're like a sculptor who picks up his clay of tones and molds the music as he goes along. All I tried to do was mold myself into the great statue of sounds you were creating."

John chuckled softly, apparently discovering in Algie DeWitt what he had seen in Pharoah Sanders, a young man of will and spirit. He said, "Algie, would you like to work with me?"

Algie replied, with enthusiasm, "I shall be your Afroic partner."

Coltrane and DeWitt did work together, on several occasions; their first engagement was a date at New York's Village Theater on December 26. Later, that same theater was renamed Fillmore East, hosting the sounds of hard rock and boosting impresario Bill Graham to several years of fame.

However, the theater on that December evening housed the most radical ensemble Coltrane had assembled since he recorded *Ascension.* People were still screaming about *Ascension,* and now the saxophonist gave his audience something further to scream about with this band. He augmented the basic quintet with Rashied Ali's brother Omar on congas, DeWitt's bata, trumpeter John Salgato and bassist Sonny Johnson. The music, as expected from such a lineup, was rawly emotional, visceral enough to cause a noticeable number of walkouts, yet valid and expressive enough to have the majority of the audience shouting, "Encore, encore!" upon completion of the concert.

As DeWitt commented afterward, "That concert spelled success. It was Trane saying, 'You don't need me any more because I've said it all.'"

> I'm an Assistant Attorney General of New York State, but I also produce a monthly jazz concert in Manhattan, and one of the reasons is John Coltrane. Not that he turned me on to jazz—I've been listening for decades—but in a way, I wanted to show my appreciation for the spiritual qualities he brought to the music. This man possessed enormous dignity; he didn't need to glad-hand or buddy-buddy the audience in order to present his music to the public. He was an artist, and you instinctively knew it. I remember attending a concert at Lincoln Center, "Titans of the Tenor," with Sonny Rollins and Yusef Lateef playing their usual excellent sets. Then Coltrane came on with a group of young musicians I'd never heard of before. I liked this new music, though I still preferred his earlier stuff. But what really impressed me was that John Coltrane, a genuine superstar and solid attraction, was showcasing new music and new musicians. He was playing the music he wanted to play, even at the cost of losing part, if not most, of his audience.
>
> JACK KLEINSINGER

Expression is the most recent Coltrane recording released, according to date, and was recorded during February and March 1967. The album has an eerie quality of finality, a carefully chosen musical refinement, that seems to sum up Coltrane's career, as if he knew that it might be one of his last recorded statements.

A journalism student named John Hollenhorst, writing in the University of Minnesota *Daily*, has reviewed—and perceived—this music so beautifully that several excerpts from his review follow:

"On the track entitled 'To Be,' Coltrane plays flute, with Pharoah Sanders playing piccolo, weaving ghostly lines around each other.

There are none of the powerful climaxes usually associated with his work, nor does he engage in any of his difficult chromatic runs. Instead, it is a quiet, reflective piece, but the emotional effect is frightening. There is something unsettled and horrifying about it, as it always threatens to bubble over into complete chaos.

"'Ogunde,' played on tenor, indicates that Coltrane's music has become simpler; he has whittled it down to a purer, more intense form, making it extremely difficult to listen to. There is no tension and release; the music is continually tight and deep, and the listener cannot come down. It is this quality that makes listening to Trane an experience rather than an activity. It purges the emotions.

"The other two tracks, 'Offering' and 'Expression,' also played on tenor, I find even more difficult. I do not fully understand this music; I doubt that anyone does. But that is one of Coltrane's greatest achievements. He makes music of fantastic subtlety and difficulty, yet his music can be appreciated, to a degree, on a lower level. Each listening brings new rewards."

A third child, Oran, was born to John and Alice Coltrane on March 19, 1967. He was their third son in three years.

> Coltrane was playing a lot of extramusical sounds at that concert, but his conception was totally different from Sanders. Coltrane played extremely technical music, then progressed to an abstraction of that, an abstraction in sound. These extramusical sounds—honking, screaming, almost crying—seemed to be an integral part of his over-all tonal structure. It was like a man who was really in control of his language; he was saying something that you absolutely understood.
>
> Billy Taylor

The Olatunji Center of African Culture, located at 43 East 125th Street, Harlem, New York, was officially opened on March 27, 1967, with Manhattan Borough President Percy Sutton in attendance.

Less than one month later, the center welcomed another honored guest whose constituency was musical. John Coltrane appeared at the center on April 23 for the first in a series of concerts on the theme *Roots of Africa.* Two shows were presented, at 4 and 6 P.M., with a door charge of $3.00 per person.

Though still sick, overweight, distracted, rehearsing, recording, and greatly worried about his present health and musical future, Coltrane heeded his friend Olatunji's call for help. He brought his musicians to the Center for their first public engagement, with minor exceptions, since the Village Theater date that previous December. They performed in a 30×100 foot loftlike room on the second floor, backdropped by colorful wall posters depicting an African village scene. The musicians turned on the audience with such tunes as "Tunji," the "Acknowledgement" section from *A Love Supreme*, "Ogunde," and the perennial crowd-pleaser, "My Favorite Things."

The crowd spilled out into the hallway and down the stairs, onto the sidewalk and around the block. It had been too long a time for most of them, and this rare Coltrane appearance was too special an event to be missed. Despite his personal difficulties, John Coltrane played, and played beautifully, his power and strength apparently undiminished, his ideas and conception as advanced as ever. With him was his regular working band of Pharoah Sanders, Jimmy Garrison, Rashied Ali, and Alice Coltrane.

Algie DeWitt and his magic drum were there, too, spreading Afroic joy and African rhythms that were experienced by all, especially the most authentic African in attendance, Olatunji himself.

It is notable that Coltrane became, as was still his custom, so passionately involved in the making of music that he had to be cued by Olatunji to conclude the first show. For there were hundreds still waiting for his second performance; and he certainly needed more than a mere five-minute break.

I believe John Coltrane wanted to learn more about African music because our music plays a much larger role in the total culture than in other places. I offered to take him to Africa with me the next time I returned to Nigeria. He said, "When?" and I suggested the following year. He said, "God willing, I will."

BABATUNDE OLATUNJI

That same month, John Coltrane renewed his contract with Impulse Records. In fact, he signed a new two-year contract at a $40,000 advance for each year.

The following month, John and Alice Coltrane were visiting John's mother at her house in Philadelphia when, on that lovely May evening, he suddenly clutched at his stomach and staggered, groaning, into his old bedroom and closed the door. He refused all entreaties from the ladies, merely mumbling that he would rejoin them shortly. It was more than an hour before he came out of the bedroom, and when he did he looked at his mother, Mrs. Alice Blair Coltrane, and his wife, Mrs. Alice McLeod Coltrane, as if neither of them were, or ever had been there in the house with him.

Shortly after returning to their Long Island home, Alice insisted on making an appointment for John with a stomach specialist. Her husband kept the appointment—alone. He also submitted to a biopsy after the physician checked him into the hospital for that purpose. But John Coltrane refused to stay for further testing; against doctor's orders, he discharged himself and phoned Alice at once.

He said, perhaps prophetically, "Come and get me; I'm ready to leave."

The last time I talked with Coltrane was my last day at *Down Beat*, June 1. I had called him to verify a date at the University of Chicago. He told me he had canceled it, saying that he was "ashamed" to be seen in public due to his weight. I asked him, "John, how much *do* you weigh?" There was a long silence. Then, he said, wearily, "Two hundred forty pounds."

DON DEMICHEAL

She dances as if weightless, a loose white scarf trailing the girl in the shimmering white dress; she moves as stately as a ballerina *en pointe;* she clutches at the sky, an expression of acquiescent melancholy on her radiant face, as if calling the Supreme One to bring John Coltrane back to earth again.

She is tall and slim, elegant and earthy; she is Judith Jamison of the Alvin Ailey Dance Theater. As she dances, she is swaying like a reed, the reed in Coltrane's saxophone, as if he is still playing it, at least inside her head.

The dance is called *Cry,* and Ailey himself has choreographed it, setting it to the music of Alice Coltrane, Laura Nyro, and the Voices of East Harlem.

Alice's song is simply titled "*Something About John Coltrane,*" with Pharoah Sanders' plaintive soprano saxophone sobbing over the crisp brushwork of Rashied Ali's drums and the extraordinary melodic inventions of bassist Cecil McBee. Laura sings, in "Been on a Train," of a lonely man sharing a train trip in her coach, shooting himself full of heroin, and ODing before reaching his destination. And the Voices are crying out, "Right On, Be Free."

> I wanted the sculptural idea of John Coltrane to stress its rhythmic quality, neither horizontal nor vertical but perpetual. It became an arch supported by two unequal parts, the arch almost developing into a motion in the shape of a circle. The emotional relevance of the sculpture to Coltrane is found in *Meditations,* Poem: Love-Consequences-Serenity and that became Coltrane-Horn-Serenity, further changing into Larger Unit-Smaller Unit-Arch. The arch is based upon the Egyptian form built to carry a man from this life into the next. There is no response here, however; the sculpture has the alertness of Coltrane's tensed neck, a forward thrust into the arch.
>
> BRADFORD GRAVES

New York sculptor Bradford Graves has created, as a memorial to John Coltrane, an abstract sculpture that was placed in the Carpathian Mountains of Czechoslovakia. It was completed during the celebrated days of Prague Spring 1968, when he and his wife, Verna, were invited to a sculptors' symposium sponsored by the Union of Slovak Artists.

"Trane's musical approach paralleled my own development as a sculptor," he explains. "It was slow and steady, working out one motif over and over again in a strongly disciplined manner. He made me realize that sculpture, which has often been compared to painting, is really closer to music, because both are three-dimensional art forms expressing fluidity and movement."

TRANE—that's what Graves called his construction. Eight tons of travertine, nine feet by six; two units separated by two inches, one representing Coltrane's head and shoulders, the other his horn.

> John was in my office the Friday before he died. He left after we discussed some business matters. I got the distinct feeling that he was dying; I could see death in his face. On my way home, I met Alan Bergman, one of ABC's attorneys, in the elevator. He asked me, "Did you see Coltrane?" I said I did. Alan said, "He looks terrible." I just said, "This man is dying."
>
> BOB THIELE

On the Sunday morning of July 16, 1967, John Coltrane was rushed to Huntington Hospital as an emergency patient. He died there on Monday morning, July 17, of primary hepatoma—cancer of the liver—at 4 A.M., again, that traditional time of meditation, sometimes called the Hour of God.

When Bob Thiele received a phone call from Jimmy Garrison later that same day, Thiele did not even have to hear the message, for he intuitively knew:

The Trane ride was over.

In 1968, John Coltrane was elected to the *Playboy* Jazz Hall of Fame. As Nat Hentoff said, "Coltrane's trademark was his unique sound, which bespoke a relentless search for perfection yet was always, even in the most elevated realms of abstraction, compellingly passionate and alive."

That same year Deborah D'Amico started listening to the music of John Coltrane.

Last year, she began studying tenor saxophone.

Once each week, a little girl carrying a big horn shows up at the Third Street Music School in New York's East Village for her saxophone lesson. As she says, "I have no plans on becoming a professional. I just wanted to prove to myself that I could learn to play John Coltrane's instrument."

FOR JOHN COLTRANE

They should have
shown you to the sun,
so he could know
his rival

you might have
made the world go mellow,

turned empty tables
golden with your sound

we are lucky, I suppose,
they let you blow at all
their love is gold
that turns to dollars

yours streamed from your mouth
as free as air,
as rare as free

still I can say
to children I don't have yet
Once upon a time, a Coltrane
walked the earth,

and hope
that they grow ears

DEBORAH D'AMICO

St. Peter's Lutheran Church at Lexington Avenue and Fifty-fourth Street, New York City, has a capacity of five hundred but can squeeze in seven hundred people in times of emergency or on special occasions.

One of each occurred on Friday, July 21, 1967, at 11 A.M. Reverend John Garcia Gensel, the "Jazz Pastor" who had ministered to the physical as well as spiritual needs of so many musicians, conducted funeral services for John Coltrane, who would never appear at the Sunday evening Jazz Vespers as Reverend Gensel had twice asked and as Coltrane had once promised.

From all over the world, people came to pay their respects to John Coltrane in death as they had previously praised him in life. A contingent of Germans occupied a front pew; a Japanese writer did not arrive until the funeral was over, but bowed as he saw the coffin placed inside the hearse; a doctor from South Africa closed his offices for three days and caught the next plane to New York upon hearing the news.

Tenor saxophonist Albert Ayler was one of several musicians performing at the service. His band was playing in the balcony, overlooking the dashiki-draped body of John Coltrane resting in his coffin at the front of the church. (Naima Coltrane had created this dashiki the night before, sewing it in a pattern of brown and white; white for the purity of his art and brown for the earth from which he came and to which he would return.) During his portion of the music, Ayler stopped, twice, and screamed; not with his horn but with his voice, the first scream like a cry of pain and the other like a shout of joy that Coltrane, though dead, would live forever.

The closing music was played by Ornette Coleman. As bassist David Izenzon recalls, "We were playing 'Holiday for a Graveyard,' with Ornette and myself ending in unison on this beautiful note, a high E-flat. Suddenly Ornette stopped playing, and for some reason I kept sustaining the note. Then, just as I released my bow from the bass, I saw the attendants close John's coffin."

John Coltrane was buried in Pinelawn Memorial Park, Farmingdale, New York. There, he remains, at rest.

Most musicians remain poor. But the music that they make, even if it does not bring them millions, gives millions of people happiness.

LANGSTON HUGHES

I think Miles Davis, not John Coltrane, was the richest jazz musician. Miles didn't put out as many records, but they sold better; that is, he had "hits." *'Round about Midnight,* for example, sold 200,000 copies the first year, and I think *Kind of Blue* sold close to half a million.

TEO MACERO

John Coltrane left an estate—insurance, mutual funds, corporate bonds, real estate, record royalties, personal property—valued in the neighborhood of a quarter million dollars.

John Coltrane . . . Buddha . . . Martin Luther King, Jr. . . . Mohammed . . . Huey P. Newton . . . Abraham . . . Bishop C. H. Mason . . . Malcolm X . . . Jesus . . . Supreme Mother Ha'qq . . .

All of the above are an integral part of the pantheon and the teachings of One Mind Evolutionary Transitional Church of Christ in San Francisco, presided over by the Servant of Truth, King Bishop Ha'qq XIX. It is a church that is devoted to, was founded for, and celebrates the music and spirit of John Coltrane, called Omnedaruth, or Compassion.

The words, the music from *A Love Supreme* form their ritual, permeate their premises with Coltrane's spirit. They compare him to Christ, who was also, they say, an artificer, a mechanic, a craftsman, as was, to their one mind, John Coltrane.

They conclude: "Therefore Omnedaruth is a Supreme Being, as is God."

I do not agree; I *cannot* agree.

Trane and Buddha, both great teachers in their differing styles and different times, suffered from similar misconceptions by far too many of their followers. While alive, they were addressed as gods; when dead, they were worshiped as God. They received not genuine respect but mindless adoration.

The romanticists might wish to remember John Coltrane, the man from Hamlet, North Carolina, in a manner comparable to Horatio's farewell to Shakespeare's Hamlet, "Good night, sweet prince." The realists might recall that Trane left as his legacy just music and memories, nothing more, nothing less.

But I believe that John William Coltrane was a mystic, a musician, and a man who changed people's lives, usually for the better. A reluctant mystic . . . a brilliant musician . . . and a decent man.

HERE WHERE COLTRANE IS

Soul and race
are private dominions,
memories and modal
songs, a tenor blossoming,
which would paint suffering
a clear color but is not in
this Victorian house
without oil in zero degree
weather and a forty-mile-an-hour wind;
it is all a well-knit family:
a love supreme.

Oak leaves pile up on walkway
and steps, catholic as apples
in a special mist of clear white
children who love my children.
I play "Alabama"
on a warped record player
skipping the scratches
on your faces over the fibrous
conical hairs of plastic
under the wooden floors.

Dreaming on a train from New York
to Philly, you hand out six
notes which become an anthem
to our memories of you:
oak, birch, maple,
apple, cocoa, rubber.
For this reason Martin is dead;

for this reason Malcolm is dead;
for this reason Coltrane is dead;
in the eyes of my first son are the browns
of these men and their music.

MICHAEL S. HARPER

DISCOGRAPHY

DIZZY GILLESPIE AND HIS ORCHESTRA: Capitol 57797, 57839, 15852, 15611, 15849, 57892

Dizzy Gillespie, Don Slaughter, Elmon Wright, Willie Cook (trumpet); Matthew Gee, Sam Hurt, Charles Greenlee (trombone); Jimmy Heath, Coltrane (alto sax); Jesse Powell, Paul Gonsalves (tenor sax); Al Gibson (baritone sax); John Acea (piano); John Collins (guitar); Al McKibbon (bass); Specs Wright (drums); Tiny Irvin (vocal).

"Say When"; "Tally Ho"; "You Stole My Wife"; "I Can't Remember" (November 21, 1949).

Floyd Smith for Collins; add Carlos Duchesne (conga), Francisco Pozo (bongo); Joe Carroll (vocal).

"Coast to Coast"; "Carambola"; "Oo-La-La"; "Honeysuckle Rose" (January 9, 1950).

DIZZY GILLESPIE SEXTET: DeeGee 3600, 3601

Dizzy Gillespie (trumpet); Coltrane (tenor sax); Milt Jackson (piano, vibes); Kenny Burrell (guitar); Percy Heath (bass); Kansas Fields (drums); Fred Strong, The Calypso Boys (vocal).

"Love Me"; "We Love to Boogie"; "Tin Tin Deo"; "Birks Works" (March 1, 1951).

EARL BOSTIC AND HIS ORCHESTRA: King 4356, 4550, 4568, 4570

Gene Redd, Joe Mitchell (trumpet); Earl Bostic (alto sax); Coltrane (tenor sax); Pinky Williams (baritone sax); Joe Knight (piano); Jimmy Shirley (guitar); Ike Isaacs (bass); Specs Wright (drums).

"Moonglow"; "Linger Awhile"; "Ain't Misbehavin'" (April 7, 1952).

Harold Grant for Shirley.

"You Go to My Head"; "The Hour of Parting"; "Smoke Gets in Your Eyes"; "For You" (August 15, 1952).

JOHNNY HODGES AND HIS ORCHESTRA–USED TO BE DUKE: Verve 8150

Harold Baker (trumpet); Lawrence Brown (trombone); Johnny Hodges (alto sax); Coltrane (tenor sax); Harry Carney (baritone sax); Jimmy Hamilton (clarinet); Cal Cobbs, Richie Powell (piano; Powell on "Autumn in New York" only); John Williams (bass); Louis Bellson (drums).

"Used to be Duke"; "Sunny Side of the Street"; "Sweet as Bear Meat"; "Madame Butterfly"; "Warm Valley"; "Autumn in New York"; "Sweet Lorraine"; "Time on My Hands"; "Smoke Gets in Your Eyes"; "If You Were Mine"; "Poor Butterfly" (August 5, 1954).

THE NEW MILES DAVIS QUINTET: Prestige 7254

Miles Davis (trumpet); Coltrane (tenor sax); Red Garland (piano); Paul Chambers (bass); Philly Joe Jones (drums).

"Stablemates"; "How Am I to Know?"; "Just Squeeze Me"; "Miles' Theme"; "S'posin'"; "There Is No Greater Love" (October 27, 1955).

PAUL CHAMBERS–JAZZ IN TRANSITION: Transition 30

Curtis Fuller (trombone); Coltrane (tenor sax); Pepper Adams (baritone sax); Roland Alexander (piano); Paul Chambers (bass); Philly Joe Jones (drums).

"Trane's Strain" (November 1955).

PAUL CHAMBERS: Jazz West 7

Coltrane (tenor sax); Kenny Drew (piano); Paul Chambers (bass); Philly Joe Jones (drums).

"Dexterity"; "East Bound"; "Easy to Love"; "John Paul Jones"; "Visitations"; "Stablemates" (March, 1956).

JOHN COLTRANE WITH HANK MOBLEY–TWO TENORS: Prestige 7670

Donald Byrd (trumpet); Coltrane, Hank Mobley (tenor sax); Elmo Hope (piano); Paul Chambers (bass); Philly Joe Jones (drums).

"Weeja"; "Polka Dots and Moonbeams"; "On It"; "Avalon" (May 7, 1956).

MILES DAVIS–COOKIN': Prestige 7094

Miles Davis (trumpet); Coltrane (tenor sax); Red Garland (piano); Paul Chambers (bass); Philly Joe Jones (drums).

"My Funny Valentine"; "Blues by Five"; "Airegin"; "Tune Up"; "When Lights Are Low" (October 26, 1956).

MILES DAVIS—RELAXIN': Prestige 7129

Miles Davis (trumpet); Coltrane (tenor sax); Red Garland (piano); Paul Chambers (bass); Philly Joe Jones (drums).

"If I Were a Bell"; "You're My Everything"; "I Could Write a Book"; "Oleo" (October 26, 1956); "It Could Happen to You"; "Woody'n You" (May 11, 1956).

NOTE: Prestige 7094 and 7129 combined in Prestige 24001—MILES DAVIS.

MILES DAVIS AND THE MODERN JAZZ GIANTS: Prestige 7150

Miles Davis (trumpet); Coltrane (tenor sax); Red Garland (piano); Paul Chambers (bass); Philly Joe Jones (drums).

"'Round about Midnight" (October 26, 1956).

MILES DAVIS—WORKIN': Prestige 7166

Miles Davis (trumpet); Coltrane (tenor sax); Red Garland (piano); Paul Chambers (bass); Philly Joe Jones (drums).

"It Never Entered My Mind"; "Four"; "In Your Own Sweet Way"; "The Theme" (Takes 1 and 2) (May 11, 1956); "Trane's Blues"; "Ahmad's Blues"; "Half Nelson" (October 26, 1956).

MILES DAVIS PLAYS JAZZ CLASSICS: Prestige 7373

Miles Davis (trumpet); Coltrane (tenor sax); Red Garland (piano); Paul Chambers (bass); Philly Joe Jones (drums).

"Woody'n You"; "Salt Peanuts" (May 11, 1956); "Half Nelson"; "'Round Midnight"; "Well, You Needn't"; "Oleo"; "Tune Up"; "Airegin" (October 26, 1956).

MILES DAVIS—STEAMIN': Prestige 7580

Miles Davis (trumpet); Coltrane (tenor sax); Red Garland (piano); Paul Chambers (bass); Philly Joe Jones (drums).

"Surrey with the Fringe on Top"; "Salt Peanuts"; "Something I Dreamed Last Night"; "Diane" (May 11, 1956); "Well, You Needn't"; "When I Fall in Love" (October 26, 1956).

MILES DAVIS AND JOHN COLTRANE PLAY RICHARD RODGERS: Prestige 7322

Miles Davis (trumpet); Coltrane (tenor sax); Red Garland (piano); Paul Chambers (bass); Philly Joe Jones (drums).

"My Funny Valentine"; "I Could Write a Book" (October 26, 1956); "It Never Entered My Mind"; "Surrey with the Fringe on Top" (May 11, 1956).

Wilbur Harden for Davis; Tommy Flanagan for Garland; Jimmy Cobb for Jones.

"Spring Is Here"; "Blue Room" (July 11, 1958).

SONNY ROLLINS—TENOR MADNESS: Prestige 7657

Sonny Rollins, Coltrane (tenor sax); Red Garland (piano); Paul Chambers (bass); Philly Joe Jones (drums).

"Tenor Madness" (May 24, 1956).

LEONARD BERNSTEIN—WHAT IS JAZZ?: Columbia 919

Miles Davis (trumpet); Coltrane (tenor sax); Red Garland (piano); Paul Chambers (bass); Philly Joe Jones (drums).

"Sweet Sue" (September 10, 1956).

MILES DAVIS—'ROUND ABOUT MIDNIGHT: Columbia 949

Miles Davis (trumpet); Coltrane (tenor sax); Red Garland (piano); Paul Chambers (bass); Philly Joe Jones (drums).

"Bye Bye Blackbird"; "Tadd's Delight"; "Dear Old Stockholm" (June 5, 1956); "'Round Midnight"; "All of You" (September 10, 1956); "Ah-Leu-Cha" (October 27, 1955).

FOUR TENOR SAXES—TENOR CONCLAVE: Prestige 7249

Coltrane, Al Cohn, Hank Mobley, Zoot Sims (tenor sax); Red Garland (piano); Paul Chambers (bass); Art Taylor (drums).

"Tenor Conclave"; "Just You, Just Me"; "Bob's Boys"; "How Deep Is the Ocean?" (September 7, 1956).

PAUL CHAMBERS—WHIMS OF CHAMBERS: Blue Note 1534

Donald Byrd (trumpet); Coltrane (tenor sax); Horace Silver (piano); Paul Chambers (bass); Kenny Burrell (guitar); Philly Joe Jones (drums).

"Just For Love"; "Nita"; "We Six" (September 21, 1956).

TADD DAMERON—MATING CALL: Prestige 7745

Coltrane (tenor sax); Tadd Dameron (piano); John Simmons (bass); Philly Joe Jones (drums).

"Mating Call"; "Gnid"; "Soultrane"; "On a Misty Night"; "Romas"; "Super Jet" (November 30, 1956).

INTERPLAY FOR TWO TRUMPETS AND TWO TENORS: Prestige 7341

Webster Young, Idrees Sulieman (trumpet); Coltrane, Bobby Jaspar (tenor sax); Mal Waldron (piano); Kenny Burrell (guitar); Paul Chambers (bass); Art Taylor (drums).

"Anatomy"; "Interplay"; "Light Blue"; "Soul Eyes" (March 22, 1957).

JOHNNY GRIFFIN—A BLOWING SESSION: Blue Note 1559

Lee Morgan (trumpet); Coltrane, Johnny Griffin, Hank Mobley (tenor sax); Wynton Kelly (piano); Paul Chambers (bass); Art Blakey (drums).

"The Way You Look Tonight"; "Ball Bearing"; "All the Things You Are"; "Smoke Stack" (April 6, 1957).

THELONIOUS MONK WITH JOHN COLTRANE: Jazzland 46

Coltrane (tenor sax); Thelonious Monk (piano); Wilbur Ware (bass); Shadow Wilson (drums).

"Ruby, My Dear"; "Trinkle, Tinkle"; "Off Minor" (April 16, 1957).

Art Blakey for Wilson; add Coleman Hawkins (tenor sax); Gigi Gryce (alto sax); Ray Copeland (trumpet).

"Nutty"; "Epistrophy"; "Functional" (June 26, 1957).

THE CATS: New Jazz 8217

Idrees Sulieman (trumpet); Coltrane (tenor sax); Tommy Flanagan (piano); Kenny Burrell (guitar); Doug Watkins (bass); Louis Hayes (drums).

"Eclypso"; "Solacium"; "Minor Mishap"; "Tommy's Time" (April 18, 1957).

MAL WALDRON SEXTET: Prestige 7341

Bill Hardman (trumpet); Jackie McLean (alto sax); Coltrane (tenor sax); Mal Waldron (piano); Julian Euell (bass); Art Taylor (drums).

"Potpourri"; "J. M.'s Dream Doll"; "Don't Explain" (April 19, 1957).

Idrees Sulieman for Hardman; Sahib Shihab for McLean; Ed Thigpen for Taylor.

"The Way You Look Tonight"; "From This Moment On"; "One by One" (May 17, 1957).

JOHN COLTRANE–DAKAR: Prestige 7280

Coltrane (tenor sax); Cecil Payne, Pepper Adams (baritone sax); Mal Waldron (piano); Doug Watkins (bass); Art Taylor (drums).

"Dakar"; "Mary's Blues"; "Route 4"; "Velvet Scene"; "Witches' Pits"; "Cat Walk" (April 20, 1957).

JOHN COLTRANE–PAUL QUINICHETTE QUINTET: Prestige 7158

Coltrane, Paul Quinichette (tenor sax); Mal Waldron (piano); Julian Euell (bass); Ed Thigpen (drums).

"Cattin'"; "Anatomy"; "Vodka"; "Sunday"; "Exactly Like You" (April 17, 1957).

COLTRANE PLAYS FOR LOVERS: Prestige 7426

Coltrane (tenor sax); Tadd Dameron (piano); John Simmons (bass); Philly Joe Jones (drums).

"On a Misty Night" (November 30, 1956).

Red Garland for Dameron; Paul Chambers for Simmons; Al Heath for Jones; add John Splawn (trumpet), Sahib Shihab (baritone sax).

"Violets for Your Furs" (May 31, 1957).

Earl May for Chambers; Art Taylor for Heath; omit Garland, Splawn, Shihab.

"I Love You"; "Like Someone in Love" (August 16, 1957).

Paul Chambers for May; add Red Garland (piano).

"You Leave Me Breathless" (August 23, 1957); "Time After Time" (December 26, 1958).

JOHN COLTRANE–THE FIRST TRANE: Prestige 7609

John Splawn (trumpet); Coltrane (tenor sax); Sahib Shihab (baritone sax); Red Garland (piano); Paul Chambers (bass); Al Heath (drums).

"Bakai"; "Straight Street"; "While My Lady Sleeps"; "Chronic Blues" (May 31, 1957).

Omit Splawn and Shihab.

"Time Was"; "Violets for Your Furs" (May 31, 1957).

JOHN COLTRANE–LUSH LIFE: Prestige 7581

Coltrane (tenor sax); Red Garland (piano); Paul Chambers (bass); Al Heath (drums).

"I Hear a Rhapsody" (May 31, 1957).
Earl May for Chambers; Art Taylor for Heath; omit Garland.
"Like Someone in Love"; "I Love You"; "Trane's Slow Blues" (August 16, 1957).
Paul Chambers for May; Louis Hayes for Taylor; add Red Garland (piano), Donald Byrd (trumpet).
"Lush Life" (January 10, 1958).

NOTE: Prestige 7609 and 7581 combined in Prestige 24014–MORE LASTING THAN BRONZE

THELONIOUS MONK–MONK'S MUSIC: Riverside 3004
Ray Copeland (trumpet); Gigi Gryce (alto sax); Coltrane, Coleman Hawkins (tenor sax); Wilbur Ware (bass); Thelonious Monk (piano); Art Blakey (drums).
"Abide with Me"; "Well, You Needn't"; "Ruby, My Dear"; "Off Minor"; "Epistrophy"; "Crepuscule with Nellie" (June 26, 1957).

JOHN COLTRANE–TRANEING IN: Prestige 7651
Coltrane (tenor sax); Red Garland (piano); Paul Chambers (bass); Taylor (drums).
"Traneing In"; "Slow Dance"; "Boss Blues"; "You Leave Me Breathless"; "Soft Lights and Sweet Music" (August 23, 1957).

JOHN COLTRANE–BLUE TRAIN: Blue Note 1577
Lee Morgan (trumpet); Curtis Fuller (trombone); Coltrane (tenor sax); Kenny Drew (piano); Paul Chambers (bass); Philly Joe Jones (drums).
"Blue Train"; "Moment's Notice"; "Locomotion"; "I'm Old Fashioned"; "Lazy Bird" (September 15, 1957).

PRESTIGE ALL STARS–WHEELIN' AND DEALIN': Prestige 8327
Coltrane, Paul Quinichette (tenor sax); Frank Wess (flute); Mal Waldrom (piano); Doug Watkins (bass); Art Taylor (drums).
"Things Ain't What They Used to Be"; "Wheelin'"; "Robbins' Nest"; "Dealin'" (September 20, 1957).

SONNY CLARK–SONNY'S CRIB: Blue Note 1576
Donald Byrd (trumpet); Curtis Fuller (trombone); Coltrane (tenor sax); Sonny Clark (piano); Paul Chambers (bass); Art Taylor (drums).
"Sonny's Crib"; "Speak Low"; "Softly"; "With a Song in My

Heart"; "Come Rain or Come Shine"; "News for Lulu" (October 9, 1957).

WINNERS CIRCLE: Bethlehem 6024

Donald Byrd (trumpet); Frank Rehak (trombone); Gene Quill (alto sax); Coltrane (tenor sax); Al Cohn (baritone sax); Eddie Costa (piano); Freddie Green (guitar); Oscar Pettiford (bass); Philly Joe Jones (drums).

"Not So Sleepy" (October, 1957).

Ed Thigpen for Jones; omit Quill and Green.

"Love and the Weather"; "Turtle Walk"; "If I'm Lucky" (October, 1957).

RED GARLAND–ALL MORNING LONG: Prestige 7130

Donald Byrd (trumpet); Coltrane (tenor sax); Red Garland (piano); George Joyner (bass); Art Taylor (drums).

"All Morning Long"; "They Can't Take That Away from Me"; "Our Delight" (November 15, 1957).

RED GARLAND–SOUL JUNCTION: Prestige 7181

Donald Byrd (trumpet); Coltrane (tenor sax); Red Garland (piano); George Joyner (bass); Art Taylor (drums).

"Soul Junction"; "Woody'n You"; "Birks Works"; "I've Got it Bad and That Ain't Good"; "Hallelujah" (November 15, 1957).

NOTE: Prestige 7130 and 7181 combined in Prestige 24023–JUNCTION

RED GARLAND–HIGH PRESSURE: Prestige 7209

Donald Byrd (trumpet); Coltrane (tenor sax); Red Garland (piano); George Joyner (bass); Art Taylor (drums).

"Undecided"; "What Is There to Say" (November 15, 1957); "Solitude"; "Two Bass Hit"; "Soft Winds" (December 13, 1957).

RED GARLAND–DIG IT: Prestige 7229

Donald Byrd (trumpet); Coltrane (tenor sax); Red Garland (piano); George Joyner (bass); Art Taylor (drums).

"Billie's Bounce"; "Lazy Mae" (December 13, 1957).

THE RAY DRAPER QUINTET FEATURING JOHN COLTRANE: New Jazz 8228

Ray Draper (tuba); Coltrane (tenor sax); Gil Coggins (piano); Spanky DeBrest (bass); Larry Richie (drums).

"Under Paris Skies"; "Clifford's Kappa"; "Filide"; "Two Sons"; "Paul's Pal"; "I Hadn't Anyone" (December 20, 1957).

ART BLAKEY BIG BAND: Bethlehem 6027

Donald Byrd, Idrees Sulieman, Bill Hardman, Ray Copeland (trumpet); Melba Liston, Frank Rehak, Jimmy Cleveland (trombone); Sahib Shihab, Bill Graham (alto sax); Coltrane, Al Cohn (tenor sax); Bill Slapin (baritone sax); Walter Bishop (piano); Wendell Marshall (bass); Art Blakey (drums).

"Midriff"; "Ain't Life Grand"; "El Toro Valiente"; "The Kiss of No Return"; "Late Date"; "The Outer World" (December 1957).

Omit everyone except Byrd, Coltrane, Bishop, Marshall, Blakey.

"Tippin'"; "Pristine" (December 1957).

GENE AMMONS AND HIS ALL STARS—GROOVE BLUES: Prestige 7201

Coltrane (alto sax); Gene Ammons, Paul Quinichette (tenor sax); Pepper Adams (baritone sax); Jerome Richardson (flute); Mal Waldron (piano); George Joyner (bass); Art Taylor (drums).

"Ammons' Joy"; "Groove Blues"; "It Might as Well Be Spring"; "Jug Handle" (January 3, 1958).

GENE AMMONS AND HIS ALL STARS—THE BIG SOUND: Prestige 7132

Coltrane (alto sax); Gene Ammons, Paul Quinichette (tenor sax); Pepper Adams (baritone sax); Jerome Richardson (flute); Mal Waldron (piano); George Joyner (bass); Art Taylor (drums).

"The Real McCoy"; "Cheek to Cheek"; "Blue Hymn"; "That's All" (January 3, 1958).

JOHN COLTRANE—THE BELIEVER: Prestige 7292

Donald Byrd (trumpet); Coltrane (tenor sax); Red Garland (piano); Paul Chambers (bass); Louis Hayes (drums).

"The Believer"; "Nakatini Serenade" (January 10, 1958).

Freddie Hubbard for Byrd; Jimmy Cobb for Hayes.

"Do I Love You Because You're Beautiful?" (December 26, 1958).

JOHN COLTRANE—THE LAST TRANE: Prestige 7378

Donald Byrd (trumpet); Coltrane (tenor sax); Red Garland (piano); Paul Chambers (bass); Louis Hayes (drums).

"Lover"; "Come Rain or Come Shine" (January 10, 1958).

Jimmy Cobb for Hayes; omit Byrd.

"By the Numbers" (March 26, 1958).

Earl May for Chambers; Art Taylor for Cobb; omit Garland and Byrd.

"Trane's Slow Blues" (August 16, 1957).

JOHN COLTRANE–SOULTRANE: Prestige 7531

Coltrane (tenor sax); Red Garland (piano); Paul Chambers (bass); Art Taylor (drums).

"Good Bait"; "I Want to Talk About You"; "You Say You Care"; "Theme for Ernie"; "Russian Lullaby" (February 7, 1958).

NOTE: Prestige 7651 and 7531 combined in Prestige 24003–JOHN COLTRANE

KENNY BURRELL–JOHN COLTRANE: New Jazz 8276

Coltrane (tenor sax); Tommy Flanagan (piano); Kenny Burrell (guitar); Paul Chambers (bass); Jimmy Cobb (drums).

"Lyresto"; "Why Was I Born?"; "Freight Train"; "I Never Knew"; "Big Paul" (March 7, 1958).

WILBUR HARDEN QUINTET: Savoy 12127

Wilbur Harden (fluegelhorn); Coltrane (tenor sax); Tommy Flanagan (piano); Doug Watkins (bass); Louis Hayes (drums).

"Wells Fargo"; "West 42nd Street"; "W.F.F.P.H."; "Rhodomagnetics"; "Snuffy" (March 13, 1958).

JOHN COLTRANE–TRANE'S REIGN: Prestige 7746

Coltrane (tenor sax); Red Garland (piano); Paul Chambers (bass); Art Taylor (drums).

"I See Your Face Before Me"; "If There Is Someone Lovelier Than You"; "Little Melonae"; "Rise 'n' Shine" (March 26, 1958).

MILES DAVIS–MILESTONES: Columbia 1193

Miles Davis (trumpet); Cannonball Adderley (alto sax); Coltrane (tenor sax); Red Garland (piano); Paul Chambers (bass); Philly Joe Jones (drums).

"Dr. Jackle"; "Straight, No Chaser" (April 2, 1958).

"Two Bass Hit"; "Milestones" (April 2, 1958).

"Sid's Ahead" (April 3, 1958).

JOHN COLTRANE–BLACK PEARLS: Prestige 7316

Donald Byrd (trumpet); Coltrane (tenor sax); Red Garland (piano); Paul Chambers (bass); Art Taylor (drums).

"Black Pearls"; "Lover Come Back to Me"; "Sweet Sapphire Blues" (May 23, 1958).

MILES DAVIS–JAZZ TRACK: Columbia 1268

Miles Davis (trumpet); Cannonball Adderley (alto sax); Coltrane (tenor sax); Bill Evans (piano); Paul Chambers (bass); Jimmy Cobb (drums).

"On Green Dolphin Street"; "Put Your Little Foot Right Out"; "Stella by Starlight" (May 26, 1958).

MICHEL LEGRAND–LEGRAND JAZZ: Columbia 8079

Miles Davis (trumpet); Phil Woods (alto sax); Coltrane (tenor sax); Jerome Richardson (baritone sax); Herbie Mann (flute); Betty Glamann (harp); Eddie Costa (vibes); Bill Evans (piano); Paul Chambers (bass); Kenny Dennis (drums); Michel Legrand (conductor, arranger).

"Wild Man Blues"; "'Round Midnight"; "The Jitterbug Waltz" (June 25, 1958).

MILES DAVIS–MILES AND MONK AT NEWPORT: Columbia 8978

Miles Davis (trumpet); Cannonball Adderley (alto sax); Coltrane (tenor sax); Bill Evans (piano); Paul Chambers (bass); Jimmy Cobb (drums).

"Ah-Leu-Cha"; "Straight, No Chaser"; "Fran-Dance"; "Two Bass Hit" (July 3, 1958).

JOHN COLTRANE–STARDUST: Prestige 7268

Wilbur Harden (fluegelhorn); Coltrane (tenor sax); Red Garland (piano); Paul Chambers (bass); Jimmy Cobb (drums).

"Stardust"; "Love Thy Neighbor" (July 11, 1958).

Freddie Hubbard for Harden.

"Time After Time" (December 26, 1958).

Art Taylor for Cobb; omit Hubbard.

"Then I'll Be Tired of You" (December 26, 1958).

JOHN COLTRANE–STANDARD COLTRANE: Prestige 7243 (Same as THE MASTER: Prestige 7825)

Wilbur Harden (fluegelhorn); Coltrane (tenor sax); Red Garland (piano); Paul Chambers (bass); Jimmy Cobb (drums).

"Spring Is Here"; "Invitation"; "Don't Take Your Love from Me"; "I'll Get By" (July 11, 1958).

JOHN COLTRANE—BAHIA: Prestige 7353

Wilbur Harden (fluegelhorn); Coltrane (tenor sax); Red Garland (piano); Paul Chambers (bass); Jimmy Cobb (drums).

"My Ideal"; "I'm a Dreamer" (July 11, 1958).

Omit Harden.

"Something I Dreamed Last Night" (December 26, 1958).

Art Taylor for Cobb.

"Bahia"; "Goldsboro Express" (December 26, 1958).

WILBUR HARDEN—JAZZ WAY OUT: Savoy 13004

Wilbur Harden (fluegelhorn); Curtis Fuller (trombone); Coltrane (tenor sax); Tommy Flanagan (piano); Alvin Jackson (bass); Art Taylor (drums).

"Dial Africa"; "Domba"; "Gold Coast" (August 18, 1958).

WILBUR HARDEN—TANGANYIKA STRUT: Savoy 13005

Wilbur Harden (fluegelhorn); Curtis Fuller (trombone); Coltrane (tenor sax); Howard Williams (piano); Alvin Jackson (bass); Art Taylor (drums).

"B.J."; "Tanganyika Strut"; "Anedao"; "Once in a While" (August 25, 1958).

GEORGE RUSSELL—NEW YORK N.Y.: Decca 9216

Doc Severinsen, Art Farmer, Ernie Royal (trumpet); Bob Brookmeyer, Frank Rehak, Tommy Mitchell (trombone); Hal McKusick (alto sax); Coltrane (tenor sax); Sol Schilinger (baritone sax); Bill Evans (piano); Barry Galbraith (guitar); Milt Hinton (bass); Charlie Persip (drums); Jon Hendricks (narrator).

"Manhattan" (September 12, 1958).

JOHN COLTRANE—COLTRANE TIME: United Artists 5638

Coltrane (tenor sax); Kenny Dorham (trumpet); Cecil Taylor (piano); Chuck Israels (bass); Louis Hayes (drums).

"Shifting Down"; "Just Friends"; "Like Someone in Love"; "Double Clutching" (October 13, 1958).

RAY DRAPER—A TUBA JAZZ: Jubilee 1090

Ray Draper (tuba); Coltrane (tenor sax); John Maher (piano); Spanky DeBrest (bass); Larry Richie (drums).

"Essil's Dance"; "Doxy"; "I Talk to the Trees"; "Yesterdays"; "Oleo"; "Angel Eyes" (November 1958).

BAGS AND TRANE: Atlantic 1368

Coltrane (tenor sax); Milt Jackson (vibes); Hank Jones (piano); Paul Chambers (bass); Connie Kay (drums).

"Bags and Trane"; "Three Little Words"; "The Night We Called It a Day"; "Be-Bop"; "The Late Late Blues" (January 15, 1959).

CANNONBALL ADDERLEY QUINTET IN CHICAGO: Mercury 20449

Cannonball Adderley (alto sax); Coltrane (tenor sax); Wynton Kelly (piano); Paul Chambers (bass); Jimmy Cobb (drums).

"Grand Central"; "The Sleeper"; "Wabash"; "Weaver of Dreams"; "Limehouse Blues" (February 3, 1959).

MILES DAVIS—KIND OF BLUE: Columbia 8163

Miles Davis (trumpet); Cannonball Adderley (alto sax); Coltrane (tenor sax); Bill Evans (piano); Paul Chambers (bass); Jimmy Cobb (drums).

"So What"; "Blues in Green" (March 2, 1959).

Wynton Kelly for Evans.

"Freddie Freeloader" (March 2, 1959).

Bill Evans for Kelly.

"Flamenco Sketches"; "All Blues" (April 22, 1959).

JOHN COLTRANE—GIANT STEPS: Atlantic 1311

Coltrane (tenor sax); Tommy Flanagan (piano); Paul Chambers (bass); Art Taylor (drums).

"Giant Steps"; "Cousin Mary"; "Countdown"; "Spiral"; "Syeeda's Song Flute" (May 4–5, 1959).

Wynton Kelly for Flanagan; Jimmy Cobb for Taylor.

"Naima" (December 2, 1959).

JOHN COLTRANE—COLTRANE JAZZ: Atlantic 1354

Coltrane (tenor sax); Wynton Kelly (piano); Paul Chambers (bass); Jimmy Cobb (drums).

"Little Old Lady"; "I'll Wait and Pray" (November 24, 1959).

"Harmonique"; "My Shining Hour"; "Fifth House"; "Like Sonny"; "Some Other Blues" (December 2, 1959).

McCoy Tyner for Kelly; Steve Davis for Chambers; Elvin Jones for Cobb.

"Village Blues" (October 21, 1960).

ECHOES OF AN ERA: Roulette RE-120
Coltrane (tenor sax); McCoy Tyner (piano); Steve Davis (bass); Billy Higgins (drums).
"Exotica"; "One and Four"; "Simple Like" (1960).

JOHN COLTRANE AND DON CHERRY–THE AVANT-GARDE: Atlantic 1451
Don Cherry (trumpet); Coltrane (tenor, soprano sax); Charlie Haden (bass); Ed Blackwell (drums).
"Cherryco"; "The Blessing" (July 1960).
Percy Heath for Haden.
"Focus on Sanity"; "The Invisible"; "Bemsha Swing" (July 1960).

JOHN COLTRANE–MY FAVORITE THINGS: Atlantic 1361
Coltrane (tenor, soprano sax); McCoy Tyner (piano); Steve Davis (bass); Elvin Jones (drums).
"My Favorite Things" (October 21, 1960); "Ev'rytime We Say Goodbye"; "But Not for Me" (October 26, 1960); "Summertime" (October 24, 1960).

JOHN COLTRANE–COLTRANE PLAYS THE BLUES: Atlantic 1382
Coltrane (tenor, soprano); McCoy Tyner (piano); Steve Davis (bass); Elvin Jones (drums).
"Blues to Elvin"; "Blues to Bechet"; "Blues to You"; "Mr. Day"; "Mr. Syms"; "Mr. Knight" (October 24, 1960).

JOHN COLTRANE–COLTRANE'S SOUND: Atlantic 1419
Coltrane (tenor, soprano); McCoy Tyner (piano); Steve Davis (bass); Elvin Jones (drums).
"Central Park West"; "Body and Soul"; "Satellite" (October 24, 1960); "The Night Has a Thousand Eyes"; "Liberia"; "Equinox" (October 26, 1960).

JOHN COLTRANE–THE COLTRANE LEGACY: Atlantic 1553
Coltrane (tenor, soprano); McCoy Tyner (piano); Steve Davis (bass); Elvin Jones (drums).
"Untitled Original" (October 24–26, 1960).
Hank Jones for Tyner; Paul Chambers for Davis; Connie Kay for Jones; add Milt Jackson (vibes).
"Centerpiece"; "Stairway to the Stars"; "Blues Legacy" (January 15, 1959).

McCoy Tyner for Jones; Art Davis for Chambers; Elvin Jones for Kay; omit Jackson; add Eric Dolphy (flute), Freddie Hubbard (trumpet).

"Original Untitled Ballad" (May 25, 1961).

THE BEST OF JOHN COLTRANE: Atlantic 1541

Coltrane (tenor, soprano); McCoy Tyner, Tommy Flanagan, Wynton Kelly (piano); Steve Davis, Paul Chambers (bass); Elvin Jones, Jimmy Cobb, Art Taylor (drums).

"My Favorite Things"; "Naima"; "Giant Steps"; "Equinox"; "Cousin Mary"; "Central Park West."

THE ART OF JOHN COLTRANE—THE ATLANTIC YEARS: Atlantic 2–313

Coltrane (tenor, soprano); McCoy Tyner, Tommy Flanagan, Wynton Kelly (piano); Steve Davis, Paul Chambers (bass); Elvin Jones, Art Taylor, Jimmy Cobb (drums); Don Cherry (trumpet); Percy Heath (bass); Ed Blackwell (drums).

"Syeeda's Song Flute"; "Aisha"; "Countdown"; "Mr. Knight"; "My Shining Hour"; "Blues to Bechet"; "The Invisible"; "My Favorite Things"; "Giant Steps"; "Central Park West"; "Like Sonny"; "Body and Soul."

MILES DAVIS—SOMEDAY MY PRINCE WILL COME: Columbia 8456

Miles Davis (trumpet); Coltrane, Hank Mobley (tenor sax); Wynton Kelly (piano); Paul Chambers (bass); Jimmy Cobb (drums).

"Someday My Prince Will Come" (March 20, 1961).

Omit Mobley.

"Teo" (March 21, 1961).

JOHN COLTRANE—AFRICA/BRASS: Impulse 6

Booker Little (trumpet); Britt Woodman (trombone); Carl Bowman (euphonium); Julius Watkins, Donald Corrado, Bob Northern, Robert Swisshel (French horn); Bill Barber (tuba); Eric Dolphy (alto sax, flute, bass clarinet); Coltrane (tenor, soprano sax); Pat Patrick (baritone sax); McCoy Tyner (piano); Reggie Workman, Art Davis (bass); Elvin Jones (drums).

"Greensleeves" (May 23, 1961); "Africa"; "Blues Minor" (June 7, 1961).

JOHN COLTRANE–OLÉ COLTRANE: Atlantic 1373
Freddie Hubbard (trumpet); Eric Dolphy (alto sax, flute); Coltrane (tenor, soprano sax); McCoy Tyner (piano); Reggie Workman, Art Davis (bass); Elvin Jones (drums).
"Olé"; "Dahomey Dance"; "Aisha" (May 25, 1961).

JOHN COLTRANE–COLTRANE "LIVE" AT THE VILLAGE VANGUARD: Impulse 10
Coltrane (tenor, soprano sax); McCoy Tyner (piano); Reggie Workman (bass); Elvin Jones (drums).
"Softly as in a Morning Sunrise"; "Chasin' the Trane" (November 2–3, 1961).
Add Eric Dolphy (bass clarinet).
"Spiritual" (November 23, 1961).

JOHN COLTRANE–IMPRESSIONS: Impulse 42
Coltrane (tenor, soprano sax); Eric Dolphy (bass clarinet); McCoy Tyner (piano); Reggie Workman, Jimmy Garrison (bass); Elvin Jones (drums).
"India" (November 5, 1961).
Omit Dolphy and Workman.
"Impressions" (November 5, 1961); "Up 'Gainst the Wall" (September 18, 1962).
Roy Haynes for Jones.
"After the Rain" (April 29, 1963).

JOHN COLTRANE QUARTET: Impulse 203 (Extended Play; Sample Album) Coltrane (tenor, soprano sax); McCoy Tyner (piano); Jimmy Garrison (bass); Elvin Jones (drums). "Greensleeves"; "It's Easy to Remember" (December 21, 1961).

JOHN COLTRANE–COLTRANE: Impulse 21
Coltrane (tenor, soprano sax); McCoy Tyner (piano); Jimmy Garrison (bass); Elvin Jones (drums).
"Soul Eyes"; "The Inch Worm" (April 11, 1962); "Miles' Mode" (June 21, 1962); "Tunji"; "Out of This World" (June 29, 1962).

JOHN COLTRANE–BALLADS: Impulse 32
Coltrane (tenor sax); McCoy Tyner (piano); Jimmy Garrison (bass); Elvin Jones (drums).
"It's Easy to Remember" (December 21, 1961); "What's New";

"Nancy" (September 18, 1962); "Say It Over and Over Again"; "You Don't Know What Love Is"; "Too Young to Go Steady"; "All or Nothing At All"; "I Wish I Knew" (November 13, 1962).

DUKE ELLINGTON AND JOHN COLTRANE: Impulse 30

Coltrane (tenor, soprano sax); Duke Ellington (piano); Jimmy Garrison (bass); Elvin Jones (drums).

"Angelica"; "Big Nick"; "Take the Coltrane" (September 26, 1962).

Aaron Bell for Garrison.

"In a Sentimental Mood" (September 26, 1962).

Sam Woodyard for Jones.

"Stevie"; "My Little Brown Book"; "The Feeling of Jazz" (September 26, 1962).

JOHN COLTRANE WITH JOHNNY HARTMAN: Impulse 40

Coltrane (tenor sax); McCoy Tyner (piano); Jimmy Garrison (bass); Elvin Jones (drums); Johnny Hartman (vocal).

"They Say It's Wonderful"; "Lush Life"; "My One and Only Love"; "Autumn Serenade"; "Dedicated to You"; "You Are Too Beautiful" (March 6–7, 1963).

THE DEFINITIVE JAZZ SCENE: Impulse 9101–Volume 3

Coltrane (tenor sax); McCoy Tyner (piano); Jimmy Garrison (bass); Elvin Jones (drums).

"Vilia" (March 6, 1963).

SELFLESSNESS–JOHN COLTRANE: Impulse 9161

Coltrane (tenor, soprano sax); McCoy Tyner (piano); Jimmy Garrison (bass); Roy Haynes (drums).

"My Favorite Things"; "I Want to Talk About You" (July 7, 1963).

Elvin Jones for Haynes; add Pharoah Sanders (tenor sax); Donald Garrett (bass, bass clarinet); Frank Butler (drums); Juno Lewis (percussion).

"Selflessness" (October, 1965).

JOHN COLTRANE–COLTRANE "LIVE" AT BIRDLAND: Impulse 50

Coltrane (tenor, soprano sax); McCoy Tyner (piano); Jimmy Garrison (bass); Elvin Jones (drums).

"Afro-Blue"; "I Want to Talk About You"; "The Promise" (October 8, 1963); "Alabama"; "Your Lady" (November 18, 1963).

JOHN COLTRANE—CRESCENT: Impulse 66
Coltrane (tenor sax); McCoy Tyner (piano); Jimmy Garrison (bass); Elvin Jones (drums).
"Crescent"; "Wise One"; "Bessie's Blues"; "Lonnie's Lament"; "The Drum Thing" (April 27, June 1, 1964).

JOHN COLTRANE—A LOVE SUPREME: Impulse 77
Coltrane (tenor sax); McCoy Tyner (piano); Jimmy Garrison (bass); Elvin Jones (drums).
"Acknowledgement"; "Resolution"; "Pursuance"; "Psalm" (December 9, 1964).

THE JOHN COLTRANE QUARTET PLAYS: Impulse 85
Coltrane (tenor, soprano sax); McCoy Tyner (piano); Jimmy Garrison (bass); Elvin Jones (drums).
"Nature Boy"; "Brazilia"; "Chim Chim Cheree"; "Song of Praise" (February 17–18, 1965).

THE NEW WAVE IN JAZZ: Impulse 90
Coltrane (tenor, soprano sax); McCoy Tyner (piano); Jimmy Garrison (bass); Elvin Jones (drums).
"Nature Boy" (March 28, 1965).

JOHN COLTRANE—KULU SE MAMA: Impulse 9106
Coltrane (tenor sax); McCoy Tyner (piano); Jimmy Garrison (bass); Elvin Jones (drums).
"Vigil"; "Welcome" (June 28, 1965).
Add Pharoah Sanders (tenor sax), Donald Garrett (bass, bass clarinet), Frank Butler (drums), Juno Lewis (percussion, vocal).
"Kulu Se Mama" (October, 1965).

JOHN COLTRANE—ASCENSION: Impulse 95
Coltrane, Archie Shepp, Pharoah Sanders (tenor sax); John Tchicai, Marion Brown (alto sax); Freddie Hubbard, Dewey Johnson (trumpet); McCoy Tyner (piano); Jimmy Garrison, Art Davis (bass); Elvin Jones (drums).
"Ascension" (June 28, 1965).

NEW THING AT NEWPORT: Impulse 94
Coltrane (tenor sax); McCoy Tyner (piano); Jimmy Garrison (bass); Elvin Jones (drums).
"One Down, One Up" (July 2, 1965).

JOHN COLTRANE–TRANSITION: Impulse 9195
Coltrane (tenor sax); McCoy Tyner (piano); Jimmy Garrison (bass); Elvin Jones (drums).
"Dear Lord" (May, 1955); "Transition, Suite–Prayer and Meditation: Day, Peace and After, Prayer and Meditation: Evening, Affirmation, Prayer and Meditation: 4 AM" (June, 1955).

JOHN COLTRANE–SUN SHIP: Impulse 9211
Coltrane (tenor sax); McCoy Tyner (piano); Jimmy Garrison (bass); Elvin Jones (drums).
"Sun Ship"; "Dearly Beloved"; "Amen"; "Attaining"; "Ascent" (August 26, 1965).

JOHN COLTRANE–INFINITY: Impulse 9225
Coltrane (tenor sax); McCoy Tyner (piano); Jimmy Garrison (bass); Elvin Jones (drums).
"Living Space" (June 16, 1965); "Joy" (September 22, 1965).
Alice Coltrane for Tyner; Charlie Haden for Garrison; Rashied Ali for Jones; add Ray Appleton (percussion), Pharoah Sanders (tenor sax), Joan Chapman (tamboura).
"Peace on Earth"; "Leo" (February 2, 1966).

JOHN COLTRANE–LIVE IN SEATTLE: Impulse 9202-2
Coltrane, Pharoah Sanders (tenor sax); McCoy Tyner (piano); Jimmy Garrison, Donald Garrett (bass); Elvin Jones (drums).
"Cosmos"; "Out of This World"; "Evolution"; "Tapestry in Sound" (September 30, 1965).

JOHN COLTRANE–OM: Impulse 9140
Coltrane, Pharoah Sanders (tenor sax); Joe Brazil (flute); McCoy Tyner (piano); Jimmy Garrison, Donald Garrett (bass); Elvin Jones (drums).
"Om" (October 1, 1965).

JOHN COLTRANE–MEDITATIONS: Impulse 9110
Coltrane, Pharoah Sanders (tenor sax); McCoy Tyner (piano); Jimmy Garrison (bass); Elvin Jones, Rashied Ali (drums).
"The Father and the Son and the Holy Ghost"; "Compassion"; "Love"; "Consequences"; "Serenity" (November 23, 1965).

JOHN COLTRANE–COSMIC MUSIC: Impulse 9148
Coltrane (tenor sax, bass clarinet); Pharoah Sanders (tenor sax,

flute); Alice Coltrane (piano); Jimmy Garrison (bass); Rashied Ali (drums); Ray Appleton, Ben Riley (percussion).
"Manifestation"; "Reverend King" (February 2, 1966).

JOHN COLTRANE—"LIVE" AT THE VILLAGE VANGUARD AGAIN: Impulse 9124
Coltrane (tenor, soprano sax); Pharoah Sanders (tenor sax); Alice Coltrane (piano); Jimmy Garrison (bass); Rashied Ali (drums); Emanuel Rahim (percussion).
"Naima"; "My Favorite Things" (May 28, 1966).

JOHN COLTRANE—CONCERT IN JAPAN: Impulse 9246–2
Coltrane, Pharoah Sanders (tenor, alto sax, bass clarinet); Alice Coltrane (piano); Jimmy Garrison (bass); Rashied Ali (drums).
"Meditations"; "Leo"; "Peace on Earth" (July 22, 1966).

JOHN COLTRANE—EXPRESSION: Impulse 9120
Alice Coltrane (piano); Jimmy Garrison (bass); Rashied Ali Coltrane (tenor sax, flute); Pharoah Sanders (tenor sax, piccolo); (drums).
"To Be"; "Offering" (February 15, 1967); "Expression"; "Ogunde" (March 7, 1967).

THE BEST OF JOHN COLTRANE VOL. 1: Impulse 9200–2
"Africa"; "Softly as in a Morning Sunrise"; "Soul Eyes"; "After the Rain"; "Afro-Blue"; "Alabama"; "My Favorite Things"; "Bessie's Blues"; "Psalm"; "Kulu Se Mama"; "Naima"; "Om."

THE BEST OF JOHN COLTRANE VOL. 2: Impulse 9223–2
"Greensleeves"; "India"; "Miles' Mode"; "Big Nick"; "The Promise"; "Chim Chim Cheree"; "Ascension"; "The Father and the Son and the Holy Ghost"; "Manifestation"; "Ogunde."

THE BEST OF JOHN COLTRANE VOL. 3: Impulse 9278–2
"Dear Lord"; "Chasin' the Trane"; "Up 'Gainst the Wall"; "Crescent"; "Nature Boy"; "Welcome"; "Cosmos"; "Dedicated to You"; "Expression"; "Living Space."

JOHN COLTRANE—AFRICA/BRASS VOL. 2: Impulse 9273
"Africa"; "Greensleeves"; "Song of the Underground Railroad."

JOHN COLTRANE—INTERSTELLAR SPACE: Impulse 9277
Coltrane (tenor sax); Rashied Ali (drums).
"Mars"; "Venus"; "Jupiter"; "Saturn" (February 22, 1967).